CHINA'S GOOD WAR

CHINA'S GOOD WAR

How World War II Is Shaping a New Nationalism

Rana Mitter

THE BELKNAP PRESS OF
HARVARD UNIVERSITY PRESS

Cambridge, Massachusetts
London, England
2020

Library of Congress Cataloging-in-Publication Data

Names: Mitter, Rana, 1969– author.
Title: China's good war : how World War II is shaping a
new nationalism / Rana Mitter.
Description: Cambridge, Massachusetts : The Belknap Press of Harvard
University Press, 2020. | Includes bibliographical references and index.
Identifiers: LCCN 2020005100 | ISBN 9780674984264 (cloth)
Subjects: LCSH: Nationalism and collective memory—China. |
Sino-Japanese War, 1937–1945—Public opinion. | Chinese—Attitudes. |
China—Historiography. | China—Civilization—1949–
Classification: LCC DS777.6 .M58 2020 | DDC 320.540951—dc23
LC record available at https://lccn.loc.gov/2020005100

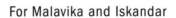

For Malavika and Iskandar

Ce sont les morts qui se relèvent
Ce sont les soldats morts qui rêvent
Aux amours qui s'en sont allés
Immaculés
Et désolés

—Guillaume Apollinaire, *Les Attentives*

Contents

CHINA'S GOOD WAR

Introduction

War, Memory, and Nationalism in China

Some eight decades after its conclusion, the Second World War still grips the imagination of large parts of North America, Europe, and Asia. Tom Brokaw's book *The Greatest Generation* (1998) and Steven Spielberg and Tom Hanks's miniseries *Band of Brothers* (2001) captivated American readers and viewers and remain cultural touchstones. British politicians use metaphors about Dunkirk and the Battle of Britain to describe the country's decision to exit from the European Union, and the sitcom *Dad's Army*, gently teasing the wartime Home Guard, still plays on television half a century after it was made. Japanese filmmakers produce movies that explore topics from home-front suffering to the mentality of kamikaze pilots. Courts in Poland adjudicate the legally correct description of death camps built during the Nazi occupation.[1] The Second World War is a long way from being all that these societies think about, of course. But in the United States, Europe east and west, and Japan, there is a continuing undercurrent of collective memory about the importance of the global conflict that does not take too much effort to bring to the surface.

Perhaps more surprisingly, the same is true of China. When outsiders think of collective memory in China, they tend to remember particular historical moments, many of them traumatic—the Cultural Revolution, or the Opium Wars of the nineteenth century. Or, more positively, the legacy of traditional Chinese thought may come to mind. In the past few decades, however, memories of another episode have become ever more prominent in China: the Second World War. Schoolchildren file by the thousands through the Beijing museum that commemorates the War of Resistance against Japan, as the conflict is known in China. Movies about topics from the massacre of Chinese civilians in Japanese-occupied Nanjing to starvation in a wartime famine in Henan top the Chinese box office. Online, netizens debate the finer points of the Battle of Shanghai in 1937, assessing the relative strength of the Chinese and Japanese troops that lined up against one another by the banks of the Huangpu River.

One particular moment in 2015 captured the way the war has entered the Chinese public sphere, with reminders of the past used to make points about the future. On 3 September 2015, Tiananmen Square, at the heart of Beijing, was filled by an enormous parade. Missiles, tanks, and marching soldiers all made their way past thousands of spectators from China and abroad. The event commemorated the seventieth anniversary of the end of World War II in Asia. It stood in stark contrast to the elegiac tone of many of the memorials in Europe the preceding spring. On the anniversary of the liberation of Auschwitz in January 1945, as on VE Day the following May, there was a strong sense that the end of a narrative had been reached—veterans and survivors attending a seventieth anniversary in the knowledge that few of them would be there for the eightieth. In China, while veterans stood at the

center of the parade, there was a much stronger sense that the military display was part of a definition of a new China rather than a farewell to the old one.

The Chinese event was distinctive in another important way. The parade was the first national, large-scale public commemoration of China's role in the Second World War. It was a major milestone in a process that had been taking place over a long period of time—some thirty years or more—during which China's attitude toward collective memory of its wartime participation changed significantly, with profound consequences for its domestic and international politics.

I was present in Beijing for the parade. Having spent around twenty years observing and writing about the changing relationship China has with its own wartime history, I found it a fascinating event that confirmed ideas I had been thinking about for some time. While researching a book I published in 2013 on the history of China's World War II experience (titled *Forgotten Ally* in North America, and *China's War with Japan, 1937–1945* elsewhere), I had become increasingly convinced that the war was very far from being long-past history; instead, it remained alive in every aspect of Chinese life, from museums to movies to new media. The generous offer to deliver the Wiles Lectures at Queen's University Belfast in 2014 gave me an opportunity to reflect on why the 1930s and 1940s have erupted back into the political and cultural life of China in the past four decades. I was also able to think about how media portrayed the conflict when I presented a television documentary on the topic titled *WWII: China's Forgotten War.*[2]

This book, which emerged from those reflections and experiences, argues that there is a strong relationship between China's memory of its experience of World War II and its present-day nationalist identity at home and global role abroad. In territorial disputes and in designing patriotic education, China refers back, again and again, to the war. Contemporary China is shaped by an assertive internationalism in the region and globally, and by an equally assertive nationalism in its domestic politics. Both of these elements are profoundly, if not always obviously, shaped by China's changing understanding of its own history during the Second World War.

China's engagement with other countries has become deeply shaped by ideas about the Second World War—both by the events and purpose of the war, and by its legacy. This is a major shift from how it previously presented itself. During the Cold War, China's primary national narrative came from its self-definition as a communist, revolutionary, anti–imperialist state. In the twenty-first century, much of China's standing and sense of itself has come from its extraordinary economic success. However, this story of growing wealth has little morally weighted content. In part, it has been tarnished by China's lack of compliance with developing norms of international behavior, for instance on human rights, although the country has sought to develop moral ballast elsewhere by entering the World Trade Organization (WTO) and by addressing climate change. China is currently both assertive, as demonstrated by its territorial claims in the East and South China Seas, and internationalist, as shown by its desire both to shape existing international institutions and to create new ones of its own, such as the Asian Infrastructure Investment Bank (established in 2015). Yet it is keen for its growing presence in the world to be seen as one of normative and moral leadership, rather than leadership defined solely by economic and military weight. One sign of this has been the almost obsessive concern with developing what Joseph S. Nye Jr. has called "soft power."[3]

The political scientist Rogers Smith has proposed the idea of "ethically constitutive stories" as a way of explaining why particular narratives take hold in a society.[4] China has recently constructed such a story of its own modern genealogy, which presents the country not only as powerful, but as just and moral—with the Second World War as the point of origin.[5] Chinese thinkers now argue that the country was "present at the creation," to use former US secretary of state Dean Acheson's phrase referring to his leading role in the formation of the postwar world. As a result, China, like the United States, should be able to draw on its record as one of the victorious Allied powers to define its own vision of the region. Like the other Allies, China also seeks to legitimize its own behavior and give itself prestige by virtue of its contributions to the wartime victory.

Yet the international aspect of China's engagement with its World War II history should not be separated from the domestic dimension. Memory of the war has also reshaped China's internal political culture. During the Mao era, class identity was central to China's self-definition; under Deng Xiaoping, class distinctions were blurred with the restoration of capitalism. A new form of non–class-based national identity was needed: World War II, with its message of shared anti-Japanese struggle across class lines, proved to be a powerful vehicle for that new nationalism.

The war-based narrative that has emerged during the past four decades is not the only historical narrative that has shaped modern China. For much of the past century, the dominant story was the rise and victory of Chinese communism. Stories about economic growth, previous instances of historical injustice (the Opium Wars, colonial occupation and extraterritoriality), and the idea of being a "responsible" actor in world society have also had a powerful influence.

Not all historical narratives are equally effective, however. Several scholars have shown that stories of "national humiliation" have been so successful in China because they allow the past experience of invasion and hostility from other powers to be turned into a discourse that demands that China be given greater status and respect. Thus the Opium Wars of the nineteenth century have been used as a powerful trope to indicate China's victim status. But this trope has a drawback: because China was defeated in those wars, they do little to project an image of strength. The warlord conflicts of the 1920s, the Chinese Civil War of the 1940s, and the Cultural Revolution of the 1960s are all poor sources of inspiration for Chinese nationalism. Appeals to traditional Chinese philosophical ideas, drawn from Confucius and other thinkers, help to promote cultural pride but do not help tie China to the formation of the modern world. In contrast, the Second World War provides for China, as it does for the other former Allied belligerent nations, an opportunity to portray the nation as both strong and victorious, as well as morally righteous. As Xi Jinping put it, "The Chinese people's victory in the War of Resistance against Japan was the first complete [*wanquan*] victory in a recent war where China resisted the invasion of a foreign enemy." In those words lies the value of the Second World War for the story of China's rise to global power.[6]

Despite its prominence in recent years, the discourse surrounding the Second World War in China has not yet been extensively analyzed. This book aims to do just that. It does not cover every aspect of how World War II appears in Chinese public life; more could be said, for example, in areas ranging from the numerous television dramas set during the war years to the contents of school textbooks. But the range of topics addressed here—diplomatic tactics, historiographical arguments, blockbuster movies, online communities, and public museums among them—will show how central war memory has become to reform-era China. As China's ambitions to reshape regional order and cement a nationalist agenda at home come together in the 2010s and 2020s, the memory and legacy of the wartime years will continue to provide an important framework for understanding an often nebulous topic: how today's China constructs ideas of its own nationhood and of its place in the international community. CCP, nat china

World War II and China's Place in the International Order

mo CCP

The Chinese government has promoted the new collective memory of World War II as a way to create a morally weighted narrative about China's role in the global order. Much analysis of China's international behavior has focused on whether the country has been following a path that is broadly within the norms of the international order or whether it is behaving like a revisionist power. Scholars such as John Ikenberry and Alastair Iain Johnston have argued that China appears to be trying to incorporate itself within the existing, largely liberal, order while seeking to revise that order to match its own preferences, for instance, on issues such as the United Nations' "responsibility to protect" or the adoption of international trade norms at the WTO. John Mearsheimer and Graham

Allison have suggested a more confrontational possibility, with a rising China seeking to displace American hegemony in Asia.[7] There is little doubt that China is seeking to exercise regional dominance in Asia, with aspirations to a more global reach.[8] One way it does so is through material, military, and economic means. Another is through discursive tactics. The former approach is more thoroughly covered in the scholarly literature. In economic terms, the period since 2000 has given rise to a narrative of China's rising global economic status.[9] Niall Ferguson's formulation of "Chimerica" expresses the idea that China's purchase of American debt has caused the two states to become intertwined.[10] The global financial crisis of 2007–2008 gave China further economic standing; just when major Western economies were on the brink of a systemic disaster, China's decision to create credit to spend on infrastructure helped to stabilize the global economy as well as to retool its own infrastructure (albeit at the price, a decade later, of a property and credit bubble). In 2013, the formal proposal of the Belt and Road Initiative put forward a bold, multiyear plan to create an integrated trading and commercial zone from Southeast Asia via East Africa and the Middle East to western Europe. This incipient project, along with the establishment of the Asian Infrastructure Investment Bank, marked China's intention to become a major economic and financial power, along with moves such as the slow internationalization of the renminbi. The decision by US president Donald J. Trump to withdraw the United States from the proposed Trans-Pacific Partnership free trade agreement in 2017 also gave more weight to China's model of the Regional Comprehensive Economic Partnership, a proposed Asia–Pacific trade agreement, as an alternative. China's economic importance to the region continues to grow. However, it does so in a context where its economic partners are concerned about the ambitions and unpredictability of China and lack trust in the country.[11] One reason for that mistrust comes from the rise in China's military spending. Between 2000 and 2019, China increased its military spending from around US$12 billion per year to US$175 billion. The People's Liberation Army has over two million personnel, by any count the largest armed forces in the world.[12] The contradictory signals given by China's foreign policy behavior are exacerbated by the lack of transparency within its decision-making apparatus. This deficiency has also made it difficult for China to project a clearly defined vision of its own foreign policy stance. Rosemary Foot has argued convincingly that missteps by Beijing have prevented it from implementing its foreign policy vision effectively in Asia.[13]

Since 1945, the United States has supported a liberal international order underpinned by a variety of international institutions intended to strengthen military and economic security. The United States has violated the liberal values underlying that order on frequent occasions, most notably in Asia and Latin America, but these same values did become norms that could then be used to criticize such behavior. China, in the 2000s, has felt the need to create an alternative international discourse while not dissociating itself from the benefits of the existing system, which it recognizes has attractions for the international community. Much of China's international discourse is very inwardly focused; that is, it defines China's place in the world to itself, rather than to others. Its outward-facing discourse is for the most part still defined in opposition to the United States: thus, it stresses no interference in the domestic politics of other countries, and no imposition of specific criteria for economic assistance. The ideological arguments for a greater Chinese role in the region are defined in terms that have little capacity to generate "thick norms," the complex web of laws, assumptions, and habits that embed a hegemon in a region. The thinness of these norms gives rise to fears that China will revert to a more power-driven, realist view of the world when it chooses to. The words of the Chinese foreign minister Yang Jiechi in 2010 at an Association of Southeast Asian Nations conference in Hanoi stoked this fear. Bursting out in anger, Yang exclaimed, "China is a big country, and other countries are small countries, and that is a fact."[14]

Even if it might be factually true, Yang's statement that other states were "small" did not begin to provide the sort of moral basis for Chinese hegemony that Beijing sought; instead, it harked back to the aggressive rhetoric which China had frequently condemned the West for using against it. Since the 1980s, however, a new discourse had begun to emerge in Beijing around the issue of the Second World War. One of its aims was to provide evidence to burnish China's claim to ownership of the post-1945 settlement. Another was to deny Japan any significant role in the region. A third was to add moral weight to China's presence in the region and the world.

China's historical revisionism seeks to provide an alternative genealogy for the contemporary order in Asia, rejecting the America-centered "present at the creation" discourse. Although it is inwardly directed, its creators hope to make it better accepted externally in due course. In the best-known version of the creation of postwar order, the United States is at the center and China features at best as an obstacle, and at worst as an irrelevance. According to this story, the United States entered the war after Pearl Harbor in 1941 and directed a strategy that placed Europe first while providing sufficient support and momentum to prevent the Japanese from consolidating control of Asia.[15] The atomic bombings of Japan brought a swift end to the war in Asia and allowed the United States to occupy Japan alone, in contrast to the kind of multipartite arrangements that marked the division of Germany in spring 1945. The original hopes that China might play a significant role in the postwar Asian order were dashed by the collapse of the Nationalist (Kuomintang / Guomindang) regime on the mainland, which was defeated and replaced by a communist government in 1949. In 1951, the Treaty of San Francisco marked the end of the American occupation of Japan, although the People's Republic of China (PRC) was excluded from signing the treaty (as indeed was the Republic of China on Taiwan).

Postwar order was then formed under two certainties. First, China was isolated from the United States and much of the Western world. Second, the United States and the Soviet Union established friendly or client regimes, with the United States dominant in South Korea, Taiwan, and much of Southeast Asia and Australasia, while Vietnam, North Korea, and China itself remained under communist control. The United States also established a formal security alliance with Japan. In the 1960s, China and the Soviet Union split, allowing the United States further to dominate the region after 1972, when it established links with the PRC. By the end of the European Cold War in 1989–1991, the existing order in Asia was still fixed in grooves that had been set in the years 1945–1952.

The Chinese alternative to this discourse has rarely been articulated as one narrative. However, its contours have become increasingly clear in recent years. In this version, the war in Asia begins not with Pearl Harbor, but with the outbreak of the

Sino-Japanese War in 1937 (or, in the official version as of 2017, with the Manchurian crisis of 1931). China fought without formal allies for four and a half years until 1941, when the United States and the British Empire entered the Asian war. In the last years of the war, and in the immediate postwar, China was given many assurances of future international assistance, an elevated global status, and a role in shaping postwar order in Asia. Yet China was isolated after the 1949 communist revolution, which allowed the United States to dominate the region and shape its structures with little interference from the Soviet Union. By the end of the Cold War, China had been partially reintegrated into the post-1945 order, particularly after it took over the United Nations Security Council permanent seat from the Taiwan government in 1971. But this interpretation of the postwar maintains that to this day, China's role and sacrifices in creating that order are mostly ignored or undervalued. If the United States could gain decades of dominance on the back of its wartime contributions to Asia, Chinese analysts argue today, so should China.

This narrative is related to an idea more frequently heard outside China: that in the early twenty-first century, China is seeking to restore its status as the traditional hegemon in the region. Yang Jiechi's 2010 outburst is a good example of this sentiment. But the way China is reinterpreting the Second World War shows that it is not just a traditional historical role in the *longue durée* that China seeks to regain. Rather, China is engaging in painstaking detail with the existing order so as to re-create it in a recognizable form, but in its own terms—to be "present at the re-creation." Finding a morally based argument has become more necessary in a post–Cold War world where American alliances in the region are based less on coercion than on the active choices of democratic polities

(Japan, Taiwan, the Philippines, and others among them). There-fore, China has to find an argument that is morally plausible but does not depend on democratic consent.

In case this sounds like an argument for hypocrisy, we should note that this type of revisionism about the origins of the post-1945 world is not merely the product of a Chinese propagandist's mind. Recent scholarly work has seriously questioned the idea that the post-1945 order was entirely created in the rooms of a small number of American and European chancelleries. Eric Helleiner, for instance, has shown that a variety of actors, from Asia and Latin America in particular, were influential in shaping the Bretton Woods settlement at the end of the war.[16]

In order to create a new genealogy of China's international status from 1945, however, China has had to grapple with the awk-ward reality that the regime that was involved in various aspects of China's postwar settlement, including the Bretton Woods dis-cussions, the establishment of economic and social organizations, and the war crimes trials, was the Nationalist regime of Chiang Kai-shek, not the Communist government of Mao Zedong. That reality has prompted an unstated, but highly visible, rehabilitation of the Nationalists' wartime role in China. That process of reha-bilitation is one of the subjects of this book.

This revisionist approach has real historical substance to it. The country's contribution to the war may not have been as central as some of its boosters now claim, but it has been seriously under-valued in the global historiography of the war. Nevertheless, I do not suggest that China's contributions to the Allied victory give it carte blanche for territorial or legal revisionism in Asia. The cur-rent order is indeed underpinned by the legacy of the Second World War—but not solely by it. The advance of democratic norms and values in the region has been in large part a product of the presence of the United States. One of the great questions raised in the 2010s, and to be answered in the 2020s, is whether the election of Donald Trump, a US president more careless of norms than his predecessor, and the rise of China, an avowedly nonliberal state, will mean that the democratization of Asia proves a more temporary moment than it might have appeared at the start of the century.

Circuits of Memory

China's treatment of its collective memory of the war draws on historical experience and political and social techniques that are in some ways similar to those of other countries, and in other ways profoundly different. This book argues that a very useful concept for understanding how collective memory flows across both time and space is that of *circuits of memory.* This idea is distinct from Henry Rousso's conception of "vectors" of memory, which describes institutions and entities that help transmit memory across time; the circuit transmits memory geographically, across national borders, as well as chronologically. Collective memory of war, or of any historical event, is rarely truly global. During the long postwar, several different circuits have emerged in which certain experiences, understandings, and judgments of the Second World War are shared (such as a core purpose of the war being to fight fascism), but the memories within them are distinct and self-contained. One such circuit exists in northwestern Europe and North America, another in Russia and some of its neighbors, a third in Japan, and a fourth in China. The Chinese circuit of memory has been highly inward-looking until recently; now the country is seeking to integrate this circuit with other more globally prominent and potent ones.[17]

There has not yet been a full-length study concentrating specifically on China's memory of its wartime experience. The need for such a study has become more compelling in recent years for two reasons. First, China has become much more similar to the other Allied, and indeed Axis, powers in the way that it has brought social memory of the Second World War to the forefront of its construction of national and international identity. But second, paradoxically, China's memory of the war is unique among the Allied powers. The United States remembers it, in Studs Terkels's evocative but ironic phrase, as "the good war," when GIs liberated Europe and Asia. The United Kingdom remembers it as a time when Britons resisted bombing and invasion and stood tall against the Nazis, with the war against Japan generally sidelined. The Soviet Union refers to it as the Great Patriotic War, and Putin's Russia has considered making it a crime to demean the Soviet war record. France has converted its story of occupation into one of resistance.[18]

China is the major Allied belligerent whose position on the meaning of the war has shifted most thoroughly during the postwar era. For the first half of the Cold War, under Mao Zedong, official China spoke in a minor key about the war years, and when it did, it concentrated on the record of the Chinese Communist Party (CCP) and the importance of the war in bringing the party to power. Only limited acknowledgment was made of the contribution of Nationalist forces.[19] From the 1980s onward, the war became a more central part of official discourse, appearing everywhere from textbooks to museums to television soap operas. During this process, the scope of China's understanding of the war expanded significantly, the most notable example being the way in which the Communists' old opponents, the Nationalists, were brought back into the narrative of the war. Many of the tropes that have become central to contemporary Chinese understandings of World War II date from the 1980s or later—the Nanjing Massacre, the bombings of Chongqing, and the disputes over the meaning of the Potsdam and Cairo declarations among them.[20]

The topic of memory has become a mainstay of historical analysis in recent decades, especially memory relating to wars. Maurice Halbwachs, Pierre Nora, and Paul Fussell are among those who laid the groundwork for what has become an immense field.[21] The Second World War, in particular, has generated a large body of scholarship on the links between memory and the politics of the postwar. Even more than the First World War, the Second has also given rise to a considerable body of scholarship that relates memory of the war itself to the experience of mass violence, and analysis of the Holocaust has become central to that particular field.[22] Assessing the ways in which memory of war has shaped postwar Europe, Jan-Werner Müller notes that "memory and power can only be fully understood if domestic and international, social scientific, historical and ethical perspectives are brought together."[23] That insight, that no one perspective is sufficient to explain the significance of memory in shaping a society, is one that informs this book.

Much of the early work on war memory, on the part of both perpetrators and victims, was centered on the Western world, but a number of studies have also focused on Japan. Carol Gluck, Ian Buruma, Franziska Seraphim, and Yoshikuni Igarashi, among others, have shown that remembering (and forgetting) Japan's period as a wartime power has profoundly shaped the country's postwar culture, to the extent that the term *sengo* (postwar) became a core part of the country's self-definition during the Cold War.[24] The memory of other wars in non-Western countries has slowly become part of the scholarship on how memory is shaped, as Viet Thanh Nguyen demonstrates in his analysis of parallel discourses in Vietnam and the United States about the war between those two countries.[25] However, the analysis of trans-Asian memory of the Second World War is still a work in progress, with China especially underexamined.

Another area that needs further analysis has to do with identifying the common factors that mark war memory in nonliberal states. The majority of the scholarship on memory of the Second World War has been either on liberal states (the United States and Britain), or states that liberalized after the war (Japan, Germany). The most thorough analysis of a nonliberal wartime belligerent that *remained* nonliberal after the war has been that of the Soviet Union, and post-1991, Russia. The concept of the Great Patriotic War was central to postwar Soviet identity. Although a more nuanced discussion of the war was allowed in some parts of the public sphere, the vast majority of the discourse about it was controlled by the state, at least until the short period of *glasnost* (openness) under Mikhail Gorbachev. The factors that shaped the development of war memory in the Soviet Union and communist Eastern Europe also influence the Chinese discourse on the war today, which is partly free and partly constrained.

The Second World War has entered Chinese life again, and shows no signs of being dislodged. The desire to woo Taiwan into reunification, the disappearance of the Cold War motivations for downplaying Japanese war atrocities and stressing Nationalist ones, and the increasing delegitimation of Marxism all contributed to a significant change in official boundaries for discussion of the war. The most obvious and perhaps startling public manifestation of this shift was the much more positive tone taken toward the role of the Nationalist government of Chiang Kai-shek in contributing to the victory against Japan, a victory that had previously been attributed almost entirely to the CCP. This reorientation could be seen in media such as textbooks, popular films, and museums. The conflict between Nationalists and Communists, endlessly recalled during the Mao era, did not disappear from historical discussion, but it began to take second place to a narrative that stressed Communist and Nationalist unity in the face of Japanese atrocities and aggression. At the same time, Japanese war crimes, especially the 1937–1938 Nanjing Massacre (widely known as the Rape of Nanking), and the representation of China as a victim of bloody Japanese aggression, became increasingly prominent. Traumatic events such as the Great Leap Forward and the Cultural Revolution, the latter much discussed in public in the 1970s and 1980s, gave way to talk of China's theater of the world war as a time of clear moral contrasts, in which noble Chinese patriots, both Communist and Nationalist, fought against Japanese devils.[26]

Although it did so particularly visibly, China is not alone in having changed its overall narrative of the war's significance during the postwar decades. Britain and France entered the war because their guarantee to Poland had been called in. The Soviet Union and the United States did not enter until attacked by Germany and Japan, respectively. Other justifications—whether saving the world for democracy or preventing the destruction of Europe's Jewish community—were only formulated later. During the ambiguities and uncertainties of the postwar, the Allied powers nostalgically reinvented the Second World War as a bomb-strewn age of gold.

The United Kingdom, in Dean Acheson's phrase, "lost an empire and failed to find a role"; the United States became entwined in Vietnam and the protests of the 1960s; and the Soviet Union became a sullen Cold War giant keeping Eastern Europeans captive with tanks, concrete, and barbed wire. For these troubled societies, the Battle of Britain, Midway, and Stalingrad provided powerful justification for what they had become. China, of all the Allied powers, had perhaps the most problematic relationship with its past because of its swift move from the Sino-Japanese War to the Chinese Civil War, during which former allies became wartime enemies. Unlike Russia's conflict with Germany, China's war against Japan was never able to provide a fount of universally resonant cultural memory.[27]

To be sure, China was not the only country that had a difficult relationship with the postwar legacy of wartime alliances. Greece, like China, plunged into a civil war between 1946 and 1949. In the Greek case, it was the anticommunist forces that won, but the unhealed fissure of that era led to highly polarized politics, a military coup in 1967, and resentments that festered for decades and are not wholly erased even now. Nonetheless, China is unique as a major belligerent Ally that had no time to absorb the shock of the war against the Axis before the conflict turned inward.

If China's civil war makes it unique among the Allied powers in one respect, its history of collaboration has some similarities with France's experience. Like France, China was both an Allied belligerent and (under a rival regime) a collaborator with the Axis. This aspect of French history has been one of the most powerful subfields of war memory. Henry Rousso's now classic *The Vichy Syndrome* (1987) suggested that there was a complex argument within France throughout the Cold War about how to remember

No deal ?

its role in the war: the country wished to portray itself as a force for resistance, but in fact it was largely controlled by collaborators. There is a parallel with the case of China. During the war, as Hans van de Ven has pointed out, "China was at war not just with Japan but also with itself."[28] In the early years of the conflict, China put up more resistance to the Axis than did France. But between 1937 and 1945, a set of collaborationist governments was established in much of central and eastern China. Unlike in France, this aspect of the war is very little discussed in China today; while there is a certain amount of debate about how much continuity of structures or legacy there was between the era of Chiang Kai-shek and the Mao period, there is almost no discussion about any similar continuity between the era of the collaborationist leader Wang Jingwei and his postwar successors.

Despite hidden stories of collaboration, and complexities beneath the heroic narratives, the Sino-Japanese War has the advantage of not being the fault of the Chinese themselves—unlike the many other wars that China endured in the twentieth century. The civil wars of the Republican era, particularly virulent in the 1910s and 1920s, culminating in the final Nationalist-Communist confrontation of 1946–1949; the massive upheavals of the Great Leap Forward and the Cultural Revolution, along with the constant mass mobilization that underpinned class warfare in the People's Republic—in all of these cases, Chinese were in conflict with other Chinese. Imperialism has been the only force that provides a seemingly uncomplicated pole of aggression and hostility, contrasted with which the Chinese can be seen as blameless; and the Sino-Japanese War is both the most recent and the most devastating example of that imperialism. World War II sits in collective memory in China as being more similar to past wars against foreign aggression, such as the Opium Wars, rather than being considered alongside World War I, as collective memory in Europe has tended to do.[29] Yet overall, the renewed interest in World War II in China merely shows China "normalizing" its experience of that conflict; it is joining an increasingly globalized discussion of the war's significance that grows stronger the further we move away from the event itself.

Sino-Japanese Relations

It may seem obvious that today's tense relationship between China and Japan is shaped by the collective memory of the conflict between them in the mid-twentieth century. Yet the connection is not straightforward. Since the turn of the twenty-first century, relations between China and Japan have fluctuated. The period from 2001 to 2005 saw a relatively passive Chinese president (Hu Jintao) and a revisionist Japanese premier (Koizumi Junichirō) generate heightened tensions. The brief first succession of Shinzo Abe to the premiership (2006–2007), despite his reputation as a "China hawk," lowered the temperature. Then, during the rule of the Democratic Party of Japan (2009–2012), Japan's attempts to warm relations with China were rebuffed. Those years saw the start of a period of tension between the two countries, including serious disputes over the Diaoyu / Senkaku Islands in the East China Sea in 2010 and 2012, which were still rumbling in early 2013, shortly after Xi Jinping's accession to power. By 2017, when both Xi and Abe had secured a further term of power, tensions once again dipped when the two sides agreed to establish a hotline to prevent clashes in the East China Sea, and Japanese and Chinese leaders have continued to hold regular, low-key meetings in subsequent years.

Yet at some level, the dispute between these two countries is not best understood as a conflict between China and Japan. Rather, it stems from a continuing debate within China about the nature of Chinese identity. While the dynamics of day-to-day, or even year-by-year, negotiations between China and Japan will go up and down, they are not for the most part relevant to the deeper discursive and ideological issues that collective memory of World War II has created within China. The areas concerning relations with Japan, while important, are instrumental and temporary; what is more, they are capable of being addressed within the context of ordinary diplomacy. Much of China's new stress on war memory is tied to dynamics that have very little to do with Japan, particularly the reality of Japan as it is today. In fact, opinion polls show that many Chinese, especially elites, have respect for certain aspects of Japanese society.[30]

This is also the reason that many of the gestures that observers and external bodies suggest for bringing about Sino-Japanese reconciliation, whether further apologies from Japan or the writing of joint textbooks, are unlikely to bring about a final resolution to the issue.[31] These are rationalist responses to what is an emotional and ideological phenomenon. They are based on the assumption that specific actions would alter a variety of elements that are deeply embedded within Chinese identity, one of which is the sense that it is safer to examine, argue about, and mourn what happened during the Second World War than to face up to the internal conflicts that have wracked China since then. China is not so much in conflict with the Japanese as with itself, over issues that include economic inequality and ethnic tensions.

The book begins with a brief account of what happened in China during World War II. I suggest that it was order, rather than the furtherance of democracy and freedom, that was the primary goal of all the main Chinese participants. The first chapter then goes on to review the Cold War years and the changing nature of the discourse about World War II in international and domestic politics. In the first, short phase of the postwar period, Nationalist China was able to draw on its wartime record to redefine its position in international society, shifting its status from a partly colonized power to a major, if weak, sovereign actor. But that strand of postwar discourse was associated with the Nationalists and did not survive their collapse on the mainland. From 1949 on, Mao's China was determined to separate itself from most of the Nationalist record, and as a result, during the Cold War, discussion of the conflict against Japan was restricted mostly to the Communist contributions to a "people's war" of anti-Japanese resistance.

The next four chapters deal with post–Cold War China's turn toward a new embrace of the memory of the war. The academic world in China, discussed in Chapter 2, was one of the first sectors to take advantage of the relatively nondoctrinaire view of research encouraged by paramount leader Deng Xiaoping and the reformists he appointed, including Hu Yaobang and Zhao Ziyang, as well as the new stress on nationalist discourse encouraged by figures such as the ideologically conservative Hu Qiaomu. One aspect of the new openness was a willingness to encourage research on a variety of previously forbidden areas of historical study, including the Nationalist war effort. I will examine the ways in which different aspects of the wartime period have been explored as part of China's changing historiography, including the role of the Nationalists and Communists, China's international alliances, collaboration with the Japanese, and crucially, the formation of the post-1945 order and China's role within that order.

In Chapters 3 and 4, I turn to public sites of memory within China in the 1990s. Since the 1980s, China has developed several strands of public remembering of the war years, a process reflected in a variety of institutions and entities that transmit collective memory, including museums, television programs and films, public art, and popular writing. These entities, in which the war against Japan is used as a foundation myth for a new vision of Chinese identity, have been highly influential in the shaping of contemporary Chinese nationalism.

Looking at public sites of war memory since the turn of the millennium, we see that much of the attention has moved from books to film and social media, with the latter providing a space for unofficial voices to comment on the contemporary significance of the conflict's legacy. Whether it is television host Cui Yongyuan discussing the fate of Chinese war veterans, or anonymous rebels swapping views on battle tactics online, the idea of the war and the postwar continues to be relevant even in cyberspace.

We then move, in Chapter 5, from the discourse dominated by Beijing to a more local exploration of wartime identity: the case of Chongqing. This city in southwest China was the temporary wartime capital of China from 1937 to 1946, where the Nationalist leader Chiang Kai-shek led the war effort in exile. In the past quarter century, Chongqing has developed its own identity in part by resurrecting the history of the wartime period. Chongqing's celebration of the Nationalist war effort has entered into unstated competition with the Beijing-centered discourse. I also examine other local stories that have recently been brought to light, including fuller accounts of Communist headquarters at Yan'an, and memories of the 1942 famine in Henan.

Chapter 6 turns from the domestic to the international, exploring the ways in which China has been using aspects of the Second World War to bolster its standing and claims in international society, particularly as it relates to regional order in East Asia. A revival of interest in topics such as the Cairo Conference of 1943 has fueled attempts to reassess the process that led to the post-1945 order. These ideas have shaped not only direct negotiating tactics, but also the discourse within which China presents itself to the wider world.

Ever since 1945, Britain has used a variety of tropes relating to World War II to shape its national identity. This was especially true during the debates leading up to and following the Brexit decision of June 2016.[32] World War II metaphors served as a substitute for those who felt that Britain's identity needed to be reshaped but could not define an attractive vision to counter the cosmopolitan, pro-European definition of the United Kingdom.

Unlike Britain, China is not suffering from status anxiety. Yet its ideological cupboard is relatively bare. It is still having a hard time defining its economic and security vision as anything other than an increasingly authoritarian not-America. Looking to the past is problematic because so many events cannot be discussed. Chinese president Xi Jinping's proscription against "historical ni-hilism" points to a new desire to close off discussion of sensitive issues such as the Cultural Revolution. It is also still immensely difficult to talk in a full and frank way about figures such as Mao Zedong and Deng Xiaoping.

The Second World War, on the other hand, provides a useful episode to look back to. It provides China with the opportunity to present itself, both at home and abroad, as being a victim of circumstances outside its control (invasion by a hostile power), but also as having been able to resist those circumstances and having contributed to international security (the global antifascist alliance). China has been attempting to re-create an identity it was forging in the 1930s and 1940s, as a rising power that took a cooperative and powerful role at a time of immense global crisis, as a key wartime ally. In doing so, it has also created a subtle corollary: the idea that China is also a postwar state. This is "postwar" in the sense of a period that defined countries by their experience of war, whether as Ally or Axis, and most crucially, by what they made of the aftermath. Today, as China rediscovers its wartime history, we can expect to hear a great deal more about the war itself and the "Chinese postwar."

To understand that postwar, we need to appreciate the significance of the war itself. To the West, the term "Sino-Japanese War" captures the period from 1937 to 1945, with the term "China-Burma-India Theater" used after Pearl Harbor. For the Chinese, the conflict has, since the very beginning of the war, been called the "War of Resistance against Japan." We turn now to the war itself and how the Chinese saw it, to lay the groundwork for examining how and why it has come back to haunt the very different China of today.

1

Hot War, Cold War

China's Conflicts, 1937–1978

Frank Capra's *Why We Fight* film series was commissioned by General George C. Marshall to win the hearts and minds of US audiences during the Second World War. The sixth film, *The Battle of China* (1944), ends with scenes of marching Chinese soldiers as the soundtrack plays the anthem "The March of the Volunteers," by the Chinese composer and revolutionary Nie Er. A stirring voiceover defines China's war against Japan as part of a "struggle of freedom against slavery, civilization against barbarism." The film closes, as do others in the series, with a caption displaying the words of General George Marshall: "The victory of the democracies can only be complete with the *utter defeat* of the war machines of Germany and Japan." The V for Victory then appears as the Liberty Bell rings.[1]

The words and ideas used in Capra's film—freedom, liberty, democracy—were mainstays of the language used among the Western Allies to explain the conflict. All of the Allied belligerents developed clear narratives about why they fought in the Second World War. Those narratives changed both during and after the war, but they have an identifiable core that is widely recognized. For the United States and Britain, the narrative was of a war to save freedom. For the USSR, it was an existential conflict for the survival of state and society. There is little recognition, at least in the West, of China's wartime narrative. Where it is mentioned at all, it is told as the story of a China that was a feeble and irrelevant partner in the war against Japan and was ultimately "lost" to communism. The historian Hans van de Ven describes it as a story of "Nationalist military incompetence and . . . a militarist and authoritarian regime mired in corruption."[2] Few in the West have explored China's wartime goals as seen through Chinese eyes. One fact, however, stands central. Despite Capra's claim, China did not portray its own efforts in terms of freedom, liberty, and democracy. During the war itself, ideas of order, rather than of freedom, were central to Chinese conceptions of the war's purpose.

Readers who come to this book with an interest in the legacy and memory of China's war may know little about the actual trajectory of the war in China, even if they have a good overall knowledge of the war in Europe and in Japan. For that reason, I give in the next section a sketch of the major events of the war. My intention is not to provide a detailed narrative of the conflict, which can be found elsewhere.[3] Instead, it is to argue that the meaning of the war for the majority of the Chinese who were fighting was significantly different from its meaning for their American and British allies. Although some Chinese ideas about wartime and postwar order were shared with the co-belligerents, they stemmed from very different assumptions on the Chinese part—assumptions which retain significance in contemporary China.

Origins and Trajectory of China's World War II

During the early twentieth century, two major ideological forces grew in East Asia: Japanese imperialism and Chinese nationalism. The former mutated into a form that demanded Japanese "leadership" through the ideology of pan-Asianism, which meant the colonization and occupation of other parts of Asia. The latter was a manifestation of a growing dissatisfaction with China's weak position in the world since the mid-nineteenth century, most obviously manifested in the Opium Wars and other acts of invasion and violence that characterized the foreign presence in China.[4]

Japan's empire expanded rapidly in East Asia, starting with Taiwan (1895), reaching into the Liaodong Peninsula (1905) and Korea (1910), and making headway in the form of an increasingly strong militarized presence in North China (1920s), though stopping short of full occupation there. A turning point came on 18 September 1931, when the Guandong Army, stationed in northeastern China (Manchuria), launched a coup that occupied the whole of the region within months.[5] During the following six years, Sino-Japanese relations became increasingly fractious. Chiang Kai-shek's government pursued a policy of avoiding active and public resistance to Japan but made it clear that further breaches of sovereignty would not be tolerated.[6]

The test came on 7 July 1937, when a relatively minor skirmish between Chinese troops and locally garrisoned Japanese soldiers on the outskirts of Beiping (as Beijing was then called) turned into a wider confrontation. Facing further Japanese territorial demands in North China, Chiang decided that the moment to resist had arrived. Chinese troops pushed back, and, within days, Chiang had ordered a second front around Shanghai. The first phase of the war was marked by fierce fighting in northern and central China. Nationalist troops were forced to retreat from Beiping, Shanghai, Nanjing, and much of the surrounding territory, but they did not withdraw without resistance.[7] During that same period the Nationalists and Communists, who had been in conflict, formed the United Front, an uneasy alliance against the Japanese.

In late 1937, Chiang's government moved its capital from Nanjing to temporary headquarters in Chongqing, in southwestern China. Chongqing was subjected to repeated Japanese air raids from 1938 to 1943 (with the years from 1938 to 1941 being particularly fierce). The first year of the war saw the Nationalist government retreat from much of eastern China, and the central Chinese city of Wuhan fell in October 1938.[8]

Wang Jingwei, a senior Nationalist politician and colleague of Chiang's, grew increasingly concerned about the seeming hopelessness of China's wartime position. In December 1938 he defected and announced that he would start negotiations with Japan to form a collaborationist government. It was not until 30 March 1940 that he was able to establish what he termed the "return to the capital" at Nanjing, where he set himself up as leader of a new government in the Japanese-occupied city. He justified this return on the grounds that he was the rightful heir of Sun Yat-sen, and that Chiang was an interloper who had betrayed the Nationalist cause—not least because of his temporary alliance with the Communists.[9]

The initial Japanese advance became bogged down in late 1938. From then on, China's territory was divided into three roughly delineated sectors. The Nationalist government was dominant in the southwest and in parts of central China, with the firmest level of control around its capital at Chongqing and surrounding

Sichuan province. In the northwest and in other parts of central China there was a strong Communist presence. The most well-integrated base area, under Mao Zedong's command, was in the Shaanxi-Gansu-Ningxia region, with its capital at Yan'an. In eastern China, beginning in 1940, Wang Jingwei's government controlled some cities, especially Nanjing and Shanghai, but it had little strength in the countryside.

In 1941, worsening relations between the United States and Japan led to the Japanese strike on Pearl Harbor.[10] This event brought the United States (and Britain) into the war on China's side. Chiang was aware that he could not hope to defeat Japan without foreign help, but the cooperation among the Allies remained fraught throughout the war. Chiang clashed with General Joseph Stilwell, his American chief of staff, and the reputation of the Nationalist government in the United States became more and more negative as reports emerged of black marketeering, corruption, and extortion of taxes and services from the population. The Chinese, in turn, became increasingly angered at China's low position on the list of Allied priorities and at the United States' unwillingness to understand that nearly five years of unassisted warfare against the Japanese had destroyed huge amounts of China's state capacity.[11]

In November 1943, Chiang took part in the Allied conference at Cairo during which the fate of postwar Asia was discussed. In spring 1944, the Japanese launched Operation Ichigō, their last major thrust into central China, which destroyed large parts of the already enfeebled Nationalist military capacity. Nonetheless, under Allied pressure, Chiang authorized troops to take part in the campaign in Burma in 1944, in which American, British Empire, and Chinese troops operated together to force the Japanese to retreat from that occupied British colony. Meanwhile, American military officials made their first visit to the Communist-controlled areas (the "Dixie Mission"), where they met Mao Zedong and other top Communist leaders. In 1944, relations between Chiang and Stilwell reached a breaking point, and Stilwell was recalled from China. Yet despite the increasingly strained relations between the United States and China, President Franklin D. Roosevelt engineered the elevation of China to the highest levels of global diplomacy in the postwar world, arguing for China to take a place as one of the permanent members of the Security Council of the new United Nations organization.[12]

The war in Asia ended very suddenly in August 1945, with the atomic bombing of Japan. When the conflict was over, China was in a strange position: simultaneously more damaged physically and psychologically than it had been for decades, but also more influential on the global stage than at any time since the mid-nineteenth century.

A Nationalist War

The war against Japan was one of the most important events in the formation of modern Chinese nationalism. It provided circumstances that ultimately helped to create a unified state bound together by an ideology of legitimacy drawn from the concept of "the people," defined as a political body in their own right: a modern nation as opposed to a premodern empire.

This was not a simple or linear process. During the war, it was hard work to turn the Chinese people as a whole—especially those who were geographically remote from urban centers, or illiterate, or unable to grasp politics—into believing ideological nationalists.[13] Chiang Kai-shek's son Chiang Ching-kuo, who worked in more rural parts of China during the war, noted the lack of nationalist sentiment in wartime Ganzhou, and Nationalist propagandists felt that they had to educate refugees in the significance of the war.[14] Among elites, however, the conviction grew that the war was forcing China to develop a powerful form of national identity.

The war against Japan forced China to concentrate on an invasion by one enemy alone. This contrasts with the situation that had existed previously, which Ruth Rogaski calls "hypercolonization." The city of Tianjin, for example, was the subject of a range of different colonial powers, including France, Britain, and even Austria-Hungary.[15] In some ways, this diffused the question of precisely who was the imperialist opponent that China wanted to resist. The Indian independence movement was strengthened by the existence of one clear invading force, the British; the Korean movement, likewise, could define itself against one colonial occupier, the Japanese. China was in the odd situation of being a country that was in part sovereign, in part colonized, but with no one clear enemy against which to unite. The British, French, Americans, and Japanese were the most important, but they were not the only opponents for Chinese patriots, and the vague enemy of "imperialism" did not, in and of itself, provide a sufficient binding glue for a debate about what sort of country China should be once it had expelled the foreigners.[16]

This changed in 1937—not at once, or completely, but substantially. The war against Japan did not create a whole new political discourse of Chinese nationalism. Many of the ideas had been discussed before the outbreak of war, but they were developed or focused in ways that presented them as being in service of the war effort. The process of creating the model of the modern Chinese nation-state was still very much in flux during the war. The view of scholars on this question of nationalist discourse has shifted over the decades. In the 1960s, the classic works of Westerners such as Chalmers Johnson, Mark Selden, and others attributed nation-formation chiefly to the war itself (identifying "peasant nationalism" as the trigger for the formation of a communist state).[17] In more recent years, there has been a trend toward arguments that nationalism was subsumed by local identities.[18] Yet there is evidence that a greater sense of nationalism was already in formation by the time the war broke out, and that the war then changed the nature of that nationalism. That emergent nationalism was real, but it was inchoate and protean.

In comparison with China, the Western powers appeared to have a clearer, better-defined narrative as to why they fought the war: essentially, to preserve liberal freedoms. To be sure, this view of the Western narrative has not gone unchallenged. Keith Lowe questioned it in his book *The Fear and the Freedom*, arguing that both Britain and the United States portrayed their war efforts as being in service of democracy, in the liberal sense of wider public consensual participation in politics, but that the reality failed to live up to the ideal in many ways.[19] The United States permitted legal segregation across nearly a third of its territory, and Britain still ran a large, nonconsensual empire. In addition, both countries were allied with the decidedly nonliberal USSR. Despite these conditions, the primary Anglophone discourse of the war centered on liberal tropes of democracy and freedom, such as Roosevelt's description in 1940 of the United States as "the great arsenal of democracy."[20]

The narratives of the United States and Britain diverged during the war years. The United States was not fighting for freedom at home; only a dire scenario would have seen a fascist takeover of the country by a foreign invader. For Britain, off the coast of occupied Europe, the notion of occupation and destruction of a liberal, parliamentary system at home (which did not extend to the empire) was a distinct possibility. This fear was reinforced by the home islands' relatively small size and the strong, London-dominated media that spread the message. Despite this divergence, both countries had strong political narratives that explained "why we fight."

Such a narrative of "why we fight" was much harder for China to construct. Chinese nationalism was a patchy phenomenon that had not yet turned peasants into Chinese—to adapt Eugen Weber's classic title *Peasants into Frenchmen*.[21] It is worth identifying the most important themes that underlay the dominant political discourse of nationalism during the war years. Some of these ideas were common to the Nationalists, Communists, and collaborationists. Others were variations on a theme; and still others separated the actors.

The Chinese discourse was not primarily about the definition of a free (in the sense of liberal) nation-state, but rather about the creation of a sovereign, ordered, and territorially united one. Perhaps the most important difference between China and its Western Allies was the sense that the first product of the war should be order, not freedom. Wartime Chinese nationalism articulated itself in two important areas: domestic political and economic order, and global order. Early on, the war was defined as a "war of resistance" (*Kangzhan*), but discussions also began to define what the purpose of the conflict was from the Chinese side as well as what the shape of the postwar order would be.

Order over Freedom

A defining characteristic of early twentieth-century China was the lack of fixed order.

China's technically sovereign status was made diffuse by concessions to imperialism as well as by the militarism that had torn apart domestic politics. The establishment of the Nationalist government under Chiang Kai-shek in 1928 provided a flawed and uneasy sort of unification. In the parts of the country it controlled, the government made advances in certain areas (transport infrastructure, regaining tariff autonomy, diplomacy) while failing in others (rural poverty, renewing the party's own structures). These prewar projects provide an outline of the kind of state the Nationalists were seeking to build: a corporatist economy with a vanguard party in charge of a constrained political and public sphere. Structure and symbolism were often as important as substance. The establishment of structures of government under an executive branch, called the Executive Yuan, was intended to add a rational-bureaucratic element to a political system underpinned by military force. Tools such as architecture, seen in the grand plans for rebuilding the capital at Nanjing, became part of this discourse.[22]

The desire for order became stronger as war with Japan approached. We can see it especially in the writings of Jiang Tingfu, one of China's most prominent historians. After returning from studies in the United States, Jiang held faculty positions at Nankai and Tsinghua Universities and then took up political service, working for the Nationalist government at home and abroad in roles that included ambassador to the USSR, representative of China at the newly formed United Nations Relief and Rehabilitation Administration (UNRRA), and ambassador to the United Nations. In 1938, Jiang wrote about China's need to modernize fast, in the face of multiple threats. He advocated natural science and mechanized agriculture as the essential elements of modernization, echoing the calls of the May Fourth Movement. That movement, whose most notable moment took place on 4 May 1919 with mass demonstrations against Japanese imperialism, held that science and democracy would rejuvenate China.[23]

Jiang advocated a centralized form of authority which would, where necessary, override the "popular will." He argued that before the First World War there had been a clearly defined single path toward industrialized modernity, and that China, Japan, Turkey, and Russia were traveling along it. "But after the Great War, thanks to the Soviet revolution and the fascist movements in Italy, Germany, and Japan, the world's political and economic system was turned upside down. . . . At the moment, the world doesn't have a common direction, and every country has its own answer as to what modern culture is." Nevertheless, he wrote, a wide range of groups—"left-wing, right-wing, imperialist, anti-imperialist, man, woman, white, yellow, old, young"—all supported "natural science and mechanized industry." Jiang characterized the alternatives of modernization and tradition in the starkly social Darwinist terms that had been commonplace since the late Qing dynasty: "Those who use [modernized] culture to preserve the national territory survived; those who can't were exterminated. This is the iron rule of modern history, and there is no nation that can violate it."[24] He went on: "In China, Japan,

Turkey, and Russia, modernization has been top-down, and has often violated the popular will. The promotion of reform has to rely on the centralization of political authority." He repeated the point: "From these four countries' modernization processes, we can obtain a common conclusion: countries where political authority is more centralized have a greater success in promoting modernization."[25] Order, that is, should trump freedom at crucial moments for development.

Later in the war Jiang Tingfu's views on political freedom and modernization would change significantly, after he spent time in the United States and became inspired by Roosevelt's New Deal. But at this point, early in the war against Japan, his was an elite voice, well connected in government, speculating on how to achieve the successful formation of the nation-state. Jiang reiterated the need for modernization, with particular reference to wartime preparation, in an essay on "national strength." In this essay, which deals with the transformation of the nation through wartime institutions and processes aimed at improving the economy and healthcare, Jiang equates nurturing bodily health with maintaining a healthy body politic. He describes Nazi Germany's Four-Year Plan and the USSR's Five-Year Plan as "national defense plans," noting that young people were being trained as warriors and that reproduction was encouraged: "Stalin and Hitler both put plenty of stress on women's childbearing, their reasons being preparation for war."[26] Jiang contrasted this view with that of Britain, citing a speech by Anthony Eden, who had resigned in February 1938 as British foreign secretary, in which Eden asked whether those who loved freedom would be as willing to make sacrifices as those in the authoritarian countries. He concluded from Eden's speech that democracies "have not greatly gone in for developing national strength." For China, the most important task was "psychological reform." This kind of reform necessitated "wholesale modernization," from the military to the educational system.[27]

At this time, Jiang strongly advocated the establishment of a polity that looked very much like the "total defense state" that had formed in Japan as the government became militarized:

> Some ask: after the war is over, do we not want to restore the situation as it was in normal times? But we have to know: at this historical juncture, war *is* the normality! So-called peace is just a period of preparing for war, a time of political and economic struggle. In times up to the present, we have no way of avoiding conflict. We cannot retreat to protect our independence. . . . This is a whole historical stage; it is not just a matter of three to five years.[28]

Jiang was not alone in expressing this sense of war as "normality." Chinese intellectuals and politicians of the era spoke of it as being an "exceptional time" (*feichang shiqi*), an idea reminiscent of the "state of exception" defined by the philosopher Giorgio Agamben, adapting the idea of the legal theorist Carl Schmitt. In this phrasing, "exceptional" implied the heightened state of crisis and expectation of conflict that marked the early twentieth century, in contrast to a perception of a (perhaps nonexistent) earlier period of peace.[29] While Jiang saw the importance of a strong economy, he understood that national feeling might also stem from causes that were not simply economic. He discussed two cases that had taken place in recent years in Germany. He noted that local Germans involved in the Ruhr crisis of 1923 had refused to accept exemptions they had been offered on indemnity taxes; he also saw the heavy vote in the 1935 Saar plebiscite in favor of return to Germany, despite financial incentives from the French to vote the other way in both cases. "This kind of national spirit depends on ourselves to develop it," noted Jiang. "Foreigners can't help us, nor can they stop us."[30] In 1938, Jiang's views were consistent with the Nationalist Party's view that the war should be used to build a sense of national identity on terms that would bring about an ordered state, rather than on the basis of individual liberties or collective democracy as the most important values.

Was the wartime Nationalist state in fact authoritarian, and, if so, what sort of authoritarianism did it espouse? At base, its ideology was defined more by values than by a system. The framework behind it was the Three People's Principles of Sun Yat-sen—nationalism, rights, and people's livelihood—but much of the language defining those ideas was general, vague, and self-contradictory. A dominant section of the party clearly had right-wing political views.[31] One critic at the time who stressed what he saw as the fascist nature of the Nationalists was Hu Qiaomu, a senior politician, theorist, and historian of the Chinese Communist Party (CCP), who wrote in 1943, as Mussolini's regime was collapsing in Italy, that the Nationalists had "received significant influence" from the Italian fascists.[32]

Although the conservative and fascist elements in the Nationalist Party were undeniably powerful, they were not the only important elements of the party. T. V. Soong (Song Ziwen), a major figure in the internal mechanics of the party, along with politicians such as Sun Ke (Sun Fo), the son of Sun Yat-sen, were relatively more liberal. The Nationalist government was a strange mixture of different political ideologies, brought together in service of a wider, but vaguely defined, national project. All of its adherents shared the desire to create a sovereign state under its control. The Communist Party expressed clearer ideas about order than did the Nationalists. It used the period when it was based in Yan'an to experiment with a new type of society, reexamining ideas on a range of issues from taxation to military strategy to women's rights. There were, of course, many alternative Communist experiments in government (for instance in Taihang and Shandong, to name just two), but Mao's base area produced a vision of what a postwar order would be like, with traditional class relationships being revised or overturned. The collaborationist governments varied greatly in their longevity and state capacity, but the most prominent of them, the government of Wang Jingwei, articulated the idea that China would have a Nationalist government that would be part of a wider, Axis-defined order.[33] Each of these models, though distinct, was posited on the idea of an integrated Chinese geobody that would have sovereignty.

Although order was key to the postwar visions of the Chinese politicians and thinkers, while ideas of democracy or freedom were more marginal, building order was not purely a matter of military control. Part of the new order was the idea of a revised social contract, in which the welfare obligations of the state would be significantly increased. China's reformers drew on ideas of their American and British mentors, who believed strongly that a postwar state should stress social security as much as military security.[34] The Atlantic Charter, for instance, issued in August 1941 by Roosevelt and Winston Churchill, included the injunction that the postwar settlement "will afford to all nations the means of dwelling in safety within their own boundaries, and . . . will afford assurance that all the men in all the lands may live out their lives in freedom from fear and want."[35]

The idea of state responsibility for aspects of social policy was not wholly new; it was a long-standing part of the Chinese imperial state. During the Ming dynasty, local elites came together with local government officials to deal with the aftermath of disaster, using identity documents and register systems to provide relief for victims of flood and famine.[36] Nonetheless, the war against Japan created new opportunities for such projects. The massive refugee crisis that spread across China spurred the creation of a network of refugee rehabilitation centers to deal with the tens of millions of people who had been forced into sudden exile. There was a clear interest in maintaining a population that could produce large numbers of healthy young fighting men, grow food, and fight disease. As a result, healthcare and hygiene became the subject of major social reform. Programs of child nutrition, vaccination, and obstetrics and gynecology were developed, along with the improvement of living conditions. After air raids, local governments were tasked with assessing damage and offering compensation.[37]

Such efforts were partial and patchy, being much more evident in the parts of China that were under strong Nationalist control (such as Sichuan) than in those where it was weak or contested. However, the wider intentions became part of a discourse that was further emphasized in media and through public education programs.[38] The idea of China as a country that valued social provision helped to shape views of what the nation-state might be. It also created a fertile environment for the Communist Party, whose promises of radical social reform quickly outpaced those of a Nationalist government that made significant plans but was unable to deliver on many of them.

A related wartime goal was to create a new economic order. A large part of China's instability in the early twentieth century had to do with its unstable finances and lack of autonomy over them. The establishment of the Imperial Maritime Customs in 1854 brought reliable flows of revenue into the country, but the price was to outsource a very significant part of China's capacity to levy tax to a body largely run by foreigners—Britons, in particular.[39] (All but one of the service's inspectors general between 1854 and 1950 were British, with the one exception being American.) Some scholars have given relatively positive accounts of the interwar Chinese economy.[40] It was, however, still highly dependent on the policies of other powers, not regaining tariff autonomy until 1930.

Because of the continuing dependency of the Chinese economy, economic and financial stability became a powerful touchstone for nationalist thinkers. Jiang Tingfu identified "warlords" and "political factions" as agents of national disunity and stressed that China needed to work toward "economic unity," in which internal economic and personal security would be linked. He noted that the United States had the advantage of operating as a single economic unit and argued that "Europe's most advanced people have long advocated studying American examples and organizing a pan-European united country. Today's economics demand a relatively large economic unit to produce efficiency."[41]

During the war, the economy was placed under unprecedented strain, with marketing networks, infrastructure, and basics such as the currency itself all threatened. The Communist response was to emphasize the importance of self-sufficiency and the development of an autarkic regional order, a tactic made more relevant in Yan'an when the Nationalists blockaded the region after

1941. The vision of Wang Jingwei's collaborationist government, by contrast, was to integrate China into a Japanese-dominated regional system.

A New Global Order

During the war years, the Western Allies gave China greater sovereignty in part as a gesture so that there would be less pressure to liberate other still-colonized societies. In 1942–1943, the United States pressured Britain to end extraterritoriality, and, in fact, Britain had been slowly reducing its imperial commitments in China since the 1920s. It did not, however, reduce its broader imperial commitments in Asia: Indian independence was not assured until immediately following the war, and Britain maintained a strong imperial presence in Malaya for years afterward. France and the Netherlands also made the recapture of their Asian colonies a key task of their postwar agenda. The elevation of China in the global community did not mark a bright new postimperialist world, but rather a deeply compromised one in which empires would be a factor for years to come.

This situation allowed the Nationalists to define themselves as anti-imperialists with a new role to play in Asia. During the war, Chiang Kai-shek wrote frequently of the need to liberate Asian colonies, and in February 1942 he traveled to India to visit Jawaharlal Nehru and Mahatma Gandhi.[42] Chiang had begun planning for the postwar period long before the war actually came to an end. Between the Japanese invasion in 1937 and Pearl Harbor in 1941, China spent much of the war on the back foot. But with the American entry in 1941, which Chiang, like Churchill, viewed as the turning point in the global war, the Chinese leader began to think about what the postwar world would look like and what China's role within it would be.

Chiang certainly regarded China as a major player in the postwar world. In his diary, he laid out a clear statement of intent. On 20 December 1941, just after Pearl Harbor, Chiang detailed what he would demand as restitution after the war: Tibet and Kowloon from Britain, Outer Mongolia and Xinjiang from the USSR, Manchuria and Dairen (Dalian) from Japan, and the end of extraterritoriality and concessions.[43] The following year he drew up further plans that included the return of additional territories, such as Taiwan, Manchuria, and independent Outer Mongolia. The plan also called for independence and a new Asian structure of support for India (at that time in turmoil because of the nationalist Quit India movement), Thailand (then essentially under Japanese domination), Burma, and Vietnam.[44] This was an intriguing mixture of anticolonial nationalism, attempts to tie America into the region (through encouraging the building of US naval bases), and the creation of a sphere of influence where China would de facto become more influential.

In December 1943, Chiang wrote about the communiqué that was issued after the conclusion of the Cairo Conference. His diary shows that he was thinking of the geopolitics of the agreements that had been made in Cairo: the promise to restore Taiwan and the Pescadores (Penghu) Islands to China and to create an independent Korea were key to a postwar settlement.[45] But the visual message created at Cairo was even more important. The photographs of Chiang Kai-shek and his wife, Song Meiling, sitting next to President Roosevelt and Prime Minister Churchill documented the first occasion at which a non-Western leader had sat in a position of equality in a wartime alliance next to the two most powerful Anglophone leaders in the world. In addition, Song Meiling was far from being simply a first lady; she was perhaps the most prominent female politician at the time, competing only with Eleanor Roosevelt for the title. The pictures symbolized the anti-imperialist goals of the war in clear terms. Like the Nationalists, the CCP also stressed the importance of anti-imperialism as a wartime goal; so, in its own way, did Wang Jingwei's government, arguing that its coerced alliance with Japan was in fact "pan-Asianism," and emphatically not a new form of empire.

The ethical compass points for mobilization in the rhetoric of wartime China were these: ideas of uncompromised sovereignty and order at home, and a moral mission to free those still colonized overseas. One other element of the narrative was the idea of China as a country that was fighting in a righteous cause. It had always been anti-imperialist, but now it was in a position to prove it. Even in the present day there is a widespread perception in the Western world, shaped both by contemporary perceptions and by the postwar "victimization" narrative, that China's participation in the war was as a victim rather than as a belligerent.[46] The counterargument has returned as an important element of contemporary discourse in China, both at the elite and the popular level. The state now has an interest in reviving ideas of China as an Allied belligerent, and the Chinese themselves have an emotional interest in bringing to mind their own stories of active resistance rather than passive suffering. The idea of China as an active anti-imperialist state became powerful during the war itself, and remains so now.

The Cold War Years

The World War mutated into the Cold War. China's relationship with the legacy of the war years during this time was quite different from that of any of the other belligerent powers because of the turbulent global events that took place. The Nationalist government stayed in office just long enough for a Western-facing China to be embedded into the international system before it collapsed, resulting in the isolation of its successor Communist regime. There had been no guarantee that the Nationalists would survive until 1945; the postwar regional order in Asia was shaped by the unforeseen fact that they did not last very long after that date.

During the Cold War, China engaged with the reality and legacy of the war with Japan in several phases. The first actually began in 1941, after Pearl Harbor, when the entry of the United States into the war in Asia made it clear that the Allies were likely to win and that China's status in Asia, under a Nationalist government, could be reimagined. This always fragile phase ended decisively in 1949 with the Communist victory in the Chinese Civil War. The next phase lasted from 1949 to the early 1980s. During this period, the war was mentioned on a range of occasions, including anniversaries, but interpretations largely centered on the war's utility in shaping the ultimate victory of the Chinese Communist Party, and it was a relatively marginal trope in the context of much fiercer class-based discourses such as the Great Leap Forward and the Cultural Revolution. The most recent phase started in the early 1980s, after the end of the Cultural Revolution, and was marked by the promulgation of the CCP's "Resolution on Certain Questions in Our Party's History" in 1981, which offered an official though partial repudiation of the years of turmoil under Mao. It was interrupted but not ended by the 1989 Tiananmen crisis. Since then, there has been a continuing emphasis on the Second World War in Chinese political discourse. The end of the global Cold War in 1989 was important for China, but less so than the opening to the United States in 1971–1972. The end of European communism did not mark a fundamental shift in China's understanding of its wartime past comparable to the change in historical perspective in Eastern Europe, where memory of the war changed profoundly with the end of Soviet domination of the region.[47]

A Global Divide on Postwar History?

One notable feature of the division of Eurasia at the start of the Cold War was the establishment of distinct circuits of memory. One narrative, centered on the role of the United States and the British Empire, dominated in the liberal states of North America and Western Europe, with Western-oriented nonliberal states such as Spain and Greece deploying rather different versions of this narrative. Another variant of this narrative developed in Japan. A different narrative, centered on the USSR's role, dominated in Eastern Europe. These two narratives had relatively little interaction with each other during most of the Cold War. They also interacted very little with the narrative of the war that emerged in China during the same period. The political isolation of China during those years had a profound effect on collective memory of the war years; it had hardly any connection to other circuits of memory, other than with the USSR in a limited fashion in the 1950s, before the split between the two communist states.

During the Cold War, Europe and Asia developed two regional orders that were superficially similar in their division between capitalist and communist regimes but were structurally distinct. In Europe, the division of the continent was settled at the Yalta Conference in 1945. One half was under US dominance (the North Atlantic Treaty Organization [NATO], the European Communities), the other under Soviet dominance (the Council for Mutual Economic Assistance [COMECON], the Warsaw Pact). Ultimately, this system proved relatively stable. The major European Cold War flashpoints were around the most anomalous part of the settlement, Berlin, in 1948 and 1961. But significant levels of communication existed between the two sides: Moscow and Washington, DC, maintained official relations, and most European capitals were linked by diplomacy across the Iron Curtain.

When Hitler's Germany surrendered in May 1945, a chapter of history—meaning one frame of historical interpretation—came to an end. The Cold War would freeze much of the continent, but both Western and Eastern blocs came to agree on one aspect of their narrative: Nazi Germany had been a menace to European security, with an exceptionally immoral domestic policy that had to be defeated. In Western Europe, an American-dominated settlement meant that the long-standing rivalry between France and Germany, and the legend of the "stab in the back" that poisoned Germany's sense of its role after World War I, was finally subsumed into a shared understanding of the past and a recognition that it must not be allowed to recur.[48]

No such realignment ever took place in East Asia. First, there was no unified epistemic framework within which to operate. The brief chimera of an American-dominated Asia, in which Nationalist China would lean toward Washington, while Japan remained under US influence and the Western empires retook much of Southeast Asia, dissipated within just a few years. The division of the region into three zones—communist China, North Korea, and North Vietnam; the nonaligned countries; and a Western-dominated zone—was one obstacle. In addition, the Western-dominated zone was not well integrated, containing within it a nascent liberal democracy (Japan), authoritarian and poor developmental states (Taiwan, South Korea), and deeply dysfunctional states (South Vietnam). Unlike in Western Europe, there was no unified liberal discourse relating to the war years.

The new postcolonial states were also hampered in their ability to talk to each other about their shared experience of the Second World War in Asia. This was, in part, another consequence of the collapse of the Nationalist regime. Chiang's aim had been to create a shared community of discourse which would have stretched from Japan to a postcolonial Southeast Asia and possibly India, as well. In that scenario, a unified circuit of memory relating to the war and its significance for shaping postcolonial Asia might have emerged.

In the immediate aftermath of the end of the war with Japan, Chiang had high hopes of establishing an Asian order with his own regime at the center. In August 1945, he was convinced that his own success in signing an agreement with Stalin meant that the CCP's guns had been spiked before they had had a chance to use them. "They don't know the contents of the USSR-China agreement," he wrote of the Communists, in his diary entry of 28 August 1945. "What a pity, they don't know that they've been abandoned by the USSR."[49] By early October, Chiang stressed in conversation with Mao that "the two parties must cooperate, otherwise it is not just bad for the country but also for the CCP. . . . If we can't pull together, then it's World War III."[50] Despite some last-minute negotiations, no real agreement was achieved. Yet Chiang observed with some confidence, "Mao flew back to Yan'an—despite his evil behavior, seeking the opportunity to rebel, and the fact that he is an obstacle to unity, I decided he has no possibility of achieving this goal and obstructing unity."[51] This turned out to be a misjudgment, to put it mildly.

Chiang's projected scenario was based on a variety of assumptions that began to unravel almost immediately. The unraveling was uncanny in its inconvenient timing, if the goal was to create a stable structure. If China's government had fallen apart immediately after the end of the war, or indeed during it, then the other Allies would not have made plans based on the assumption that the Nationalists would continue in power. If they had continued in office for a longer time, a different, more stable order in East Asia would have been more likely to develop.

In retrospect, most analysts have concentrated on the factors that caused the downfall of the Nationalist government, supplemented by some speculation about whether or not Chiang could have taken an alternate path. At the time, however, there was an expectation that the existing regime, in some form, would continue for a long period. The bargain struck by the United States was that China's wartime contribution entitled it to a role in shaping the postwar world; the United States clearly expected this situation to last, since it would not otherwise have awarded China a permanent seat on the UN Security Council. Despite the brevity of the Nationalists' postwar spell in power, China did influence a variety of international organizations—notably the United Nations, but also the institutions of the Bretton Woods system.[52]

Nationalist China also had strong views about its role in shaping the postcolonial world, particularly when much of it was not "post" at all, but still colonized. The Roosevelt administration was strongly opposed to traditional empires, and this opposition was translated into a project to raise the status of China in the world order. This was by no means a wholly altruistic attempt. The British realized that a key aim of the United States was to end the British imperial presence in Asia, which would boost American commercial prospects in the region in the postwar.[53] China being thrust into global status was an honor, but it was also a great burden to load onto the shoulders of a country that was much poorer and less industrialized than any of the other powers that fought in the war, and had been torn apart by bombing, refugee crises, and economic blockades.

The nomination of China as one of Roosevelt's "Four Policemen" (with the United States, the USSR, and Britain) was a major elevation for a country that had still been subject to colonial rule on significant parts of its territory at the outbreak of war with Japan in 1937. The American position helped to define a vision of postwar Asia in which China would play a major regional role. Japan, of course, would be under American control, and in the immediate postwar period, the British and French expected that they would regain control of the colonies that had been seized by Japan (including Malaya, Singapore, and Indochina). In one sense, the proposed postwar settlement in Asia was like that at the end of World War I in Europe, in that it created new spheres of influence and confiscated colonies from the powers that had lost the war, which it then redistributed.

But a significant difference between the world of 1919 and that of 1945 was that one of the major Allied belligerents was a strongly anti-imperialist, non-European power: China. In 1919, Japan was non-European, but it rejected Western imperialism rather than imperialism in principle. In 1945, the expectation of the world's leaders—including Stalin—was that Nationalist China (under Chiang Kai-shek) would remain a major power in the region for decades to come and would act as a force critical of empires, even though some of China's desire for influence in the region looked like creating an empire by another name. This outcome would have meant an Asia-Pacific region where the United States would be dominant—allied to China, controlling Japan, and influencing South Korea. Much of the area not under American hegemony would find itself still tied to one European empire or another. The USSR would be confined to a marginal presence in areas such as North Korea and Manchuria. This Asia would have been very different from the one that emerged in practice.

Of course, it never came to pass. Those who were envisioning Asia's future failed to realize that liberation from imperialism was not simply something to be bestowed from above. The forces that had been unleashed by the Japanese occupation (and by the humiliation of the British and French in 1941) could not be reversed, and within a decade, wars against colonialism would shape the region. But the major factor that changed the whole dynamic of the region was the fall of the Chinese Nationalists and the establishment of the People's Republic of China (PRC) under Mao Zedong. The subsequent policy of nonrecognition between the PRC and the United States, followed by the Korean War, set the stage for an uneasy status quo that still affects the region today.

Nonetheless, the 1945–1949 period did see the Nationalist government attempt to create a regional and global role for itself, even though the Civil War was undermining it fatally by the latter part of that period. This period also marked the start of China's creation of an "ethically constitutive story" (to use Rogers Smith's

term for narratives that unite members of a community around a
core, ethically shaped identity) about its own performance in the
war, as well as the first foundations of a circuit of memory that
would have created a narrative relating to the creation of a postwar
Asia centered on Nationalist China. The international architecture
and vectors of memory were being moved into position by 1949.
Unfortunately for the Nationalists, their regime then collapsed.

War Memory during the PRC Years

Between 1946 and 1949, China was embroiled in a vicious civil
war. After uneasy attempts between the Nationalists and Communists to come to an agreement on a coalition government, and
a mediation process led by General George C. Marshall, full-scale
war broke out in late 1946. China had not even begun to recover
from the destruction wreaked during World War II, and now it
found itself torn apart again. During the three years of the Civil
War, the Nationalists lost their initially favorable military position.
The CCP's army was better trained and was able to draw on Soviet assistance, which went some way to counter the US assistance
given to Chiang Kai-shek. Just as important was the increasing lack
of trust in the Nationalist government, which was seen as cor-
rupt, vindictive, and with no overall vision of what China under
its rule should look like. The military situation for the Nationalists had deteriorated beyond recovery by early 1949. Later that year,
Chiang's regime fled to Taiwan, never to return. On 1 October
1949, the CCP declared the establishment of the People's Republic
of China, under Mao Zedong's leadership.[54]

The CCP's victory against the Nationalists was immensely
important for China's future, but it also profoundly affected the

way the country told the story of the recent past. The only me-morialization of the Civil War in China after 1949 was a strident public celebration of the Communist victory. The CCP did not utterly demonize all former enemy soldiers; the regime sought to rehabilitate a range of Nationalist and Japanese prisoners of war in the 1950s. But there was no space for formal commemoration of the Nationalist dead. This space would come to be partially filled, eventually, by the rehabilitation of the Nationalist record in the war against Japan, but that process would not begin until the 1980s, more than three decades later. Meanwhile, the Cold War froze Asia into a particular set of shapes, a set of ideas that congealed into half-formed positions around 1950, meaning that the scope for heroic reinvention of a grand narrative of history was narrower than in Europe.

Europe settled down after 1950 to a "cold" Cold War. Aside from incidents such as the Berlin Wall crisis of 1961, few events occurred to provide a trigger for conventional military conflict. There was time and space in Western Europe, then, to consider the war—the most powerful event influencing discourse within the region—as an important part of the shaping of national iden-tity. This was not a straightforward process: from the French struggle to come to terms with the legacy of the Vichy govern-ment to the changing debates about the nature of the German path to Nazism, there was a vast realm of memory and forgetting about the war.

Reference back to World War II was less frequent in Asia because the Cold War kept turning hot. Even the People's Re-public, keen to find areas of dispute with the capitalist world, did not draw on the idea of an unfair postwar settlement as a primary source of political capital. The outbreak of the Korean War in 1950

triggered circumstances that would profoundly reshape the still nascent circuits of memory in Asia. Mao was pressured by Stalin
and Kim Il-Sung to invade South Korea, but eventually China
joined the war of its own accord, thereby triggering an unneces-
sary crisis in Asia. After the armistice of 1953, the United States
refused to accord recognition to the PRC, thereby lengthening the
crisis through stubbornness.[55] The problem lay not just in the fact
that the PRC was ideologically opposed to the United States (as
was the USSR), but that it was isolated from it diplomatically, and
therefore scientifically, educationally, and culturally, as well; after
the Sino-Soviet split in 1960, China and the USSR were also effectively separated. This circumstance placed China firmly onto a
track where its memory of wartime was almost entirely internally
generated, with little opportunity for its understanding of the wartime years to be affected by an interchange of memories and experiences from beyond China.

During the Mao years, the war against Japan shifted from being
a central part of the project of national self-definition to becoming
a more secondary, though by no means absent, part of the political
and public culture. Discussion of the war did not disappear from
public life, but there was distinctly less in China than in almost
any other country that had made a significant contribution to the
war. Chan Yang's fine study of the period from 1949 to 1982 shows
that memory of the war was used at official and more grassroots
levels, for instance in 1965, when a major commemoration of the
Nanjing Massacre took place in that city. Kirk Denton's detailed
account of Chinese museum culture since the 1980s also demonstrates that there were numerous films, paintings, and events that
drew on the war against Japan to bolster nationalism during the
Mao era.[56] However, most wartime memory was still promoted

by official state channels, which tended to emphasize the CCP's role in the war rather than that of "China" as a whole. While mentions of Nationalist contributions to the war did exist, there was no overall assessment of that contribution; still less was there any rehabilitation of Chiang Kai-shek, who was, after all, still on Taiwan waiting for a comeback.

Significant changes happened in the last years of the Cold War, in the 1980s, stimulated by changes in both the domestic and international spheres. On the domestic front, the politics of China had changed significantly after the death of Mao in 1976, with a new era of economic reform. In addition to the problems of the economy, the party felt an urgent need to address questions of ideology. In 1981, the CCP promulgated the "Resolution on Certain Questions in the History of Our Party Since the Founding of the People's Republic of China," which repudiated the policies of the Cultural Revolution, even while praising Mao as a great leader. It provided an endpoint to the charismatic policies of the Mao years that demanded mass mobilization of the population and set the stage for politics over the following three or four decades that would be more economistic and technocratic than those of the Cultural Revolution.[57]

CCP leaders were aware that it was undesirable to end up with a vanguard party that had no real ideological impetus behind it. By the early 1980s, there were a variety of reasons that a new emphasis on the Second World War seemed to have weight. First, the idea of reunification with Taiwan had garnered new interest. Chiang Kai-shek had died in 1975, and Mao Zedong in 1976. The two states were both authoritarian but liberalizing entities at that point, making it more plausible that they might find common ground. Praising the war effort of the Nationalists was now politically prudent for the CCP. Second, there was now more interest in placing pressure on Japan. Up to 1972, the PRC had been keen to detach Japan from the embrace of the United States and had soft-pedaled Japan's war crimes, although it did not ignore them completely. By the early 1980s, when it looked as though Japan might become not merely the strongest power in Asia but part of a G2 (a leading group of two states) with the United States, it was useful to remind Tokyo of unsettled issues from the past. In 1982, a row erupted between Japan and China over Japanese history textbooks, which China alleged were minimizing Japanese war crimes.[58] Above all, there was a profound feeling of ideological malaise in China after the end of the Cultural Revolution. A new emphasis on a war in which the Chinese people united against a foreign invader (collaborators were not mentioned) provided much needed ballast, an ethically constitutive story of the most powerful sort.

It was not until the 1980s that China's memory of war came explicitly into conflict with that of Japan. In some ways, the PRC's decision not to emphasize the war with Japan in the postwar decades was a continuity, not a contrast, with the policy of the Nationalists. Even during the war, Chiang had used the phrase "repay evil with good" to describe his aims for postwar relations with Japan. Chiang's postwar regime made a huge effort to protect elements of the Japanese army that had invaded China. General Okamura Yasuji, commander in chief of the China Expeditionary Army (i.e., Japanese forces in China), was acquitted of war crimes by a Chinese court in 1949, and the Chinese repeatedly intervened to prevent Okamura from testifying at the Tokyo War Crimes Trial, regardless of repeated American requests.[59]

In the other Asian countries that had been invaded by Japan, attitudes toward the Japanese were more varied than were attitudes (almost invariably negative) toward the Nazi regime in Europe.[60] In Korea, as in China, anti-Japanese sentiment was strong. However, in some former colonies, including Indonesia and Burma, the colonial elite had more sympathy for the idea that an alliance with the Japanese might be an appropriate way to counter Western imperial power. This was the logic, for instance, of Subhas Chandra Bose, whose formation of the Japan-oriented Indian National Army has done his long-term reputation no harm in his native India, and certainly not in his home province of West Bengal.[61]

Furthermore, there was little if any sense of the personalities or ideas that would create an "Asian project" of the sort that bound postwar Europe: no Japanese Schuman Plan, no Korean Jean Monnet. Chiang Kai-shek's wartime plans had included a wide range of interventions by China to shape the settlement that would follow the end of the war against Japan. But the PRC had very different views about intervention in the region: for the Communist Party leaders, the Korean War was the most obvious example of a communist internationalist view that drew little on the legacy of World War II. Additionally, the non-communist parts of the region had more that divided them than united them. Although Japan and South Korea were both under American protection, relations between the two societies remained frosty, even after the 1965 Treaty on Basic Relations. Much of the 1950s and 1960s in Southeast Asia was marked by wars of liberation and the formation of new, distinct nationalist states. Taiwan was fixated on minimizing the effect of its fast-ebbing international standing. All this meant that there was little space in which to create a shared sense of the significance of the war years. By the 1980s, the circuits of memory in Asia were national, not transnational: Japanese, Koreans north and south, Indonesians, Taiwanese, and

Chinese had very different ideas of what the Second World War had meant.

Unlike in Europe, 1945 remained unfinished business in Asia. Conditions in the region prevented the creation of a common narrative of reconciliation and mutual understanding. Part of the necessary architecture, mutually agreed-upon treaties that would lead to robust institutions within the region, was absent. Even the date of the war's end in Asia was not collectively agreed upon between the major actors. The official end of the hostilities between the United States and Japan was declared in San Francisco in 1951. But the Chinese were not present, since the United States recognized the government of the Republic of China (RoC) on Taiwan, whereas Britain had recognized the PRC in 1950. The two major signatories could not agree on which China to invite, with the result that neither one attended. (The RoC later signed the separate Treaty of Taipei.) The absence of the new PRC had great significance. Although Cold War tensions between the USSR and the United States remained grave during much of this period, the two sides were always at least in diplomatic contact. The absence of contact between the United States and China made the establishment of shared norms, or even areas of mutually acknowledged difference, impossible.

The situation was complex, but the results were clear. No system of institutions emerged in Asia comparable to NATO and the European Union, the Warsaw Pact and COMECON. Instead, US influence, which was growing in the region, became increasingly defined in opposition to a Chinese state that was gaining strength and importance but was constrained, not just by the American presence but also by the breakdown of relations with the USSR after 1960. Japan, South Korea, Taiwan, and South Vietnam became American Cold War allies. Institutions such as the Association of Southeast Asian Nations and the Southeast Asia Treaty Organization did not have the robust structure of NATO. Elsewhere in the region, the hopes that had emerged at the 1955 Bandung Conference for a new nonaligned Afro-Asian bloc of postcolonial powers produced more rhetoric than substance. In the 1970s and 1980s, following China's rapprochement with the United States and Nixon's visit to the country in 1972, the Chinese were relatively restrained in terms of seeking dominance in the region. This restraint was fueled by the desperate need for reconstruction at home after the Cultural Revolution, and the fear that displacing the balance in Asia might assist the USSR, with which China's relations in the 1980s were correct, but hardly warm.

These circumstances set the stage for a powerful new revision of the history of China's wartime experience. The place where the shift was most immediately visible was in the academy. Yet this change did not take place just in the ivory tower: a crucible of fierce debate took place at the highest levels of the Communist Party.

2

History Wars

How Historical Research Shaped China's Politics

The 1980s opened up new ground for historians in China. The country had begun to transform since the ascendancy to power of Deng Xiaoping in 1978. China's "new era" was in full swing. This era of reform and opening up brought with it new economic theories, cultural freedoms, and an interest in objective, scientifically driven higher education. And the year 1985, the fortieth anniversary of the end of the Second World War, provided an opportunity for historians to assess the meaning of the war.

The writing of history and the practice of politics have always been closely intertwined in China. In the Han dynasty, Sima Qian used his position at court to pioneer the composition of official histories. In the twentieth century, the historian Hu Shi became the Nationalists' ambassador to the United States, while another historian, Jiang Tingfu, would serve as head of the Chinese National Relief and Rehabilitation Administration as well as ambassador to the United Nations. Both Hu and Jiang were significantly shaped by their experience of higher education in the United States.

Historians in China played an important role in one of the most significant intellectual shifts that informed the politics of the era: the rehabilitation of the war record of the Nationalists. During the Cold War, this inheritance had been neglected, if not entirely lost. The first iteration of China's social memory of war, in which the Chinese Communist Party defined the war as one of "people's liberation" led by the party, had huge gaps; there was no Nationalist war effort, no US or British alliance, and no serious engagement with collaboration. It is not surprising that the Nationalists were cut out of the narrative in the immediate aftermath of the Civil War: the Communist Party was hardly likely to give any credit to its opponents.

The new historical interpretation that started in the 1980s implicitly acknowledged the legitimacy of the Nationalist regime's war effort without explicitly stating that it had changed positions. The redefinition of the central political fissure of the mid-twentieth century as being about national loyalty rather than class division, as well as the rapid economic development of the reform era that was capitalism by another name, made this shift less problematic than would have been the case in earlier years. But this change did not happen in a vacuum. It could not have happened without the remarkable relationship between Chinese politicians and Chinese historians working together to alter the narrative, albeit with rather different purposes in mind.

The cliché about academic historians in China, as in the West, is that they are a closed-off bunch who are obsessed with the minutiae of footnotes and combative debates over specific areas of historical interpretation. These qualities actually stood the historical profession in China in good stead as the reform era took off, and they continue to do so today. The changing interpretation of

World War II has always been fiercely political in China. It has also always been deeply connected to new developments in cutting-edge historical research in the academy. The interpretations and arguments developed in academic debates, as we will see later, are eventually transmitted into the public and party sphere in China. In areas such as the assessment of the relative burden of fighting shouldered by the Nationalists and Communists, or even the seemingly simple question of how long the war itself lasted, the academic debates were the starting point from which much less nuanced and brasher certainties about the war and its significance became widely spread into the public sphere.

War History on Two Sides of the Pacific

To understand the changing historiography and its significance, we need to return to the relationship between the United States and China and the way the history of that relationship was written after the war. There is a stark contrast between the story of US–China relations and that of the United States and Japan. In the case of Japan, the story could be seen as a continuous one: two enemies fought; one defeated the other and promptly took the vanquished nation in hand and re-created it in its own image. Much of the history that was written in both the United States and Japan after the war drew on the new closeness between scholars (as well as politicians) in the two countries.

The very different relationship between the United States and China, an alliance rather than an enmity, was, and still is, at the heart of debates about the war in Asia, because the other Allies were ultimately secondary to the struggle against Japan. Yet although there was a US–China alliance during the war, the postwar historiography of their joint effort was decidedly not a shared enterprise, unlike in the case of the Americans and the Japanese. The thin, in many areas nonexistent, relationship between the West (particularly the United States) and China during the Cold War prevented much opportunity for historiographical engagement across borders on any topic, including the history of the war. This contrasts with the situation in some fields of global non-Western history. In the history of India, for example, there was a slow but perceptible engagement between practitioners in a newly independent India and the Western academy in Britain, the United States, and France, as well as a powerful involvement with new theoretical models, a notable example being Ranajit Guha's redefinition of Antonio Gramsci's concept of the subaltern, which spread quickly beyond the history of South Asia to the history of other areas, including South America.[1] This sort of transnational, cross-field scholarly engagement with the liberal world did not happen with Chinese history in the mainland, and happened only to a limited degree with the scholarship that developed in Taiwan.

For Anglophone readers, the major innovations in the study of the wartime period in China occurred in American universities. The Cold War made Chinese wartime history a powerful analogy for American policy in Asia that academics could draw on to make arguments linking the recent past with the present. One of the most important books to appear during that period was actually by a political scientist, not a historian: Chalmers Johnson's *Peasant Nationalism and Communist Power* was published in 1962, just seventeen years after the war had ended and just thirteen after the Communist victory.[2] Nonetheless, this book remains one of the few works on China's recent past that has had a transformative influence outside its own field. This was partly because of its thesis that the Communists' ability to inspire nationalism among the peasantry during the war against Japan allowed the Chinese Communist Party to rise to power. In the early 1960s, the book's power also derived from its status as marking an end to a McCarthy-era assumption—that the success of the Chinese Communist Party must be attributed purely to geopolitical forces or to subversion within the United States, not to any inherent qualities of the movement itself.[3]

With the heightening of the Vietnam War in the mid-1960s, many in the American academy become increasingly critical of US policy in Asia. In this context, Mark Selden's monograph *The Yenan Way in Revolutionary China* (1971), which analyzed the social basis of the Communist revolution in the Shaanxi-Gansu-Ningxia base area controlled by Mao, had a major impact. Selden agreed with Johnson that it was necessary to take account of indigenous factors shaping the Chinese revolution, but he argued that social policy, not nationalism, was of primary importance to the peasantry.[4] An implicit analogy with the Vietnam War ran behind much of this debate, which projected the events of the Second World War onto the war in Southeast Asia. The sight of Southeast Asian countries being bombed on the basis of the domino theory (which held that communism, if unchecked, would spread from country to country) provoked academics who wished to demonstrate that indigenous factors, not geopolitical ones, were better explanations for revolutionary change. The debate in the American academy about the peasant revolution in China would remain lively for another decade and a half.[5] The market reforms pioneered by Deng Xiaoping after 1978, however, made the question "Why did the Chinese peasant revolution succeed?" less relevant to understanding China. Starting in the mid-1980s, fewer studies on the war years as the pathway to Chinese Communist revolution appeared in the West. This shift was influenced by events in the previous decade. Nixon's visit to China in 1972 heralded the beginning of a new engagement with China; also influential was a 1971 book by one of the most important popular American historians, Barbara Tuchman: *Stilwell and the American Experience in China*. Drawing mostly from materials on the American side, Tuchman gave a damning account of the Chinese theater of World War II, suggesting that a brave American individual, General Joseph Stilwell, could do little in the face of the massive corruption and incompetence of Chiang Kai-shek's regime.[6]

The missing voice in the Western discourse for the three decades from the 1950s to the 1970s was that of the Chinese mainland. While there were works of history and historiography published in China during that period, for the most part, they stuck to a closely defined and somewhat sterile view of the inevitability of Communist victory. The wartime period appeared as a foil to that inevitable victory rather than being analyzed in its own right.

The rather sparse historiography on the Chinese side began to fill out during the reform era of the 1980s, when the atmosphere became more open. One important Chinese review of the state of scholarship on the war, written by senior Chinese scholars led by Huang Meizhen of Fudan University and published in 1987, outlined in precise terms what the problem had been and how to address it, reviewing the trajectory of historical research since 1949. Huang noted that there had been some promising historical research on the war after the Communist victory, but that the Cultural Revolution had largely put an end to it. "Therefore, we could say of this stage of research on the War of Resistance," the review declared, that "it gained some preliminary results, but progress was relatively slow."[7] Some major works from that earlier period, such as Hu Qiaomu's *Thirty Years of the Communist Party of China* (1950), did include some discussion of the War of Resistance, but usually as part of a larger argument about the rise of the Communists.[8] The review noted that the most important area of research during this period was the history of the Chinese Communist Party (CCP) during the war, with key topics being the tactics of the CCP, the contribution of Mao Zedong to victory, the development of the CCP's Eighth Route Army and New Fourth Army, the Rectification campaigns in Yan'an, the level of autonomy that the CCP had as part of the United Front, and other topics relating to the formation and fortunes of the Communist Party. Research on the war was taken seriously by the Central Committee of the CCP; for instance, in April 1952, a documentary collection of wartime CCP edicts was published.[9]

Contrasting with this positive interpretation of the CCP was the very hostile analysis of the record of the Nationalists. "Many essayists argued that because the Nationalists were representatives of big landlords and capitalists," wrote Huang and his coauthors, "at the start of the War of Resistance, the Nationalists carried out a one-sided war of resistance, dependent on the government and the military, leading to the loss of large amounts of territory." This strain of scholarship also denigrated the ultimate war aims of the Nationalists: after the war, the previous historical interpretation had maintained, "they wanted to lock China up in a semicolonial, semifeudal dark society. During the war, the Nationalists strengthened their policies of fascist dictatorial control . . . and were sternly criticized by historical workers."[10]

Chinese historians also read the international relations of the wartime period through the lens of the Cold War. "In the 1950s, the key point in research about the USSR and China was the assistance given by the USSR to China during the War of Resistance," noted the review, citing the Soviet declaration of war on Japan in August 1945 as an important example. In this view, "if there had not been Soviet assistance, the Chinese victory in the War of Resistance would have been impossible." Huang ended by noting drily, "In the 1960s, when relations between the USSR and China became more tense, this research topic was suspended." In contrast, in the same era, all analysis of the American role was framed as if the United States had been an enemy during the war; in this interpretation, "Americans helped Japan to invade China, supported Chiang Kai-shek to oppose the CCP, and pretended to help but really invaded."[11] Starting in 1966, the Cultural Revolution essentially closed down all serious historical scholarship in China.

The 1960s, a time of tension in the Western academy, saw important scholarly debates on World War II–era issues such as the nature of the Nazi regime and the responsibility of the Chamberlain government in Britain for the failures of appeasement.[12] Such debates did not take place in China (although they did in Taiwan). Western scholars had only a vanishingly small chance of engaging with scholars in the mainland.[13] Archives and libraries in the mainland were also closed to Western scholars, who had to rely on materials in Taiwan, Japan, or Western libraries.

The Ambivalence of Hu Qiaomu

Serious historiography on the war in China began in the reform era, in the 1980s, particularly around 1985, the date of the fortieth anniversary of the end of the war. This first decade of the reform era was associated with major changes in the production and analysis of knowledge. The Cultural Revolution had allowed few serious scholarly endeavors to take place, but this changed after 1978; Deng Xiaoping's promotion of the Four Modernizations, building on modernizing developments in Mao's last years, was predicated on the assurance that scientific experts would be given freedom to do research without having to bow to ideologically driven viewpoints.

The definition of "science" was a broad one (closer to the German concept of *Wissenschaft*) that included social sciences such as history. The more objective revisionism on China's wartime period became associated with scholars from several institutions; one of the most important was Nanjing University, whose historians have become closely associated with innovative scholarship on the Republican period (1912–1949) as a whole. Another important institution was the Chinese Academy of Social Sciences, and one particular, perhaps surprising protagonist: the theoretician and propaganda chief Hu Qiaomu, who became its first president in 1977.

When Hu died in 1992, the *New York Times* referred to him as a "hardliner" because of his association with repeated purges within the CCP.[14] An early member of the party, he had become close to Mao in Yan'an during the years of the Rectification campaigns. He criticized the great writer Lu Xun after his death in 1936, suggesting that Lu's unwillingness to accept direction by the party was a severe failing. In the 1950s, Hu became one of the foremost theoreticians of Chinese communism and its view of the sweep of modern history, encapsulated in his book *Thirty Years of the Communist Party of China,* published in 1950. Like many senior party figures he was persecuted during the Cultural Revolution, but after his rehabilitation in the 1970s, he became closely involved in the development of a new historiographical model for the party. He played an important role in discussions on how to address the Cultural Revolution as part of the narrative of the party's rule and was centrally involved with the influential 1981 document "Resolution on Certain Questions in Our Party's History."

Hu had a long history of dedication to the party and a particular concern with historiography. This gave weight to his decision in the early 1980s to advocate a more inclusive attitude toward the role of the Nationalists in China's wartime effort. One senior Chinese historian gave three major reasons for Hu's desire to raise the standing of the war in the Chinese political scene. "He was really concerned with party history," this historian noted, "and he felt that the history of the War of Resistance was part of party history." Hu also thought it was appropriate because of then "current circumstances with Japan," as tensions had begun to rise in the early 1980s. Also important was "his own individual personal experience" as a participant in the war.[15]

Another figure with significant influence on the formation of the new interpretation of wartime history was the veteran historian Liu Danian.[16] Liu was born in 1915 in Hunan and was classically trained in Changsha. In 1938 he joined the CCP's Eighth Route Army, and he joined the party later that year. Over the next decade, he became involved in the party's efforts on education, and after the CCP came to power he became a research fellow in history at the Chinese Academy of Sciences, at points standing in for the senior historian Fan Wenlan. After his rehabilitation, following persecution during the Cultural Revolution, Liu became the president of the Institute of Modern History at the Chinese Academy of Social Sciences in 1978, a position he held until 1982.

Liu's experience as a soldier and scholar in the CCP's armies gave him high standing within the academy and the political world. The historian Zhang Haipeng noted that Liu first started writing about the War of Resistance in the aftermath of the "textbook crisis" of 1982, when the Chinese government protested against the publication of history texts in Japan that they felt obscured the reality of Japanese war crimes in China. Liu went on to write important articles and edit collections on war history and was one of the first scholars to write in impartial terms about the importance of Nationalist collaboration with the CCP. He also suggested a shift in interpretation of modern Chinese history from the revolutionary paradigm to the "modernization" one, which gave more emphasis to the balance between the Nationalist and Communist contributions.[17]

Hu Qiaomu visited the Northeast in 1982 to discuss proposals for a museum commemorating the Japanese invasion. Liu Danian and the Chinese Academy of Social Sciences (CASS) then became involved in the discussions, and Liu suggested that a comprehensive museum should be founded at Wanping, near the site of the Marco Polo Bridge, where the first battle of the Sino-Japanese War occurred in 1937. By 1985, as the construction of the museum was well underway, Liu sought to stress the level of collaboration between the CCP and the Nationalists in the displays. The museum, opened on 7 July 1987, the fiftieth anniversary of the outbreak of the conflict, as the Memorial Museum of the Chinese People's War of Resistance against Japan, was endorsed at the highest level, with Deng Xiaoping providing calligraphy for it.[18] The academic community read the signals and began to produce a new type of historiography. One important milestone was the publication in 1987 of the three-volume document collection *KangRi zhanzheng zhengmian zhanchang* (Key battlefields of the War of Resistance against Japan) under the direction of the historian Zhang Xianwen of Nanjing University.[19] In the previous year, the new historiography had also begun to penetrate popular culture, with Yang Guangyuan's 1986 movie *Taierzhuang xuezhan* (The bloody Battle of Taierzhuang) showcasing a heroic account of a battle fought by the Nationalists early in the war.[20]

But Hu Qiaomu's willingness to open the interpretative window on the CCP went only so far. The beginning of 1987 saw a hardening of the political atmosphere as the liberal-minded general secretary of the party, Hu Yaobang, was forced to step down from his post in January under pressure from conservative party forces, and a new campaign in favor of "spiritual civilization" and against "spiritual pollution" was invoked.[21]

In that same year of highly febrile politics, the review essay by Huang Meizhen and colleagues that I discussed in the previous section was published in the major scholarly periodical *Minguo dang'an* (Republican archives). The journal was associated with some of the most important revisionist scholarship on the Republican era, including the war, and many of the scholars in the group were from major universities, such as Nanjing and Fudan, that were associated with new, archive-driven scholarship on what had previously been a sensitive period.

In the April 1987 edition of *Minguo dang'an*, Huang and his colleagues laid out a review of past scholarship and an agenda for the future that seemed, at times, more like a manifesto. This report was not the first example of the revisionist scholarship about the war that emerged in the reform era. But it presented an important analysis of the issues facing scholars of the wartime period in the early phase of historiographical permissiveness. It also shows the boldness and anger that underlay their challenge to the orthodoxies of the Mao era. Many of these scholars had themselves been victims of the Cultural Revolution. A sense of personal injury, along with the urgency of making up for time lost through no fault of their own, runs through the piece. The authors were careful to use the political shibboleths of the time, observing that since 1979, there had been a policy of "seek truth from facts, liberate thought," which "has swept away the former depressing situation, and has opened up scholarly discussion on some important issues, making research on the War of Resistance very lively."[22] When discussing future research, they proposed a scientific Marxist attitude that would "enthusiastically explore and contend." They added:

> The period of the War of Resistance is not too distant a historical period from now, and this period has plenty of historical significance for issues such as Sino-Japanese, Sino-American, and Nationalist-CCP relations and other issues. . . . But precisely because the War of Resistance is not that long ago, we must pay attention in our research to avoid emotion and carry out an analysis based on scientific reason. Only thus can we follow "seeking truth from facts" to summarize our historical experience, explore new questions, and explore new topics.[23]

They dutifully added, "If we want to complete this 'system engineering' [*xitong gongcheng*], then we must do it under the direction of Marxist-Leninist dialectical materialism, exploring modern scientific methodologies."[24] But between the political bromides, the scholars placed a depth-charge under the CCP's traditional historiography of the war years:

> Of course, looked at with today's eyes, the history of the War of Resistance written in the thirty years since the foundation of the PRC is clearly inadequate, and has serious flaws. First, the field of research was too narrow. This did not just reflect the choosing of narrow research fields, or the many "blank spaces"; the whole of the research on War of Resistance history was bound in with the framework of CCP history or revolutionary history.[25]

Huang did not deny the important link between the CCP and the history of the war, but he argued that "it should not become a restrictive relationship." As an example of that sort of restriction, he observed that mainland Chinese research on the United Front between the Nationalists and Communists had tended to stress "the contradictions and struggles" between the parties, while neglecting to explore the "aspect of cooperation between the two." Nor was the previous scholarship inclined to show much nuance in its analysis of the Nationalists: "There was not enough differentiation between . . . the Nationalist [political] faction and the faction that would surrender to Japan, and the broadly patriotic Nationalist generals."[26]

Huang also pointed out the many areas that were not discussed because of contemporary political difficulties. The Hundred Regiments Campaign of 1940, led by General Peng Dehuai, a senior military figure of the Communist Party, was one of the relatively few examples of a traditional battlefield campaign (as opposed to guerrilla warfare) carried out by the Communist armies during the war. This campaign had been overlooked, however, because of Peng's loss of status. At the Lushan Conference of 1959, during the depths of the Great Leap Forward, Peng had challenged Mao Zedong over the policies that were causing mass starvation in the Chinese countryside. Infuriated, Mao banished Peng from leadership circles, and the latter's many military achievements were no longer politically safe to discuss. Huang summarized the situation for Chinese scholars during much of the Cold War: overall, "'forbidden zones' [jinqu] were many, and many important areas could not be explored; the scholarly atmosphere was very depressed and as a result the level of research naturally couldn't be raised." He did not hesitate to assign blame for this situation: this "abnormal" (*bu zhengchang*) form of politics was because of the "severe influence of the 'left.'"[27]

Huang brought up for particular praise one book still regarded as a classic piece of revisionist scholarship, the collection of documents from the national-level No. 2 Archive in Nanjing, edited by the senior historian Zhang Xianwen. Huang singled out Zhang's editing of *KangRi zhanzheng zhengmian zhanchang* (Key battlefields of the War of Resistance against Japan), suggesting that Zhang and his collaborators "threw off the 'left' influence and relatively objectively pursued the battlefield situation of the Nationalists, confirming the contribution of the patriotic Nationalist generals toward the War of Resistance."[28]

Huang also considered a topic which was distinctively politically sensitive: the question of which party had led the resistance during the war. Huang was not unaware of the political danger surrounding this issue, noting that "during the era when the 'left' tide of thought influenced historical scholarship, raising this sort of question would have been unimaginable."[29]

He argued that there were four main viewpoints on this question: (1) the war was fought under the leadership of the CCP; (2) the CCP had been instrumental in the politics of developing the wider "people's war"; (3) the war was led by the Nationalists in form, but in practice was a Nationalist-Communist cooperation; (4) the war shifted from Nationalist to Communist leadership, with 1943 as a turning point when the major anti-CCP campaigns came to an end.[30] He also added that some foreign and Taiwanese scholars went so far as to "claim that the Nationalists 'really led' the War of Resistance." This viewpoint, however, is "completely different" from ours, he wrote. Whether a touch of dry irony characterized the latter statement is unclear.

Huang's essay emphasized that there was a wider goal for revisionist scholarship, which was to secure a clearer idea of "the question of the historical position of the War of Resistance in the world antifascist war. However, for a long time now, because [foreign] scholars researching the history of the Chinese War of Resistance haven't yet [extended their analysis by linking China's domestic war experience] to the Second World War, and scholars of the Second World War have had their eyes on battlefields outside China, this important aspect has therefore been overlooked."[31]

Huang also noted that "foreign scholarly circles still have a prejudice that looks down on the Chinese War of Resistance." In 1987, it was still the case that the vast majority of Western scholarship on the wartime period was shaped by what the historian Hans van de Ven has termed the "Stilwell-White paradigm"—that is, a negative view of the Nationalist government's wartime record (informed by the hostile postwar interpretations of the American general Joseph Stilwell and the journalist Theodore White) that extended to dismissing the China-Burma-India Theater's relevance to the trajectory of the Second World War.[32] Huang is clear about the case he wishes to make: "China's War of Resistance from start to finish lay in the way of the force of Japan's army, [and] shattered Japanese imperialism's stated plan to conquer Asia and overcome the world." He went on:

> The War of Resistance delayed the outbreak of the Pacific War, so that the Western democracies could strengthen their strategies and gain precious time; it created an obstructive factor for the militaries of Japan, Germany, and Italy; it reduced the burden of the USSR's defensive war; it provided strong support for the war of the British and Americans in the Pacific; and it protected an important supply line to the USSR for the US and Britain.[33]

He argued that, because of the work being done by Chinese scholars, there were now more foreign scholars who were interested in the topic. "But there are some who maintain their prejudices," he warned, "with an attitude of denial toward the new results of Chinese historical scholarship, and they attack it."[34]

Huang made it clear, however, that progress in encouraging historians to understand the Chinese conflict as a mainstream part of the global history of the war would require abandoning the old frameworks derived from the CCP's worldview. "There has been a lot of discussion of the place of the War of Resistance in the history of the CCP and the history of the Chinese revolution," noted Huang. "But up to now we have not seen these sorts of results in a wide and systematic exploration of what position the War of Resistance has in the wider tide of modern history."[35]

He also noted areas where the field in China was still lacking at the time: "The [wartime] history of the Nationalist-controlled areas still has plenty of weak spots, such as cultural history, social history. . . . Therefore opening up these new fields of research is very necessary." In the field of international history, he observed that there were far more works on US-China relations than on those between the CCP and the USSR, or between China and the UK, France, or Germany.[36]

Huang concluded his piece with a pointed plea for change: "Speed up the arranging and publishing of historical materials about the War of Resistance. In recent years, although . . . some collections of materials have been published, they are far from being usable as research material. . . . The length of time it takes to arrange and publish the specialist and archival material is seriously affecting the progress and development of the history of the War of Resistance. . . . The fact that some fields are blank cannot be separated from this. . . . We certainly hope the No. 2 Historical Archives, which are very rich in holdings, can be made more convenient for research on the war, to develop historical science in China, and to make a greater contribution to 'spiritual civilization' in China." He ended by calling for the writing of a multivolume history of the war.[37]

During this period, there was a clear connection between the revisionist view of the Republican period more broadly and the specific history of the War of Resistance. A senior Chinese historian, looking back thirty years later, was clear that this revisionism was driven by "political needs," but also that individual scholars within the system could push at the edges of historical interpretation. One senior CASS scholar had argued at the time that the Communists and Nationalists both nurtured centers of resistance during the war; while this was not an "official view" early on, it shows the extent to which carefully phrased challenges to the political framework could open the historiographical range. The primary political reason that this interpretation was permitted for academic discussion was to open up relations between the mainland and Taiwan, which led to some lighthearted moments when the first mainland scholars were invited to the island in the early 1980s. One of them remembered some of the Taiwanese scholars muttering on their arrival, "The Commies are coming! The Commies are coming!"[38] During this period, there were few specific orders from the party as to how far mainland scholars could go with revisionist views on the relationship between the CCP and Nationalists during the war, but there was "self-control" about how far to stretch the boundaries.

These limits could be felt not just in terms of political edicts, but in terms of the emotional freight that many people still carried in relation to the war. Huang's essay expressed this thought explicitly:

> First, when the historical scholars of New China started research on the War of Resistance, the conclusion of that war was still not very distant, and the huge emotional wounds that the war had made on people were hard to overcome in just a few years. Also at that time, there was a hostile situation between the two sides of the straits and with the US, so when doing research work, emotional criticism rather than rational analysis couldn't help but influence scholarship.[39]

One of those "historical scholars of New China" was Hu Qiaomu. While he was rather more than a mere academic, he clearly regarded himself as someone seeking to provide historical as well as political weight to the contemporary questions that China was facing in the early reform era. Yet Hu was not willing to pose the sort of direct challenge that was being put forward by revisionists such as Huang Meizhen. Having played a very significant role in opening up the range of historical interpretation to include the Nationalists, he now declared publicly that it was important not to go too far in that new direction.

On 7 August 1987, Hu published a major editorial in the *People's Daily*. The piece, titled "The Great Significance of the War of Resistance," was a review of Sino-Japanese relations from the late Qing dynasty to the present. Hu declared that "the eight-year War of Resistance not only greatly sped up the progress of the Chinese revolution, but also changed the last hundred years of the unfair situation between China and Japan." He continued with a long description of the many occasions in the early twentieth century when conflicts between China and Japan had come to a head. After a lengthy preliminary, he then gave a forthright statement about what he regarded as the politically accceptable version of the history of the war, with no doubts about the leading role of the CCP and the reactionary nature of the Nationalists:

> This is how the War of Resistance began. Before the war . . . the CCP seized the right to political mobilization. We completely acknowledge the wartime contribution of the Nationalist government's army's patriotic generals [and officers], but before the war, Chiang Kai-shek's government was carrying out the mistaken policy of a partial [*pianmian*] war of resistance (that is, just the military, without the people). From 1939 onward, it carried out a . . . War of Resistance, pursuing a reactionary policy that was anticommunist, anti-people, to the point that its military nearly lost all of its fighting strength.[40]

Even in the Mao era, the CCP had been willing to note the sacrifices of a few Nationalist figures and military heroes.[41] But Hu was not willing to let this interpretation extend to his old enemies, the people who had besieged him in Yan'an nearly half a century earlier. In 1943, he had written a piece discussing the fall of the Mussolini regime, arguing that "clearly the Nationalist Party received significant influence from it," referring to the CC Clique, the highly authoritarian faction within the party which was indeed significantly shaped by European fascist ideology.[42] Now, over four decades later, the elderly Hu reminded readers of the Nationalists' strategic failings: "In 1944, a year before the Japanese surrender, Japan's invading armies could still attack from Henan; [heading south], they attacked Guangxi and Guizhou, causing panic in the wartime capital of Chongqing."[43]

He even brought the old enemy, the United States, into the indictment, although General Stilwell, the figure he cited, had always been more sympathetic to the CCP than were many of his fellow Americans:

> Because of the reactionary Nationalist clique's corruption, it not only aroused the wrath of the democratic parties and the patriotic people, but even caused China-Burma-India Theater commander and commander in chief for Chiang, General Stilwell, as well as many American diplomats stationed in China, to advocate that they ought to reduce assistance to Chiang Kai-shek (the assistance was all being used by Chiang to prepare for a new civil war and not to fight the Japanese), and to give help to the CCP instead.[44]

The historian Arthur Waldron has noted the way in which Zhang Zizhong, the Nationalist general who was killed in action against the Japanese in Hubei, had been rehabilitated in the 1990s as a less politically problematic figure than Chiang Kai-shek.[45] Hu also cited Zhang, "the famous patriotic general whom Chiang deeply trusted," in his criticism of the Nationalist regime. "You can see that the crisis of the Nationalists was very great," he wrote. "This was a commonly known fact both domestically and internationally."[46]

In contrast, claimed Hu, the Chinese Communist Party provided a powerful example of leadership during the war years: "Who would not work hard to recover and promulgate that outstanding spirit of the time of the War of Resistance?!"[47] Hu claimed that during the eight years of the conflict, the Communist Eighth Route and New Fourth Army troops, in addition to other troops led by the CCP, made up 64 percent of anti-Japanese forces and

95 percent of the forces fighting the forces of the collaborationist governments. "Therefore after eight years of the War of Resistance," Hu concluded, "the CCP really had outdone the Nationalists."[48]

Hu wrote in the impersonal style common to editorials in the *People's Daily*. Yet it is not farfetched to see him as drawing on resentments built up during his years in Yan'an as Mao's political secretary. The Hu Qiaomu who had written eloquently in 1943 about the similarities between Italian fascism and the Nationalists' policy was not likely to grant his old foes any more than a bare minimum of political legitimacy. In early 1987, Hu had a hand in a partial purge of the Chinese Academy of Social Sciences; having been instrumental in founding the academy, he maintained a strong interest in keeping it pure. He was also one of the last of the generation of political thinkers and historians who had lived through the war. There was an undoubtedly personal element to his hardline tone in 1987. As one senior historian put it, "he participated in the War of Resistance; he was in Yan'an."[49]

Yet Hu's ideological firmness masked a real weakness in the party's grip; he was not expressing unquestionable orthodoxy but rather trying to intervene in a debate which he feared he was losing. The body of scholarly work, based on new archival material that started to emerge in the 1980s, could not easily be altered. The 1980s, up to 1989, marked a high point of liberalism under the CCP, and Hu's intervention was something of a conservative thrust in a dynamic between views such as his own (or that of economic socialist-conservatives such as Chen Yun) and that of economic liberals such as the new general secretary, Zhao Ziyang, whose followers were willing to support a livelier public sphere in pursuit of their more radical economic ideas.[50] Since the only real solution to Hu's criticism would be to force scholars once again to write purely propagandistic history, it was a warning that seemed to hark back vaguely if menacingly to the past, rather than representing a future-facing, more objective attitude toward writing history.

In fact, 1987 proved to be Hu's last hurrah in terms of prominence in Chinese life. That autumn, he was not reelected to the Central Committee of the party. The liberal tide, however, was ebbing. The Tiananmen Square confrontation and killings in June 1989 led to a major hardening of attitudes in history, as in many other areas of Chinese intellectual life, at least for a while. The War of Resistance was very much present in the new political atmosphere. During this time, plans were made for CASS to establish a new journal, entitled *KangRi zhanzheng yanjiu* (Research on the War of Resistance against Japan), that would showcase research on the war years but would also provide academic ballast for the party-state's new emphasis on nationalism. In the period leading up to the journal's inaugural issue in 1991, there was political pressure both from Chinese politicians and from figures in the Chinese diaspora in the United States, recalled one scholar who was involved in the planning.[51]

Wartime History and Contemporary Politics, 1990s–2010s

The tensions between the political sphere and the academy in interpretations of the War of Resistance continued over the next two decades. The fiftieth anniversary of the end of World War II in 1995, extensively commemorated around the globe, was influenced in China by the storm that erupted in June of that year when the president of the Republic of China on Taiwan, Lee Teng-hui, visited the United States. China, which did not recognize Lee's claim to presidential status, was angered by the impression that he had been received in his official status, rather than as a private citizen, and the incident led to a dampening of relations between the mainland and Taiwan.[52]

But that year also saw the publication of a special issue of the new journal that had been established at CASS. The journal had started publication in 1991, in the intellectually chilly aftermath of Tiananmen, but was distinguished by carrying rigorous, empirically rich research essays on wartime history, mostly of a political and military nature.

In the aftermath of the 1989 killings, the state became increasingly concerned to promote "patriotic education." In 1989–1990, Hu Qiaomu kept up a correspondence with the veteran (in both senses) historian Liu Danian, in which Liu expressed his wish for Hu to take the title of head of the research group underpinning the journal, if only on an honorary basis. Liu also approached the prime minister, Li Peng, seeking funding of some RMB 700,000 for the journal; he argued that it would provide a means to examine Japan's historical record in wartime China and engage with Japan in the present. The funding appears to have been granted.[53]

Five years later, as the fiftieth anniversary of the end of the war approached, Hu wrote to CCP general secretary Jiang Zemin, suggesting that 15 August should be marked every year as a commemoration of victory against the Japanese, and that Jiang himself should go to Lugouqiao (the Marco Polo Bridge, where the war had broken out) on that date. "Every great power is using the opportunity to commemorate victory in the Second World War," Liu noted, observing that other countries had been organizing events intended to show off their survival and later development: these included President George H. W. Bush's "important" speech at Pearl Harbor in December 1991, the visit of Queen Elizabeth and Presidents Clinton and Mitterrand to Normandy in June 1994 for the fiftieth anniversary of D-Day, and the ceremony in May 1995 for VE Day with Russian, British, French, and American representation. This might be the last opportunity, he pointed out, for China to use the memory of the war "to enable our socialist homeland to gain a more beneficial international environment."[54] Liu was clearly concerned that commemorations of the war should burnish China's global standing, not just fuel domestic nationalism.

To mark the anniversary, the journal put out a special edition. The frontispiece of the 1995 volume included calligraphy from prominent political figures, starting with Vice President Rong Yiren, the founder of CITIC (China's major state-owned investment company) and one of the rare figures who had risen to high office under the PRC despite being related to an extremely prominent Nationalist business family. Rong's presence in the volume hinted at the wartime connections between the Nationalists and the CCP, as well as China's extensive international connections, neither of which were favored in pre-1980s historiography. Two other signatories, Xiao Ke and Zhang Aiping, had impeccable military credentials as a general and CCP official, respectively, who had fought both the Japanese and the Nationalists; yet they were associated by some with reluctance to send troops into the center of Beijing during the Tiananmen crisis, and Xiao Ke was also associated with the founding of the liberal journal *Yanhuang Chunqiu* in 1991 (which was closed down in its original form under Xi's government in 2016).[55] Song Renqiong, another signatory, was one of the "Eight Immortal" senior figures of the PRC and had been a hardliner in 1989. One Westerner (a naturalized Chinese citizen) who signed was Israel Epstein, a long-standing sympathizer with the party. The volume itself showcased essays by senior historians on a range of topics, including Jin Chongji on United Front politics during the war, Liu Danian on the conflict as the point of origin for China's revival, and Cheng Siyuan on Zhou Enlai's role in the victory at the 1938 Battle of Taierzhuang.[56]

A decade later, on the sixtieth anniversary of the end of World War II in 2005, the atmosphere was less tense. China had cautiously begun to reemerge into the world. In 2001, two events, the country's entry into the World Trade Organization (WTO) as well as the award of the summer Olympic Games to Beijing for 2008, created a sense of limited liberalization in the public sphere. Wartime history was one beneficiary of the new atmosphere when in 2006, the foreign ministers of China and Japan, Li Zhaoxing and Tarô Asô, declared that they would establish a joint Japan–China Historical Research Commission featuring scholars from both sides, who would attempt to provide a mutually agreeable version of various historical controversies relating to the relationship between the two countries.[57] After some three years of study, however, the two sides were unable to come up with a joint report on the most controversial areas of interpretation, notably the Second World War period.[58] From 2010 on, relations between China and Japan began to deteriorate over the disputed Diaoyu / Senkaku Islands in the East China Sea.

In 2012, Xi Jinping came to power. Sino-Japanese tensions, after rising alarmingly during his first year in office, began to calm down as Xi and Japanese premier Shinzo Abe agreed to lower the temperature and avoid any risk of armed conflict. Sino-Japanese history, however, did not disappear from the agenda. One notable aspect of Xi's rule was increased restriction of academic freedom.[59] Another was the strong political direction of many fields, including history. The War of Resistance was a primary target for such top-down management.

On 31 July 2015, Xi Jinping spoke at the Academy of Military Sciences on the continuing importance of academic research on the War of Resistance. He tied that work firmly to the current political messages of the PRC:

> The goal is to reconsider the great path of the Chinese people's War of Resistance, to confirm the great contribution that the war made to the victory in the world antifascist war, and to show our upholding of the results from the victory in the Second World War and determination for international peace and justice.

Xi's stress on China's contribution to the ultimate Allied victory underpinned the idea that the country deserved a continuing role in creating the contemporary international order. He also noted the war's significance to China's project of national renewal:

> This great victory thoroughly smashed the Japanese militaristic plot to colonize and enslave China; it once again confirmed China's position as a great power [*daguo*] in the world, and the Chinese people received the respect of the peace-loving people of the world; it opened up the bright prospect of the Chinese nation's great revival [*zhonghua minzu weida fuxing*], opening up a new path for the Chinese phoenix.

Xi's statement that the war turned China into a *daguo* was a tacit endorsement of at least some of the wartime contribution of the Nationalists. By stating that China had achieved "great power" status in 1945, rather than 1949, Xi was pinning that important turning point on the moment of Chiang and Mao's joint victory, rather than on Mao's solo revolutionary triumph at the end of the Civil War.

However, Xi acknowledged that the Chinese role in shaping the global understanding of the world war's significance was still inadequate. This made it necessary to promote further academic research on the topic:

> The propaganda and cultural circles and all circles of society have worked very hard. However, in comparison with the historical position and significance of the Chinese people's War of Resistance, in comparison with the influence of this war on the Chinese nation [*zhonghua minzu*] and the world, our research on the War of Resistance is still not nearly sufficient, and we must continue to pursue deep systematic research.

For Xi, a greater international recognition of the war's significance was not just a scholarly matter but a political one, relating to China's international standing and to the Taiwan question:

> We must encourage international society accurately to recognize the Chinese people's War of Resistance position and role in the world antifascist war. We must strengthen the international interchange of research on the War of Resistance. And we must encourage the mutual sharing across the Taiwan Straits of scholarly materials and jointly written books.[60]

The comments on Taiwan were made in the last months of the presidency of the Nationalists' Ma Ying-jeou, who had overseen eight years of relative warming in relations between the mainland and the island. At the end of his remarks, Xi declared that there would be "national-level social science funding and publication funding" of research on the war. In fact, CASS is engaged, at the time of writing, in putting forward major new collections on the topic. Academic research on the War of Resistance continues to be a topic of real significance for the Chinese leadership.

Controversial Dates

The continued political interest in the war years has had a noticeable effect on the nature of the academic debate. One notable example occurred in 2017, when the government announced that the War of Resistance against Japan would officially be dated as lasting for fourteen instead of eight years—from 1931 to 1945, starting with Japan's invasion of Manchuria on 18 September 1931. The government reportedly wanted new materials revising the timeline to be in use within months, and textbooks were supposed to stress "the instrumental function of the Communist Party in the resistance against aggression" as well as China's role as a major antifascist battlefield.[61]

This decision placed a political imperative on what had, up to then, been a question of historical interpretation. At the conclusion of the war itself and for decades afterward, the term *banian kangzhan* (eight-year War of Resistance) had been a mainstream term in China, with the Marco Polo Bridge incident on 7 July 1937 marking the start of the war. Even Hu Qiaomu's 1987 essay critiquing what he viewed as excessive concentration on the Nationalists referred in its title to the "eight-year" war.[62] Over the years, however, perfectly reasonable historiographical arguments for an earlier start date had emerged. Huang Meizhen and his colleagues' 1987 historiographical review essay stated,

An issue closely related to the position of the War of Resistance is the question of the war's starting point. The traditional viewpoint is to use the 7 July incident [the Marco Polo Bridge incident] as the outbreak of the War of Resistance of the whole nation [*Quan minzu kangzhan*]. But recently, there have been six or seven essays that take a different viewpoint and argue that the start of the war was the 18 September incident [the invasion of Manchuria]. . . . So some argue "During the 18 September event, the Chinese people fired the first shot in the antifascist war; the War of Resistance of the whole people [*Quanmin kangzhan*], begun on 7 July, was the first battlefield of the antifascist war." Therefore, China's War of Resistance should be considered the starting point of the Second World War, but there is still dispute over the starting point of that War [of Resistance].[63]

This interpretation was paralleled by the postwar debate in Japan on the issue of what was called the *jyugonen sensô* (Fifteen-Year War), a (slightly anomalously calculated) term that covered the period from Manchuria to the atomic bombing, incorporating the China War and the Pacific War, with interventions from left and right about the significance of the term.[64] Proponents of a fourteen-year interpretation in China could point to the invasion of Manchuria as the moment at which Japanese imperialism in China entered a new, more aggressive mode, which foreshadowed what would become an all-out war. This view allows even longer timeframes to be used, in which a "Sino-Japanese War" lasts from 1894 to 1945—from the defeat of the Qing fleet by the Meiji state to the atomic bombings. Hu Qiaomu's 1987 essay points to a long strand of Japanese interference with and invasion of China, beginning with the late Qing.[65] Recent interpretations of European history have also posited the idea of a "European civil war" that lasted from 1914 to 1945, or indeed until 1991, and there is now rich scholarship on the wars that flowed on after the end of the Great War.[66]

Yet 1937 is still a more plausible starting point for the war between China and Japan than 1931. Between 1931 and 1937, Chiang Kai-shek's government made many agreements to try to contain Japanese aggression, including the Tanggu Truce of 1933 and the He-Umezu agreement of 1935.[67] People in China and Japan did not perceive themselves to be at war between 1931 and 1937, nor did their leaders, although some intellectuals regarded the era as a "period of exception" (see Chapter 1). Indeed, one of the primary sources of domestic resistance to Chiang Kai-shek consisted of groups opposed to his supposed policy of "nonresistance." In 1937, Chiang saw himself at a turning point between peace and war, as his diary makes clear, and the Japanese response, in terms of troop deployments, was on a much greater scale than their previous actions in China.[68]

The government edict of 2017 to change the start date of the war was not put forward as a suggestion or debating point; rather, it was a declaration at the highest political level that textbooks and official interpretations of the war would have to use the "fourteen-year" definition. The redefinition was undertaken for political rather than scholarly reasons. Political pressure from the Northeast, which felt that its experience under Japanese occupation was downplayed by the "eight-year" framework, was one significant reason for the extension of the timeline.[69] A push for recognition of the Northeast's contribution had started at least as far back as 1987, when construction began for a museum to the 18 September incident (i.e., the invasion of Manchuria in 1931) in Shenyang. Legal issues might also have been a consideration; if a state of war is officially recognized over a particular period, it becomes easier to declare that atrocities during that period are war crimes, with all the legal implications of that term.

Discussion of the "fourteen-year" framework took further shape in the first years of the twenty-first century. One senior Chinese scholar observed drily, "Political figures in China can influence war memory, rather like Shinzo Abe. . . . What they decide becomes a fact." He added, "Politicians' and national leaders' influence is huge," noting that "there's a process" [of discussion], since at least one very senior academician opposed the change in a conference held at CASS, and the early parts of the debate were openly reported; but the overall trajectory is "not very clear" and "the final decision is in the hands of Xi Jinping."[70]

Xi gave his own verdict in his speech of 31 July 2015, in which he declared:

> We need to grasp the connections between the regional War of Resistance [*jubu*] and the national-type [*quanguoxing*] war, the frontline battlefields and the battlefields behind the lines, and the Chinese people's War of Resistance and the world antifascist war. We do not just want to study the eight-year history of the total war after the Marco Polo Bridge incident, but we must also seriously research the history of the fourteen-year War of Resistance after the September Eighteenth incident, and [the concept of] "fourteen years" should link up and unite our research.[71]

A year and a half after this speech, the edict was promulgated that "fourteen years" would now be the official version, with the 1931–1937 period designed as the "partial" (*jubu*) war, and the 1937–1945 period being the "total" (*quanguo*) war. One senior historian remained unhappy, noting in an interview, "Now all the textbooks say—you can't say 'eight years,' you have to say 'fourteen years.'" He also remarked that the number of nationally accepted textbooks would be reduced from four to one. He lamented that space for scholarly discussion of the historiography had been shut down: "Previously scholars could discuss this, but now they can't."[72] What had been an obscure issue of definition became a tool in the creation of a more unified domestic propaganda message, along with an increased capacity to criticize Japan for war crimes in Asia.

The State of the Field in the 2010s

Serious revisionist work on the history of the War of Resistance has been under way in China for some four decades. The contours of the historiography are now clear, but since the 1987 historians' "manifesto," how far have interpretations really changed in China's academy? Some areas of specialization have emerged: in particular, a revisionist political and military history of the Nationalist and Communist Parties, the internationalization of China's wartime experience, and a history of mass violence. Other areas, though, including the history of collaboration with the Japanese, have been less well covered.

Western scholarship on China's World War II has benefited immeasurably from engagement with academic work from within China. In turn, some work from overseas has influenced the Chinese writing of their own wartime history. This phenomenon is not unprecedented; France's examination of its period of Nazi occupation was heavily influenced by the publication of the American scholar Robert Paxton's book *Vichy France: Old Guard and New Order, 1940–1944* in 1972.[73] While no single non-Chinese work has had quite that effect in China, Japanese scholarship as a whole has had considerable influence on Chinese interpretations. This may seem surprising in light of hostile headlines in China about Japanese distortions of history, but one senior Chinese scholar was at pains to point out to me that "differences over Nanjing are political differences, not scholarly differences." He acknowledged that interpretations that reduced the sense of Japanese responsibility might be tolerated if they came from Western scholars, but not if they came from the Japanese: "The difference is that the Westerners were not our enemy during that time, so whatever they argue won't be criticized by us." Even scholars, he acknowledged wryly, "are influenced by some political feelings."[74]

Despite these international influences, the majority of the debate around China's wartime history continues to be a Sinophone discussion within the academy in China and Taiwan. In the remainder of the chapter, I outline some of the areas of major research progress.

Nationalist and Communist political and military history

Before the 1980s, academic analysis in China treated the war against Japan largely as a guerrilla war dominated by the CCP. This changed in the next three decades, so that the war came to be seen as a conflict in which the Nationalist government played a significant role. This revisionism has produced a new framework for the military history of the conflict. Broadly speaking, this history runs from the outbreak of war at the Marco Polo Bridge in 1937 to its sudden conclusion in August 1945 with the atomic bombings of Japan. Among the important staging posts of this history are the Battle of Shanghai (1937), the capture and despoliation of the capital at Nanjing (1937–1938), the Battle of Taierzhuang and the subsequent Xuzhou campaign, the fall of Wuhan

(1938), the entry of the United States and Britain into the war after Pearl Harbor (1941), the Burma campaigns (1942, 1944), and the Ichigo campaign (1944).[75]

The first wave of revisionism in the 1980s and early 1990s dealt mostly with the Nationalist armies rather than with the government or its leader, Chiang Kai-shek, enabling the construction of a new historiography covering the successes as well as the failures of the Nationalist troops. One example was new scholarship on the April 1938 Battle of Taierzhuang in Shandong province, which marked a rare occasion when the Nationalist armies were able to repel a Japanese advance. Troops under Li Zongren and Bai Chongxi blocked the Japanese assault on Taierzhuang, which was supposed to clear the way for an attack on Xuzhou, one of the major railway junctions of east-central China. Taierzhuang was a shrewd topic to choose for revisionism. It was a military campaign that had no substantial connection with the actions of the CCP, but it was a Chinese victory, making it ideologically more acceptable for discussion. It was also a victory for Li Zongren, a senior figure in the Nationalist government who eventually defected to the People's Republic. The publication of documentary collections relating to Chiang Kai-shek's armies also served to bring Nationalist military performance into academic discussion in the mainland.[76] The body of work on this topic is now immense, and it is a well-established part of the current scholarly debate in China. Yet the Nationalist military record, while now openly acknowledged within China, is still subject to the waxing and waning that marks official permission for broaching certain sensitive topics. On the other hand, it would take a tremendous amount of effort to remove the voluminous scholarship on the Nationalist wartime contribution from the Chinese academy altogether. One senior researcher in this field acknowledged the constant negotiation needed to progress, noting that as an editor of scholarly work, "I know what you can publish—and what you can't."[77] The reorientation of the war narrative toward the Nationalists has partially eclipsed scholarship on the Communists. One reason has been the attraction of a relatively unexplored field; many researchers find it more appealing to head toward new historical horizons than to revisit old debates. However, political considerations have also played a role. Material relating to the history of the CCP in wartime, in the words of one senior historian, has a "complicated" status, and "the openness of materials is a big problem."[78] Previously there was more direct access to the archives on matters relating to the CCP, but now the majority of scholars are denied permission to visit them, and the institutions in charge of the material tend not to publicize what holdings they have. Nonetheless, a significant amount of (carefully preselected) material is published with official financial sponsorship. Both Huang Meizhen in 1987 and Xi Jinping in 2015 mentioned the importance of "materials," data which could provide the basis of a more objective research agenda on the war.[79]

Yet while studies of the CCP became less prominent, scholarship in the new millennium on the Nationalists went beyond reassessment of the military and began to focus on a central personality who had previously been taboo: Chiang Kai-shek himself. During the Mao era, it was nearly impossible to give any positive account of Chiang's period in power. One of the signs of an expansion of boundaries appeared in 1988. An image of Chiang was shown as part of the controversial television series *River Elegy* (*Heshang*), a liberal-minded documentary that was broadcast nationally; at that time, this was still daring. By the 1990s the taboo was lifting, and in the 2000s, a significant event took place that shifted scholarship on the period. The Chiang family arranged for one of the most important historical resources of the period to be relocated to the United States: Chiang Kai-shek's diaries. Chiang maintained a diary almost daily for over half a century, and a set of the materials, which had been held in Taiwan, was moved to the Hoover Institution at Stanford University and opened to scholars in 2006.[80] An ironic result of this shift was that scholars from China came to California to examine these crucial materials on their own country's history. One of the most prominent of them was Yang Tianshi of the Chinese Academy of Social Sciences, whose major study, *Searching for the Real Chiang Kai-shek* (*Zhaoxun zhenshi de Jiang Jieshi*), became a standard volume in the field. Yang's interpretation of Chiang was a measured one, drawing substantially on the diary entries to paint Chiang as a flawed but major historical figure. It also marked a certain convergence between scholarship on the topic in the mainland and on Taiwan. Lu Fangshang, a senior historian whose own work includes major projects based on Chiang's diary, wrote a foreword to Yang's book, emphasizing the cross-straits nature of the topic.[81]

International history of China's war

Since the 1980s, much more attention has also been given to the international role of China in the war as part of a global "antifascist alliance." A great deal of political significance lies behind this shift in historiography, since it relates to a wider project in which China wishes to project itself as having been "present at the creation" of today's international order. The newly internationalized interpretation of the conflict has also encouraged the argument that China was itself the major battlefield within the Asian war. Most non-Chinese historians, even those sympathetic to the upgrading of China's contribution to the war, would be uneasy at this claim. China was certainly the first Asian battlefield (or battlefield of any sort), and its role in holding back some 600,000 Japanese troops was very important, but the United States' defeat of Japan in the Pacific was ultimately the deciding factor.

The new internationalization of the war has also allowed a reassessment of one of the most fraught topics relating to the wartime period. the relationship between the United States and China. During the Cold War, there was an imbalance between the two sides. In the United States, the "Who lost China?" debate shaped much of the early Cold War period, with a division between the "China Lobby," associated with the right wing of the Republican Party, that argued for continued support for Chiang Kai-shek's regime on Taiwan, and a growing liberal group that argued for a rapprochement with the PRC. With President Richard Nixon's visit to China in 1972, the last emotional link with the uneasy World War II alliance with the Nationalists was essentially ended, even though Chiang lived on for a few years, and Madame Chiang lasted until 2003, when she died at the age of 105.

The situation in China during the early Cold War, however, was quite different. The War of Resistance did not shape China's perception of its relations with the United States. There was no "America lobby" within the CCP leadership, nor was there a relationship between the two countries that might have allowed aspects of the wartime relationship to be discussed or even disputed. American and Chinese diplomats, scholars, and students simply did not meet during most of the period up to the 1970s. Even after that, Track II (semi-official) meetings through agencies such as the National Committee on United States–China Relations provided only a limited opening for discourse.[82] As a result, Chinese academic discussions of the wartime relationship with the United States were limited and stylized. The opening up of space for new scholarship from the 1980s has meant a much richer body of work relating to the US-China relationship in wartime. In addition, there is a wide body of scholarship on the relationship between China and other Western powers during the same period, and a smaller but growing field of work on China's relationship with non-Western actors during that time.

The relationship between the United States and China has developed into the single most important bilateral adversarial relationship of the twenty-first century. Historical work on the nature of that relationship during the war years has provided the basis for a discussion of the current antagonism between the two countries. In the United States, the relationship between Chiang Kai-shek and General Joseph Stilwell is not much remembered. But in 2012, the senior Chinese historian and CCP member Zhang Baijia wrote an assessment of the breakdown of relations between Chiang and Stilwell during the war in terms of its significance for the present-day relationship with the United States. Zhang served as deputy director of the Party History Research Centre, and his views had the authority of a senior figure within the CCP. "Many people feel there exists today between the United States and China a sort of mutual attraction, but also a force of rejection," he observed; "so the friendship between the two countries is in a zigzag shape." He went on to ask, "Why did the wartime experience not only not bring about closer understanding but actually foment opposition between the two?"[83]

Zhang saw the years before and after the Second World War as the crucial ones for the US-China relationship. He saw Stilwell's role as important because he was the first major American figure to advocate a turn away from Chiang Kai-shek; Zhang described Stilwell as "naïve" and "rash," but he also acknowledged that the general wanted a "world that was totally different." In the end, "he tried to use American methods on Chinese problems, and failed." Yet, Zhang argues, he did understand that the United States should leave China swiftly, that is, not try to prop up Chiang's regime during the Civil War. His fellow Americans did not see that, and so after the revolution, the two countries, which had formerly been friends, became enemies. Zhang concluded: "The causes and the effects of the tragedy are much longer lasting than was the [Stilwell] tragedy itself."[84]

In a 2019 article, intended for Western readers, Zhang made a related point that addressed contemporary international relations much more explicitly:

> Historically, the evolution of China-US relations was affected to a large extent by third-party or multilateral factors. For example, in the 1930s and 1940s, Japanese aggression and expansion was the most important factor driving China and the US together. From the end of the 1940s through the early 1970s, the US-Soviet Cold War, the Korean War, and the Vietnam War fueled a China-US standoff and confrontation—the Sino-Soviet split and the US withdrawal from Vietnam created conditions for China-US reconciliation.

In other words, the US-China relationship had in some way been mediated through a series of confrontations or collaborations relating to other states; after normal relations were restored in 1979, "bilateral considerations gradually became dominant in their policies towards the other nation. . . . The influence of any individual country as a single third-party factor in China–US relations decreased."[85] The tragedy was that it had taken some three decades to recover from one of the great diplomatic anomalies of the modern era, the lack of direct contact between the United States and China after the formation of a tentative basis for postwar engagement in 1945, despite the tensions exposed by the Stilwell affair. Now, at last, US–China relations could be restored at a bilateral level.

Atrocities, casualties, and the history of mass violence

In the West, there has been a significant shift toward a history of war that incorporates the experience of mass violence. This is in part because of the "social turn" toward a history of warfare that incorporates the experiences of those beyond the battlefield, but also because of the interest in reparations for war, which has made the histories of the effects of war more politically relevant.[86]

Chinese academic work in the past had not generally examined China's wartime experience within the framework of mass violence. Recently, however, there has been a noticeable shift toward studying war damage, rather than simply classic military campaigns and political history. First, and perhaps most prominent, has been the growth in studies of Japanese war atrocities in China. One notable aspect of this is work on the Nanjing Massacre of 1937–1938, when the invading Japanese army took the Chinese capital and killed many thousands of civilians.[87] The production of critical scholarship and primary materials on the massacre has become part of a wider political trend that is linked to official Chinese government criticisms of Japan's role in Asia. There has also been a growth in the study of other war crimes, such as Japanese bacteriological warfare in China; an important example of this is the work pioneered by the late Bu Ping of the Chinese Academy of Social Sciences (who was also a leading figure in the 2007–2010 Japanese-Chinese History Commission).[88]

The broadening of the acceptable areas for historical investigation have also encouraged scholars in the Southwest, which was a particular target of Japanese air raids, to compile a series of volumes on the damage to lives, property, and infrastructure in Chongqing and the surrounding areas under Nationalist control.[89] There has also been a slow but steady growth in work examining the wider social impact of acts of destruction carried out not by the Japanese, but by the Nationalists, such as the destruction of the dikes on the Yellow River at Huayuankou and the Henan famine of 1942.[90] For many years, these phenomena were little discussed because of the historical ambiguity surrounding them. This might appear puzzling. These events were not indictments of the Communist contribution to the war (the CCP was irrelevant to both), and one might think that criticism of the Nationalists would be unproblematic in today's China. Yet there was clearly a sense of unease about criticizing any Chinese government for inhumane acts of commission or omission in the midst of a war caused by Japan. More troublingly for the CCP, there were also parallels with events during the Mao era, such as the Great Leap Forward, that made subjects such as famine very touchy.

Collaboration

One area of historiography that has been only lightly developed is analysis of the wartime regimes that collaborated with the Japanese.

This is in marked contrast with the experience of France, where new academic work in the 1960s finally opened up one of the most difficult questions on the occupation period. While major controversies still exist on many topics regarding Nazi-occupied France, there are active discussions on the nature of collaboration.[91]

That debate is far more limited in China. The regime which has been the most studied is that of Wang Jingwei, which was established at Nanjing in 1940 and collapsed at the end of the war in 1945 (after Wang's death in 1944). The discourse on Wang Jingwei has generally categorized him as a *hanjian,* or traitor, closing down rather than opening up any lines of discussion. Yet his self-presentation was significantly different from that of the men who established the Vichy regime in France. Philippe Pétain and Pierre Laval rejected the legacy of the Third Republic, whereas Wang made it clear that he regarded himself as Sun Yat-sen's heir and that the establishment of his regime in 1940 was a *huandu,* or "return" to the Nationalist capital, rather than a change of regime. (In making this claim, he was seeking to erode the legitimacy of Chiang's regime in exile in Chongqing.)

However, the Wang regime was not the only collaborationist regime in China during the war years. The first prominent one was the Manchukuo regime, set up in 1932 after the invasion and occupation of the northeastern region of China by the Japanese Kwantung Army in autumn 1931; this regime has further significance if one accepts the argument that the Sino-Japanese War began in 1931 rather than 1937. The Manchukuo regime's ideology of *Wangdao* (the Kingly Way) was very explicitly not the type of modern nationalism which Wang, Chiang, and Mao all espoused in different forms. Instead, it sought to create a premodern and backward-looking pseudo-Confucian view of how the polity should be understood. In addition, there were other short-lived regimes with little ideological basis to them, sponsored by the Japanese in part to engender rivalries between the different collaborators; one such government was that of Liang Hongzhi, which has been analyzed by Timothy Brook.[92]

There have been scholarly studies of these regimes, in particular that of Wang, in China.[93] But these studies have not been comprehensive, nor is there a sense of the regimes as being much more than a dark and anomalous chapter in modern Chinese history. A few popular writers and media figures have mentioned Wang Jingwei in more thoughtful terms, and their interventions seem more pointed or even taboo-busting in the absence of a wider historical debate in China about wartime collaboration influenced by an academic discussion, unlike the discussion on the partial rehabilitation of the Nationalists. One senior academic told me that the topic of collaboration remains "a very difficult topic to research" with "very few people publishing in it," and that those scholars are concentrating on factual topics, such as the numbers of troops under control of the Wang regime. Overall, he explained, scholars can research the topic, but it would be forbidden to argue that the collaborators were in any way "patriotic"—that is, to take seriously the terms in which Wang, Chen Gongbo, Zhou Fohai, and other leading collaborators, as well as their local counterparts, saw themselves. For that reason, the major internal conflict analyzed in academic discussion remains the Nationalist-Communist conflict. There is far less work on the conflict, or indeed contacts, between either of these groups and the collaborationist regimes.

The scholarly discussion in China on the history of the war is specialized, and the majority of it takes place in an academic context.

This does not mean that it is rarefied or irrelevant, however—far from it. The writing of history has always been political in China, and the understanding of the Second World War is no exception. The initiation of a new, expanded discussion of the war and its significance was authorized at the highest political levels in the early 1980s, and it continues to be the subject of direction and control in the era of Xi Jinping. The memory and legacy of the war have risen to the surface in many ways in China's domestic public sphere. Yet none of the very public interpretations of the war in Chinese politics or media would have appeared had it not been for the remarkable surge of energy in the study of the war itself over the past four decades, since the death of Mao. The academic debates around the war were the wellspring from which a powerful new discourse emerged that has come to shape China's society. Let us turn now to the effects of that discourse on China's public sphere.

3

Memory, Nostalgia, Subversion

How China's Public Sphere Embraced World War II

In her book *The Unwomanly Face of War,* the Belarusian writer Svetlana Alexievich provided firsthand accounts of Soviet women's experiences during World War II.[1] These harrowing stories of young women being forced to the front lines ran up against decades of Soviet-inspired narrative of a glorious war in which a united people confronted the Nazi invaders. The women she interviewed, three decades or more after they had fought, complained that their stories had been erased from most official narratives of the war, subsumed beneath a sanitized and highly masculine account of resistance to Nazism. Although the women's stories are constructions, distant memories that have been shaped by political constraints, they provide a remarkable variant on the official version of Soviet wartime history.

The same kind of ambivalence and return of hidden histories has been central to the formation of Chinese identity in the post–Cultural Revolution and post-1989 years: the telling of new, previously forbidden stories in a variety of sites supported by the official system as well as in more nebulous public arenas. In China, the state and the wider public interact with each other as they undertake this reclamation, often without acknowledging that they are doing so.

The state's reclamation of the war years began before 1989, with actions such as the construction of huge museums commemorating important events of the wartime period. Although the confrontation in Tiananmen Square ended a period of relative liberalism in political discourse, the closing down of discussions of democracy and political freedoms served to redirect the continuing sense of uncertainty over identity rather than to eliminate it. Instead of concerns about political pluralism, attention turned to ideas of national identity. At the same time, there was an unease that a growing economy and more comfortable lifestyles were failing to provide a sense of greater purpose beyond the purely individualistic. Neither the state nor the wider public sphere at that time could rebrand the Mao era as a positive period. But social memory of the war provided a potent source from which to create a sense of identity, particularly at a time when the state was promoting a new campaign of patriotism.

By the 1990s, memory of China's experience during the Second World War was becoming a prominent part of a new political consciousness. This was a period of immense political change both in China and globally. The Cold War ended in the late 1980s, more suddenly than many anticipated, and the Chinese Communist Party had a near-death experience with the 1989 Tiananmen crisis and killings. Yet within a few years, by the mid-1990s, China's rapid economic growth had resumed, and by 2008, China had the second largest economy in the world.

During these remarkable and turbulent years, a growing discourse around the Second World War in China remained a constant. At a time when many of the other building blocks of the global environment, notably the Cold War structure, had changed beyond recognition, there was a remarkable continuity in the institutions and individuals involved in building a broader narrative of the war, a continuity that has extended over more than three decades and is still evident today.

We have seen that changes—often controversial—in the Chinese academic sphere profoundly reshaped the way in which the war was understood in scholarly circles in China, both before and after 1989. In this chapter, we will focus on collective memory of the war and its significance in China's state and public spheres at the national level, and explore how it was shaped by academic discourse but developed in new directions from the mid-1980s to the turn of the millennium (although some of what I describe does stretch into more recent years). It is not that there was a monolithic understanding of the experience of the war years during that period—a "totalitarian" model fails to capture the complexity of the discourse even at the national level. Yet the sense of a distinct collective memory certainly does exist.

The 1990s was a particularly important decade for the discourse about wartime China. It was a time of newfound state concentration on patriotism as well as uncertainty, after Tiananmen, about identity among China's intellectuals and the public. Social media and the internet were still in the future. In those years, social memory was created through a variety of "vectors," to use Henry Rousso's term.[2] Museums have been one of the most obvious means by which the state has sought both to control public memory of the war and to reflect changing official views of history. The patriotism of the 1990s was reflected in institutions such as the War of Resistance museum in Beijing. The messages of the campaign were also reflected in the way in which writers and intellectuals engaged with the memory of the war. Popular writers absorbed the patriotic, state-defined view of the war's significance and used it to reflect on their own personal experiences or on the changing nature of contemporary Chinese society.

The new social memory has not been created in a vacuum. The primary purpose of its creators—politicians, cultural figures, and the media under the CCP's control—is to forge a moral discourse related to Chinese domestic identity and intertwined with the country's international role. This makes the portrayal of wartime history in the public sphere (museums, popular books, films, video games) distinct from its portrayal in the academic texts discussed in Chapter 2. Ostensibly, the discourse is centered on Chinese virtue in the face of Japanese savagery, as in the work of the writer Fang Jun and in the film *The Flowers of War,* directed by Zhang Yimou. But much of this discourse also reflects on the nature of Chinese identity. The Japanese are a foil, while the real target is some perceived sense of Chinese moral weakness, whether it is succumbing to the contemporary temptations of consumerism or the historical ambiguities surrounding wartime collaboration, as shown in the writing and museum curatorship of Fan Jianchuan, or the television work of the presenter Cui Yongyuan. Much of the discussion of the war in the public sphere is not really about Japan at all; it is about China and what it thinks about its own identity today, rather than in 1937 or 1945.

The Chinese public sphere now includes a major strand concerning the memory of the Second World War and acknowledgment of its significance for present-day China. This revived discourse about the memory and legacy of the war is by no means the only element that is shaping contemporary Chinese politics.

Many elements of the nationalist narrative have emerged in China since the 1980s, from the reappropriation of traditional philosophy to the valorization of "socialist values" as part of the Chinese Communist Party's reinvention of itself in the era of Xi Jinping.

Nonetheless, the war discourse is an important element. China's relationship with the Second World War is a distinctive aspect of the country's multifaceted cultural and political environment. It is distinctive both in the way that it contributes to the formation of the wider discourse of Chinese nationalism, and in its contrast with the memory and legacy of the war in the other major belligerent powers.

The War of Resistance Museum

For a concrete expression of the growing importance of memory of the War of Resistance in China, an obvious place to go is one of the three major museums on the conflict. All three were built in the 1980s and 1990s, and they have since been expanded and further developed. In Nanjing, the museum to the Nanjing Massacre opened in 1985; in Beijing, the Memorial Museum of the Chinese People's War of Resistance to Japan opened in 1987; and in Shenyang, the September 18th History Museum, a museum commemorating the date, 18 September 1931, that marked the start of the Japanese occupation of Manchuria, opened in 1991.

The idea of a public museum is a relatively recent phenomenon in China, going back only to the early twentieth century. In the 1920s and 1930s, the Forbidden City was converted by the Republican governments into a National Palace Museum as a means of inculcating a new sense of citizenship rather than subjecthood.[3] The People's Republic was more stable than the Republican governments, yet the museums that it sponsored became subject to rapid changes in historical interpretation inspired by political change within the Communist Party. The Museum of Revolutionary History in Tiananmen Square remained closed for much of the 1960s and 1970s as a result.

During the Mao era, the war against Japan was a secondary theme in public history; it was eclipsed by the divide between the Communists and Nationalists, not least because the Nationalists were perceived as a current threat, whereas the war with Japan was clearly in the past. This did not mean that the War of Resistance was entirely absent from the public sphere. In Fushun, a war crimes museum was set up in the 1950s to tell the story of the grisly Japanese atrocities in the region, along with accounts of the political "reeducation" of Japanese prisoners of war after 1945.[4] The new museums established in the 1980s saw a shift in emphasis and tone.

The War of Resistance museum was the product of a significant national-level initiative by a figure who certainly knew about the problems inherent in modern Chinese history: the theoretician and hardliner Hu Qiaomu, who was so instrumental in promoting the War of Resistance as a topic within the academy. Following discussions between Hu, the historian Liu Danian, and the Chinese Academy of Social Sciences (CASS), the town of Wanping, near the site of the Marco Polo Bridge incident, was chosen as the site for the museum. In 1983, Hu gave a speech on the importance of building museums to commemorate major historical events, declaring himself an "outsider" when it came to artifacts and curating, but an outsider who strongly supported the development of China's museum culture. He noted that the previous year, it had been reported that the government in Tokyo was producing school textbooks that altered the description of the

Japanese invasion of China in the 1930s.[5] "The War of Resistance is very recent," he said, "but today we don't have a museum of the war." His tone was measured; he advocated the building of another museum which would celebrate the much longer history of Sino-Japanese cooperation (a museum which, as it happens, has not yet been built). He also observed that there were relatively few specialist museums of any sort in China, whether on topics such as the history of women, or on Chinese "celebrities" from history such as Confucius, Du Fu, Yue Fei, and Sun Yat-sen—an intriguing list coming just a few years after the end of the Cultural Revolution, which had rejected such icons of the past.[6] Yet it was the War of Resistance museum that took priority.[7]

The Beijing Memorial Museum of the Chinese People's War of Resistance to Japan, to give it its full name, opened in 1987. It is a low-rise modernist building, surrounded by gardens and supplementary exhibition halls. The displays, rather than the building itself, are what draw visitors' attention. In the first few years after opening, the museum showed the shift in historiographical emphasis that would become even more pronounced over the next two decades. The Hall of Martyrs contained four large relief sculptures. Two were generic images of "generals, patriotic soldiers, and the wider people and masses," and the other two showed specific events. One represented the "Five Heroes of the Langyashan [Wolf's Tooth Mountain] Incident" of September 1941, during which five soldiers from a unit in the communist Jin-Cha-Ji base area on guerrilla maneuvers in Yi county, Hebei province, were said to have held back two thousand Japanese soldiers. The 1997 printed museum guide declared, "Finally, because all their bullets had run out and they had been cut off from all help, they collectively sacrificed themselves and jumped off a cliff, showing an exalted revolutionary spirit, courage, and ardor."[8] The fourth relief commemorated an example of Nationalist heroism, the defense of the district of Haibaoshan in Shanghai by a garrison of the Ninety-Eighth division of the Eighteenth Army under Yao Ziqing in August 1937. Yao and his garrison "bravely laid down their lives," but not before dispatching eight hundred Japanese soldiers. Near the reliefs, tablets to the martyrs of the war contained 296 names, from "high level commanders of the [CCP] Eighth Route and New Fourth Army troops, Nationalist troops . . . and Northeast United Army, who sacrificed themselves during the War of Resistance." Their names are listed in order of "the time of their sacrifice during the War of Resistance," with no differentiation as to which army they served.[9]

The Beijing museum, not surprisingly, gave the Chinese Communist Party a central role in the museum's narrative. The guidebook noted that "independent, autonomous guerrilla warfare was one aspect of the people's war, and was a concrete example of troops under CCP leadership opening up the people's war under the conditions of the anti-Japanese national United Front," further observing that close relations between the people and the CCP were "the basic guarantee of victory in the people's war."[10] The Nationalist government earned some praise, with one display stating that in the "political, economic, cultural and foreign relations fields," it did carry out some "effective policies relating to resistance to Japan and the establishment of reforms." Similarly emollient treatment of the Nationalist government could be seen at the exhibition "Modern China 1840–1997" at the Museum of Revolutionary History in Tiananmen Square in 1997, which was timed to coincide with the handover of Hong Kong and included displays of engineering and scientific projects carried out under Chiang Kai-shek's government in the 1930s.

The turn to patriotic education after the 1989 crisis provided a new opportunity for the museum of the War of Resistance to show that it could be a useful ideological tool. The museum managers believed that they had a responsibility to counter some of the morally corrupting effects of peacetime prosperity. Yu Yanjun, of the museum's educational activities staff, explained that it was important to teach children about the war years, because "the . . . 1980s one-child generation of students, both boys and girls, with their luxurious lifestyles, have grown up in an environment in which they have always been placed at the center of things." Yu also worried that students might not be aware of the historical record of China's neighbor: "There are many young people whose understanding of Japan is just from . . . television and the brand names of household appliances, and they do not know the historical tendency of the 'Japanese imperialists' to invade, as well as the hegemonic nature of the Western world today." In this sentence he managed to combine the twin fears of an unfriendly neighbor with the danger of commercialism.[11]

The idea that peacetime consumerism was having a negative effect on postwar society is not distinctively Chinese. Similar ideas circulated in other victor nations. The play *Plenty* (1978) by the British playwright David Hare is a powerful expression of this idea. In the play, which is based on real events, former Special Operations executive agent Susan Traherne finds that her peacetime life married to a diplomat does not match the excitement of her experiences in wartime France; her disillusionment at the banality of her postwar life destroys her own life and her husband's as a result. In China, the idea of empty and banal consumption ("plenty") did not proliferate until the 1980s. While urban consumption increased somewhat in the 1950s, the 1980s was really the first time since 1949 that widespread capitalist-style consumption had been seen. Criticism came along with this consumerism—which the likes of Hu Qiaomu termed "spiritual pollution."[12]

The desire to educate China's youth led the museum's management to make a particular effort to involve schoolchildren in its activities; in 1994, they made up over 60 percent of the one million visitors during that year. In the early 1990s the museum worked with local schools, including the Fengtai and Changxindian high schools and the Lugouqiao primary school, to find out which techniques worked better to influence young audiences. The dioramas were the most popular of the regular exhibits, and a variety of activities were scheduled. School history lessons were relocated to the museum, and special activity days for students were held for two weeks each month, when former Red Army and Eighth Route Army soldiers acted as guides to the exhibits. The primary school students were also taken through a special exhibition on children who had shown bravery during the war.[13]

The most original approach, however, was to establish a summer school on the theme of "Life during the War of Resistance." Established in 1993, the program lasted five days, with over six hundred pupils participating. The summer school took a different approach from the main museum exhibit, which deals mostly with the Communist and Nationalist combined war effort against the Japanese, concentrating instead on the Japanese-occupied areas. The children were first shown documentary films and then were taken to a reconstruction of an occupied zone, in effect a massive diorama. Yu Yanjun described what happened there:

We chose a hillside about two square kilometers in area, about five kilometers south of Lugouqiao. . . . Using simulated installations, we created an "occupied zone" of the War of Resistance era, with "Japanese devils" [*Riben guizi*] with loaded rifles, "collaborationist interpreters" making menacing gestures, Japanese military jeeps and motorbikes shuttling back and forth continuously, ruins giving off thick smoke, houses burnt and derelict, . . . people's heads running with blood, compatriots trussed up and beaten, laborers being savagely oppressed by bayonets, the noise of planes bombing in the sky, the sound of gunfire on the ground, and . . . salted vegetables being eaten by the refugees, while the "devils" and "collaborators" ate bread and roast duck. . . . A lifelike scene, realistic props and situations, to bring the history of the occupied zones from books and films to reality; the students wore refugees' clothes and straw hats, carrying their residence passes and undergoing ID checks.[14]

The summer school concluded with a student military corps drill. Its aim was to "contrast the past and the present . . . and strengthen [the students'] consciousness of national defense." Yu Yanjun felt that the scheme's success lay in its combination of lessons about the past with new methods of presentation. In the future, he suggested, policymakers should "get rid of the traditional model of patriotic education" and use new methods that would "make patriotic education more visible, tangible, and no longer just empty slogans and hackneyed inculcation."[15]

These summer camps (which were discontinued after a few years because of cost) were an expression of the politics of the 1990s, not the 1930s. The story told was a simplistic narrative which did not express the reality of how people felt about austerity in wartime China; the version of history they presented had a teleological trajectory that was simply not possible to foresee at the time.

How the War Museums Portray the Global War

From the 1990s onward, the War of Resistance museum in Beijing reflected the academic scholarship that portrayed the conflict as part of a global struggle. "The War of Resistance was an important constituent part of the world antifascist war," noted the guidebook published by the museum in 1997; the same phrasing was present in the 2018 version. A wall chart was on prominent display, with lights placed in Southeast Asia and North America showing significant overseas ethnic Chinese communities that had made contributions to the war effort. The text next to it was designed to appeal to a contemporary diaspora community, as was the wording of the guide describing an illuminated globe with areas lit up to show concentrations of overseas Chinese communities "all over the world during the period of the War of Resistance . . . their hearts all linked to the swelling patriotic sentiment of their homeland."[16]

The museum has had periodic updates since its foundation in 1987, notably in 1997 and 2005. Its incarnation in 2018, shortly after the eightieth anniversary of the Marco Polo Bridge incident, showed significant continuity with the original displays, including those on the importance of the Chinese Communist Party's role in winning the war.[17] Yet one change in phrasing reflected the growing political importance of the war in China's claims to a role in defeating fascism: publicity material declared that "China was the main Eastern battlefield for the global war against fascism," clearly placing the Pacific Theater in second place.[18] The museum also featured new displays that provided evidence for a much more globalized view of China's war experience and its legacy. The section on the end of the war featured a large panel on China's involvement in the formation of the United Nations, with prominent references to key Nationalist figures at the 1945 San Francisco Conference, such as T. V. Soong and Wellington Koo, along with the Communist delegate, Dong Biwu. During the long years when China's place at the United Nations was taken by the ROC on Taiwan (1949–1971), mention of the United Nations as a product of the wartime alliance would have been out of bounds. The appropriation of the Nationalists' efforts by the CCP means that there is, instead, an elided history which suggests a continuity between the "China" of 1945 and that of 2018, an elision that is easier to present in popular history, which does not demand great nuance.

The simplified narrative presented in the museum obscures a more complex history of China's relationship with the United Nations. Contemporary Chinese discourse also includes a great deal of anger at the legacy of that period, particularly the 1951 San Francisco Treaty, which excluded Beijing (as well as Taipei, which had to sign a separate treaty). The legacy of the period that gave rise to the United Nations is not accurately reflected by an unbroken continuity. Continuity with the past and fractures with it vie for discursive space: China's historical discourse claims on the one hand that it is the inheritor of 1945, and on the other that it has spent the past eight decades unjustly severed from the world created at that moment. At a speech at the UN offices in Geneva in early 2017, Xi Jinping made the link with the creation of the new global system in 1945, including the UN, quite explicit, declaring, "China is a founding member of the United Nations and the first country to put its signature on the UN Charter. China will firmly uphold the international system with the UN as its core, the basic norms governing international relations embodied in the purposes and principles of the UN Charter, the authority

and stature of the UN, and its core role in international affairs."
His speech associated China's UN activities closely with the development of the idea of a "Community of Shared Future" (sometimes rendered as "Community of Common Destiny"), a political framework that China has been developing in the 2010s to
create a sense of a Chinese mission that is beneficial for countries
other than China itself. Other Chinese politicians have made the
same point in public, for instance, foreign minister Wang Yi at the
2020 Munich Security Conference.[19]

The museum's displays about the wartime alliance are also used
to make points about the contemporary global order. There was
little mention of the Soviet contributions to the war effort from
the 1960s onward in China because of the split within the Communist bloc between the Soviets and the Chinese. But even when
relations between the two countries became better in the 1980s,
it was hard empirically to demonstrate a significant Soviet contribution to the war in China, since the USSR was neutral in the
Asian war between the time of the signing of the Soviet-Japanese
Neutrality Pact on 13 April 1941 and the declaration of war on
Japan on 8 August 1945. The museum does include a display on
one major Soviet contribution from an earlier period, however.[20]
During the first phase of the Chinese war against Japan in 1937–
1938, Stalin provided assistance and even fighter pilots. These pilots were helping the Nationalist, not Communist, forces, but
they were crucial in supporting a Chinese resistance that had almost no other air cover. This episode serves as a reminder that the
Russians are still able to offer support in the present day, although
China is now in the stronger geopolitical position.

The Beijing museum's displays have also changed to reflect engagement with one of the most powerful narratives of the war-

time years: the Nazi Holocaust. As of 2018, the museum features Chinese figures who helped Jewish refugees escape Europe. By creating its own array of non-Jews who aided Jewish victims—known in Israel as the "Righteous among the Nations"—the museum is able to connect itself to the wider discourse of this global atrocity.

The Holocaust also provides a touchstone for the Nanjing Massacre Museum, established in 1987, which was built on the site of one of the mass killings carried out during the Japanese invasion of the city in 1937. The museum, whose architect, Qi Kang, has noted the influence of Holocaust museums on his thinking, is significantly different in design from the Beijing museum. It has been upgraded every decade, with new displays added on each occasion. The museum grounds feature sculptures that represent scenes from the massacre, such as mothers mourning their lost children and a husband dragging the corpse of his wife. The museum's garden includes a bell that symbolizes memory of the massacre, and within the complex there are candles and water features. "The new space," wrote the literary critic and specialist on Chinese museology Kirk Denton in 2014, "with its huge triangular exhibition hall and vast, open square, gives the site a scale that transforms the original modest space into something monumental, ramping up its visual rhetoric and magnifying the victimization narrative."[21]

The museum contains a variety of features that reflect the influence of other institutions, including the US Holocaust Memorial Museum in Washington, DC, and Yad Vashem, the Holocaust museum located near Jerusalem. The reflecting pool, for example, is reminiscent of the one at the Israeli museum. Links between these two museums have become stronger over the years. In 2011, for example, a workshop was held at Yad Vashem for twenty-nine Chinese educators, one of whom declared a feeling of commonality: "With this new knowledge . . . I will do my best to tell the spirit of the Holocaust and the Jewish people, to promote the friendship between China and Israel."[22]

The city of Nanjing has found other ways to commemorate the atrocity, especially in relation to the Chinese American author Iris Chang. In 1997, Chang published *The Rape of Nanking,* an account of the killings that attracted significant attention both from the media and from readers in the global Chinese diaspora.[23] Chang's book highlighted the massacre at a time when both Chinese and Chinese American political identities were becoming stronger, and it became the basis for a broader conversation about the legacy of the war in Asia. Chang tragically took her own life in 2004. In the years since, commemoration of her work has become incorporated into the narrative of the war in China, and she is given credit as an important figure who bridged the Western and Chinese worlds with her writing.

Chang's work received some criticism from scholars. The historian Joshua Fogel, for example, challenged her argument that there was a deliberate, planned massacre of the population comparable with the Holocaust. Fogel pointed out that such errors of interpretation gave fuel to people in Japan who had an interest in denying that the massacre ever took place.[24] Yet in the Asian American community, Chang's work has turned her into a symbol of a determination to preserve the memory of a historical atrocity. Several books assessing Chang's legacy have been published, and her work inspired a 2018 play by the Asian American playwright Christopher Chen, *Into the Numbers.*[25]

In Nanjing itself, Chang has been venerated for her contribution. A statue of her was erected inside the Nanjing Museum in 2005. She is also commemorated at the former house of John Rabe, the head of the Siemens company in Nanjing, who created a "safety zone" for Chinese civilians during the occupation of the city and whose diaries recorded his horror at the killings and destruction visited upon the population. A statue of Chang was placed in the garden of the house, linking her legacy directly to that of those who tried to save lives in 1937–1938.[26]

The commemoration of Japanese war atrocities in the Nanjing Museum contrasts sharply with the lack of official memorialization for other events of mass violence and death in recent Chinese history, such as the Civil War (1946–1949), the Great Leap Forward (1958–1962), and the Cultural Revolution (1966–1976). These other events are sometimes remembered at one remove, through the acceptable lens of memory of the war against Japan, whether in private museums or through films and other creative works.

The Literary War in the 1990s

The war museums in Beijing, Nanjing, and Shenyang demonstrate the state's interest, starting in the 1980s, in promulgating a new historiography of the war. Other cultural phenomena in that decade also brought the war to a wider audience; for instance, in 1986, Mo Yan's novel *Red Sorghum* (*Hong gaoliang jiazu*), adapted as a film in 1988 by Zhang Yimou, told the story of a family caught up in the violence of the war against Japan. (Mo was awarded the Nobel Prize in Literature in 2012.) The growth of writing on the war years as a reflection on Chinese identity began a little later, in the 1990s. It was at this time that the idea of China's Second World War as a "good war" became widespread. The term "the good war" was popularized in the United States by Studs Terkel, in his Pulitzer Prize–winning oral history of hundreds of people's memories of World War II.[27] Terkel's use of the term was layered with irony, since the war had been devastating for so many Americans, and the "goodness" of its overall narrative stood in sharp contrast to the Vietnam War that had followed just two decades later. Nonetheless, his account of the "good war" became one of the most prominent ways in which personal experience has come to the fore in explaining the wider cultural significance of that and other wars in the Western psyche.

In China, the highly personalized style that marked literary nonfiction about the war in the 1990s, assessing it as a positive, nation-building exercise, was not wholly new. Nonfiction texts written in a literary style and reporting on current events (*baogao wenxue,* or reportage) had flourished within China's media culture in the early twentieth century, as the press became more established.[28] A distinctive journalistic voice in this mode during the Republican period was that of Du Zhongyuan, a nationalist business entrepreneur and journalist who fled the Japanese occupation of the Northeast in 1931.[29] The reportage style was revived in the era of "scar literature" in the late 1970s, when writers were given more leeway to deal with the personal traumas of the Cultural Revolution. Liu Binyan, author of pieces such as "People or Monsters?" explored that politically traumatic period in a highly personal style.[30] This type of reportage became an important aspect of China's reorientation around memory of the war as part of its refashioning of identity after the Cold War.

It would be too much to say that the writers who have recorded their own experiences of the war, or their reactions to its legacy, speak for an entire generation; the fact that they have chosen or been chosen to make their views public automatically categorizes them as unusual. But because they are educated and self-expressive, and they write in the public domain, they are able to craft accounts that reflect the realities they see in society and, in turn, to affect that society. One notable phenomenon in the West has been a rise of interest in the world wars as the events become more distant and fewer people remain to recall them. In that sense, China is catching up with a worldwide phenomenon.[31] World War II becomes a "good war" not just in terms of the cause for which it was fought, but in contrast with what came afterward. In much of Europe, World War II was followed by the Cold War and its shades of gray. China's postwar history was one of radical politics written in the primary colors of historical traumas such as the Cultural Revolution that are now politically problematic.

An example of the new literature describing memories of the war is the collection edited by Song Shiqi and Yan Jingzheng entitled *The War of Resistance to Japan through the pens of journalists* (1995).[32] On the fiftieth anniversary of the end of the war, the People's Daily Publishing Company in Beijing asked sixty-two former war correspondents, many of them long-standing party members and former employees of the predecessors of the CCP-controlled Xinhua (New China News Agency), to write short memoirs of their experiences during the war. The most famous contributor, perhaps, was Lu Yi, a frontline correspondent who had worked for the Tianjin newspaper *Da gongbao* in the 1930s.[33] In some ways the collection is rather bland; the accounts, although told in the first person, generally use formulaic and standardized language. Yet the topics covered include many of the battles and campaigns that took place in the Nationalist-controlled areas of China (such as Taierzhuang and Xuzhou), and it is clear, despite the official editing of the pieces, that the former correspondents valued the opportunity to put the most significant events of their lives in the public record and to chip away at some of the certainties of the CCP's version of history.

The journalist Zhang Menghui's contribution deals with his time in wartime Chongqing, when he helped write a patriotic song. A Sichuanese native, Zhang had become editor of the *National Gazette* (*Guomin gongbao*) in Chongqing in 1943 and continued to work as a writer and publisher in post-1949 China. He reminisced about the old days:

> The voices of the youths in the Nationalist areas grew ever louder. They had not yet gone to the frontline and joined up, but they weren't just sitting there and waiting for victory. They used their strength to the utmost to provide fuel for the fire of the War of Resistance.
>
> Half a century has gone by. China has gone through massive changes. But the songs of national salvation in resistance to Japan still remain deep in the hearts of us old people.[34]

Compare that sentiment with the following extract by Du Zhongyuan about his visit in 1937 to the local National Salvation League (one of the locally organized anti-Japanese resistance organizations) in Taiyuan:

> The meeting place for the league was the National Normal School, and the place where they had asked me to lecture was the school's auditorium. The auditorium could hold over 1,000 people; at 7 o'clock, I mounted the stage, and after the league's leader had in-

troduced me, I gave a special talk on the determination for resistance at the center, and on the words that Chairman Chiang had personally uttered in Shanghai, and in Nanjing. . . . In their applause and welcoming voices, I saw their warm enthusiasm for resistance to the enemy and saving the nation. Afterwards, all the League members sang inspiring songs about national salvation; their spirit strengthened mountains and rivers, their voices shook the tiles on the walls, and it made you very emotional.[35]

The two pieces, written some five and a half decades apart, have remarkable similarities. Retrospect and romanticism surely affected the way in which Zhang Menghui recalled the events of the early war period from a distance of more than fifty years. Yet many of the linguistic conventions and tropes remain the same. The expression "War of Resistance to Japan" was officially adopted early on in the war, and the idea that unity against Japan was constant, enthusiastic, and unquestioned is explicit in both of these pieces.

This similarity in language and ideas makes it appear as if the understanding of the wartime experience remained constant across the sixty-year gap between the composition of these two texts. As we saw in the previous chapter, this time period actually saw major changes in the trajectory of historical interpretation. But even though it was published after the historiographical changes of the 1980s, Song and Yan's collection of memoirs continued to stress the CCP's role in the war and to glorify events such as the Hundred Regiments Campaign, in which legendary Communist military figures such as Peng Dehuai were involved. The publication of the memoirs, officially constrained though they were, did, however, mark a significant change in emphasis. Although most of the sixty-two participants were CCP members, or sympathizers before 1949, the range of the pieces acknowledges the spread of the conflict well beyond the classic Communist base areas. Furthermore, there are implications throughout the memoirs that the participants were glad to have a chance to speak of matters that they felt had been unjustly ignored. (Participants in the project *Going to the Interior* [*Qu da houfang*], discussed in Chapter 5, expressed a similar sentiment.) In his conclusion to the collection, Zhang Menghui takes care to note that however many decades have passed, the events in which he took part during the War of Resistance continue to be significant. More than a decade later, as we will see in the next chapter, the television presenter Cui Yongyuan would express a similar view, using one of his media projects to criticize the public invisibility of those who served in the Nationalist armies.

Zhang Menghui's essay refers to a theme that is threaded through the new discourse about the war: justice. In the official discussions, "justice" usually refers to the need for China to achieve more recognition in international society, particularly for its role in the war against the Japanese and in shaping the postwar order. Ding Fuhai, who had been a journalism student between 1942 and 1945 and went on to work for the storied *Da gongbao*, ends his piece in the same collection on this note: "Half a century has gone by, and our country has produced massive changes. But the history of Japanese imperialism invading us, we will never forget! The Chinese people's brave spirit of resistance to Japan will eternally stimulate us forward!"[36] But, he suggests, justice must be done within China itself, by acknowledging the contributions to China's ultimate victory from the Nationalist side. Youth in the Nationalist zone, as Zhang said, "weren't just sitting there and waiting for victory."

Repeatedly, the writers in this collection recall the importance of the war period; while they do not explicitly contrast it with the Mao era, the terminology they use, all of which has changed little from reports from the 1930s—war to the end, enemy, imperialism—stresses the sheer significance of the events to the shaping of their own lives as well as that of the country, and shows the continued downgrading of the Mao-era conflict with the Nationalists.

Baby Boomers and Confucian Tropes

It is logical enough that a generation that lived through the war, and found its political commitment at that time, should look back to those years with nostalgia. But why should the war have such significance for generations born after the conflict was over? The work of writers born in the years of high Maoism, such as Fang Jun and Fan Jianchuan, shows that the reclamation of the war against Japan as a "good war," one that justified both the existence of the nation and the lives and experiences of those who lived through it, has also shaped the postwar generations who are looking back to a war they never saw, rather than to their own experiences, to find legitimacy in post–Cultural Revolution and contemporary China.

Demographically parallel with the Baby Boomers of the West, writers born in the 1950s had a very different trajectory from their counterparts in the United States and Europe. Born during the Great Leap Forward period, they grew up during the Cultural Revolution and came of age during the reform era, when economic and educational opportunities opened up in a way that would have been unimaginable under Mao's rule. In the 1980s, rather like their counterparts in Eastern Europe, they experienced socialism with consumerist characteristics. In 1989, they lived through the greatest crisis of the Chinese reform-era state, the Tiananmen Square protests and killings; but unlike in Eastern Europe, as they entered their thirties, they were confronted not with an entirely new liberal political discourse, but rather with economic loosening and a reworked version of the existing model of political control. It was in this context that they wrote about the war as a vehicle for the ideas and sentiments that resonated with 1990s China. The War of Resistance came to be seen as parallel to events such as the Cultural Revolution and the May Fourth Movement; it was considered important not so much because of the details of particular campaigns, social phenomena, or other events, but rather as a means of reinterpreting the present.

One prominent example of this reinterpretation is the book *The "Devil Soldiers" I Knew* (1997) by Fang Jun.[37] Fang Jun was born in 1954 in Beijing. The son of an Eighth Route Army veteran, he became a steelworker and then joined the military and the CCP in 1973. He studied Japanese at night school in the 1980s and became an assistant at the newspaper *Yomiuri Shimbun* and then at the Japanese consulate, before going to Japan as an overseas student from 1991 to 1997. While in Japan, Fang found out that three to four hundred thousand Japanese soldiers who had taken part in the invasion of China were still living. Stimulated by the memory of conversations with his father about the war years, he decided that he would interview some of these Japanese "devil soldiers" before they died.[38] His book, a highly personal and emotional account of self-discovery, recounts his interviews with these Japanese army veterans.[39]

Fang's choice to write in a first-person narrative is noteworthy. Autobiography as a genre has been influenced in China by the Confucian tradition, which disapproved of accounts that pushed the subjective self forward, deeming them arrogant, self-promoting, and untrustworthy.[40] A more modern sort of persona emerged in the twentieth century, as journalists and writers, often drawing on the conventions of mass-market fiction, began to project themselves as personalities via newspaper columns. To avoid accusations of self-aggrandizement, they did so not in a celebration of themselves, but in the Confucian style of men who, though self-declaredly uneducated, nonetheless had to speak out at a time of national peril.[41]

The writings of Du Zhongyuan provide a clear example of a precedent to the writing of the 1990s. From 1934 to 1935, Du was editor of the *Xinsheng* (New life) magazine of political commentary; week by week, the strong, personalized voice of his "Honest talk" (*Laoshihua*) column connected the periodical with its readership. Du's long opening letter in the first issue of *Xinsheng* points out some of the different aspects of his identity and displays both premodern and modern conventions of self-presentation:

> I should introduce myself and the motivations behind producing this journal. I am not a cultured man [*wenxuejia*], and I'm not a news reporter, nor am I a famous or great character. Formerly, I was an entrepreneur in Shenyang. . . .
> I don't know what country I am from. Can I say I am Chinese? My home village clearly is no longer part of China's territory. Can I say I'm not Chinese? But I was nurtured and raised in the same environment with 450 million compatriots; only because it is the cause of the Chinese people do I feel the pain and shame. . . .
> There are people who are stray curs, like the slaves of a lost country, and now I have become a stray cur.

> But as I have experienced the pain of a lost country [*wangguo*],
> I therefore have the authority and the necessity to call out a war-
> cry to the masses of the whole country.[42]

Much of Du's language and political analysis is modern, shaped by notions of nationalism. Yet it is also implicitly, and on occasion explicitly, informed by Confucian norms. One particular feature that draws on premodern tropes is Du's reiteration of the role of the writer as moral authority. In the words of the scholar Pei-yi Wu, "To cultivate the person, to examine the self, to develop each individual to the utmost—these are among the themes most frequently discussed in classical Confucianism."[43] Also dating from the premodern period is the declared modesty of the author. Du emphasized that he was neither a cultured man nor a news reporter, and another contributor to the first issue of the magazine started his open letter by declaring, "Why don't I write essays but instead write 'letters'? . . . I could never write essays. Even when I was little and at school, I couldn't write essays well."[44] The moral imperatives of national salvation are also embedded everywhere in Du's writings, along with his exhortations to his readership to turn away from their own apathy and resist Japan.

Du Zhongyuan was a member of the generation that had made the transition from the empire to the republic. Fang Jun was not born until a decade after Du's death, but much of his self-presentation bears a resemblance to Du's account of why he chose to write about the Sino-Japanese conflict. In his concluding chapter, Fang addresses the question of why he wrote such a personal book in the first place. He protests, "I'm not a politician, I'm not an artist, I'm not an educator, nor am I an essayist, and moreover, I've never thought of doing such stuff."[45] Earlier, he had declared: "I really have no talent for writing. . . . If the Japanese were like the Germans, would I still need to write? . . . [Yet] I feel that it is a sort of historical responsibility that I sense driving me on."[46] Fang's reference to the Germans was meant to suggest that they had acknowledged their war guilt in a way that the Japanese had failed to do.

The most significant difference between the two writers is that Du was writing at a time when China was actually under attack from Japan, while Fang Jun was writing in the 1990s, a time when Sino-Japanese tensions were high but China was a strong sovereign power and Japan was firmly under its postwar "peace constitution."

Both writers, despite their protestations of simplicity, wrote works full of literary artifice, deployed with great skill. Fang, for example, uses repetition very effectively when he explains why he began to weep when he learned of Japanese war atrocities: "My tears were for the humiliation of the Chinese people half a century before; my tears were for the blood shed in struggle by . . . the Chinese people half a century before; my tears were for the heart of a former soldier . . . who risked death for his country."[47] He ends the book by answering his own question as to why he wrote it: "I hope that our motherland will be rich and strong, I hope that our children will be healthy and strong. When it was not rich and strong, when they were not healthy and strong, then we let the Northeast [Manchuria] go, we lost Lugouqiao [the Marco Polo Bridge], we retreated from Shanghai, and the blood flowed in Nanjing."[48]

With a nod to the social Darwinism that has informed most nationalist discourse in China over the past century, Fang Jun connects his own personal *Bildung* with the fear, prevalent at the time, that neo-imperialism might once again make China vulnerable. Though he is careful to acknowledge the Japanese students and veterans who have recognized their country's war guilt—this is a sophisticated book, despite the author's protestations of lack of culture—Fang Jun positions himself as part of the discourse that sees China, even in its current prominent position in East Asia, as always on the verge of victimhood.

This theme of victimization is prominent in the first chapter of Fang Jun's book, titled "Human flesh dumplings." In this chapter, which uses one of the most powerful images in Chinese culture, Fang writes that one of the Japanese veterans he interviewed reported having heard that guards at a certain prison had cooked up body parts of Chinese prisoners, especially women, and eaten them.[49] With seeming disingenuousness, Fang Jun claims in the first sentence of the chapter that he originally intended to place this section at the back of the book, rather than at the beginning. But why give priority to the one incident in the book that is reported at second hand? Yamashita, the veteran, does not claim that he ate human flesh himself, but that he had heard that others knew of it being done. Considering how many well-documented atrocities the Japanese did commit in China during the war period, why does this one have such power that Fang places it before the more "mainstream" atrocities reported at first hand later in the book?

Fang may have chosen to highlight the chapter on cannibalism because of the importance of the taboo against this practice as a recurring theme in Chinese culture. Lu Xun is perhaps the most famous writer to have used this image in the twentieth century. In his *Diary of a Madman* (1918), the metaphor used by the "madman" for the pervasiveness of Confucian thought in Chinese culture is that of a society where people eat each other.[50] The theme itself goes back centuries in China and is also present in many other cultures; it is almost always associated with a premodern sense of atrocity in contrast with the image of modern warfare, which tends to be mechanized and impersonal.[51]

After Fang hears Yamashita's story, the idea of cannibalism affects his encounter with the Japanese people around him. As he and Yamashita are cooking a meal together while chatting, Fang says he is suddenly revolted by the dumplings in front of him: "I felt that the meat on the plate I was holding was bright red human flesh! . . . I put the plate on the table and said to the old Japanese devil: 'This is human flesh! Old man . . . I can't make dumplings out of human flesh for you!' "[52] Later, he visits Mount Fuji and hurls accusations at the mountain: Why did it not speak out and tell the truth about this awful practice?

Cannibalism is presented here not in terms of a historical phenomenon, but as a means, constructed through an essentially literary mode of writing, through which to examine Chinese society. Fang's treatment of the subject has some similarities with one of the more notable exposés of cannibalism in the past few decades, Zheng Yi's *Scarlet Memorial* (*Hongse jinianbei*), which was published in Taiwan after the author escaped from post-Tiananmen China.[53] *Scarlet Memorial* is a reportage account of the phenomenon of cannibalism in Guangxi autonomous region during the Cultural Revolution, at the most extreme period of internal conflict. As in the most radical works in the antitraditional May Fourth tradition, Zheng uses cannibalism as a means of focusing on trends in China that led to metaphorical, as well as literal, self-devouring.

Fang Jun does not make an explicit reference to the May Fourth trope of cannibalism, but like Zheng Yi, he stresses the cultural significance of the idea. Unlike Lu Xun or Zheng Yi, however, Fang uses the cannibalism trope not to criticize China from within, but instead to find a way to portray China's invaders as truly evil, in some way culturally beyond the pale. The chapter on "Human flesh dumplings" is an extreme example of the way in which writing on the Sino-Japanese war has been used to reconstruct the twentieth-century Chinese as positive, patriotic figures who are at the same time victims of unspeakable savagery by others, rather than the authors of their own misfortunes.

Fan Jianchuan is a different sort of writer from Fang Jun. Born in 1957, Fan grew up during the Cultural Revolution and was sent down to the countryside before he joined the army. He then served as a teacher and deputy mayor in his hometown of Yibin before becoming a real estate developer. In an interview with the *South China Morning Post,* he declared that by the year 2000, he was running one of the top five property firms in Sichuan. At around that time, he began to concentrate full-time on creating what would become China's largest private cluster of museums. These museums deal with some of the most sensitive topics in Chinese history, including the Cultural Revolution. One of them commemorates the War of Resistance and is the subject of Fan's book *One Person's War of Resistance (Yige ren de kangzhan)* (2000).[54]

Fan Jianchuan's book title and subtitle indicate his sweeping aims. The title, "One Person's War of Resistance," suggests that it is a participant's memoir, but the subtitle, "Using one person's collection to look at a war of the whole nation," reveals something rather different.[55] Fan informs readers that his book was inspired by Fang Jun's memoir, and indeed his book is a variant of the exercise Fang Jun was carrying out. Fan is also reconstructing the war experience, but in his case, via the artifacts that he has collected. He declares that he has been a collector of memorabilia since childhood, with a particular interest in the ceramic goods of the Cultural Revolution and the War of Resistance, and that his collections from these two periods are among "the leading examples in the country."[56]

Each short chapter of the book starts with a description of a particular item from Fan's collection—a cup, a helmet, an ID card—and then moves into a reflection about the item's significance during the war and in society today. Fan's framework is rather different from Fang Jun's. Fang's narrative is in some ways a fairly typical expression of nationalist sentiment, oriented toward the role of the CCP in the war and dismissive of the Nationalists. Fan puts the Communist and Nationalist leaders on the same side, in contrast to the collaborators: "On the one side were Mao Zedong and Chiang Kai-shek in the camp of resistance to Japan; on the other were Wang Jingwei and Puyi, representing the camp of treachery."[57] Looking at his collection of memorabilia, he notes, "From the few . . . Chiang Kai-shek items [I have], we can say they are the proof that he made a contribution to the War of Resistance to Japan."[58]

He reflects further on collaborators like Wang Jingwei:

We Chinese often call ourselves descendants of the dragon. . . . With Wang Jingwei's . . . type, we gnash our teeth in hatred, and look on them as fleas produced by the dragon. In fact, rather than saying that they are a variant type of the dragon seed, say instead that our Chinese nation closely resembles . . . a group of ants . . . among whom a certain proportion are fleas. The strong proof of this is the 800,000 puppet soldiers who were willing to sell themselves to the Japanese. . . . Of the bad things that happen in the world, half are done by bad people, and the other half are the result of the apathy, indifference, tolerance, and even support of people who don't care about the bad people. If those 800,000 puppet troops (and not every one of those puppet troops was a follower of the big collaborators or evildoers) had not produced Wang Jingwei, then they could instead have produced Li Jingwei or Zhang Jingwei; if they had not produced Chen Gongbo, then they would have produced Wang Gongbo or Zhao Gongbo.[59]

On the surface, there is nothing much in this passage that the CCP-endorsed version of the new public memory of the Sino-Japanese war could find fault with. Nonetheless, the view that Fan puts forward here, that Wang Jingwei's lust for power was such that he was exploited easily by the Japanese, indicates a small shift in attitude toward the collaborators.[60] Chen Gongbo was one of Wang Jingwei's closest colleagues in the collaborationist wartime Nanjing government. By creating characters with the same personal names as Wang and Chen (rather like saying, for Vichy France, "if we hadn't had Pierre Laval, we might have had Pierre Lebrun or Pierre Leblanc"), Fan steps away from any idea that Wang Jingwei's actions were uniquely evil, instead arguing that Chinese society and human nature meant that cooperation with the enemy might not be so unexpected. (A decade later, the television presenter Cui Yongyuan would offer similar views, as we will see in Chapter 4.)

However, there is another interpretation of this passage about ants and fleas: it could refer not just to the war against Japan, but also to the Cultural Revolution, or other periods where Chinese society has produced "fleas" as well as "ants." Fan Jianchuan has, over the decades, spent enormous sums of money on China's only private museum commemorating the Cultural Revolution. The

Cultural Revolution was officially blamed on the Gang of Four, a convenient scapegoating that allowed wider questions about the nature of Chinese society, such as those raised in Zheng Yi's *Scarlet Memorial,* to go unasked by the CCP.[61] Similarly, in his writing about the war, Fang Jun demanded that the responsibility for China's wartime crisis be diverted from the Chinese themselves to the imperialist invaders. Although there is nothing explicit in this passage from Fan Jianchuan's book that contradicts that interpretation, there is a strong hint that something within Chinese society made it easier for the Japanese to exercise control. The hint that perhaps an analogy with the Cultural Revolution is intended is made clearer in a later chapter in the book.

The most direct point of connection between the Cultural Revolution and the Sino-Japanese conflict in Fan's book does not date from the war period at all. It occurs in a chapter that is entitled "An 'appeal' on an earthenware cup: the fate of a Sichuanese old soldier of the war of resistance." Fan says of the featured artifact, "It's an ordinary earthenware cup, not very old . . . but it's one of the most precious items in my collection of War of Resistance items." The cup has written on it, "I only remember the eight years of the War of Resistance. I fought the Japanese, and I took a bullet in my leg. I determinedly fought to the end and never left the line of fire! 15 September 1966."[62]

Fan explains that the owner wrote this on the cup just a few months after the Cultural Revolution broke out. During the period of what Fan terms the "red terror" (*hongse kongbu*), the owner probably came under attack because he was a Sichuanese former soldier in the Nationalist army whose record now counted against him. The owner could not have been well educated, as the relatively short sentences contain four badly written characters. Fan's deduction that he was persecuted in the Cultural Revolution means that he must have been a soldier in the Nationalist army, not the Eighth Route Army or a local guerrilla force. Fan writes,

> Looking at this string of characters, I felt saddened and angry. In the eight years of the War of Resistance, he had dodged death and had for many years been considered to have had an honourable experience, and suddenly, overnight, it was considered shameful?! He . . . had no place to appeal, in the political high temperature of that era, the majority of people didn't believe him . . . so all he could think of was to write on this cup, and write down some words from his heart; he was surely sad and angry.[63]

Worse still, Fan wondered, perhaps he was sent down and made the cup while serving a sentence of reform through labor (*laogai*). But the cup, which Fan not only makes the subject of a lengthy reflection but also uses as the image for the front cover of the book, suggests that one reason for his interest in the War of Resistance may be that as a "just war," it provides a contrast with the Cultural Revolution and the Mao era more generally, during which the importance of the nation and the identity of China's regions were downplayed. Fan's work shows how the more flexible boundaries for interpretation of the war allowed new and daring analogies.

In the twenty years since Fan published his book, he has developed his museum complex yet further. The Jianchuan complex now holds over two million artifacts and is a major tourist attraction.[64] In 2018, the Jianchuan Chongqing museum opened, commemorating that city's resistance to Japan when it served as the temporary wartime capital for the Nationalist government.[65]

The books by Fan Jianchuan and Fang Jun were products of the late 1990s, when Jiang Zemin held power and the post-Tiananmen campaign of "patriotic education" was taking effect. Two decades later, it is much easier to see the two books as outriders of a phenomenon that has become ever stronger in the twenty-first century, a new public remembering of World War II, and to recognize how they exemplify two contrasting strands within this trend. The first strand, exemplified by Fang Jun, is the move toward a "victimology" culture in which China's suffering and sacrifice, along with a revival of the CCP's standing, are brought to the fore. The second, exemplified by Fan Jianchuan, is an ambivalent attitude toward the official discourse. It tends to stress the Nationalist contribution but also, more broadly, the changes in Chinese identity that were engendered by the war.

Problematic Memories—Forbidden or Forgotten?

Fang Jun's and Fan Jianchuan's books take quite different positions on the importance of the Sino-Japanese war in contemporary Chinese life, even though they deal with many similar topics and tropes, as well as taking a strongly individualistic and personalized stance. In other words, there is no monolithic post–Cold War interpretation of the War of Resistance; there is not one new Chinese memory of the war, but rather a variety of diverse memories. In a way that is common in Chinese political writing, Fan uses his book to make more critical and self-reflective observations about contemporary Chinese life, but is rarely explicit in doing so, preferring to rely on hint and inference. The boundary between memories that are permitted and those that are frowned upon is often deliberately left vague.

Probably because of his family connections with the Eighth Route Army, Fang Jun hews much more to a traditional CCP-driven historiography, which downplays the contribution by

Chiang Kai-shek and the Nationalist government to the victory over the Japanese. Fang's father, a veteran of the (Communist) Eighth Route Army, tells him that "the reason that Chiang Kai-shek had to withdraw to Taiwan was that he didn't fight the Japanese." Fang then regrets that he never took the opportunity to ask his father, "If Chiang had begun to fight the Japanese, what then?"[66] One entire chapter (entitled "Your Dad was in the Eighth Route Army?") deals with an interview with a Japanese veteran who talks about his respect for this most legendary of Communist forces during the war.[67]

Even in Fang's work, there are some references that suggest a widening of the agenda beyond the hagiography of the CCP's contribution. One of these is Fang's discovery of the story of the Manchurian resistance leader Ma Zhanshan, who was only later involved with the Communists: "When I left China in 1991, almost all the anti-Japanese heroes whom I had in my heart were CCP people," he notes, but finding out about Ma Zhanshan changed that view. He also writes of the desire of a Japanese army veteran, Kobayashi, to return with Fang to Beijing, where he served during the war; he wants to visit the street named after a respected enemy, the Nationalist general Zhang Zizhong, who was killed in battle against the Japanese during the war.[68] These changes are also visible in sites such as the Beijing Museum of the War of Resistance; the official widening of viewpoints on the war has been a gateway for exploration of figures not so tied to the state.

The War of Resistance has now become China's "good war." In a world where the Cold War definitions of Chinese identity no longer hold, the history of the war plays an important role in redefining what it means to be Chinese. But many issues—generation, gender, regional affiliation, experience of the war itself, of the

Cultural Revolution, and of the reform era—shape group and individual understandings of exactly why that war was "good." Museums and books are not the only ways that such understandings can be transmitted. In the next chapter we will see how visual media have also provided a powerful arena in which to explore the boundaries of China's changing memory of war in the new millennium.

4

Old Memories, New Media

Wartime History Online and Onscreen

The Second World War became ever more prominent in China's public sphere in the 1980s and 1990s. In the new millennium its visibility increased yet further as a result of one of the most significant transformations of the era: the changing nature of China's media. During the first decade of the 2000s, China's middle class became larger and more prosperous, with more disposable income, and a celebrity culture emerged. Movie and television stars began to appear not just onscreen but in magazines and on billboards advertising lifestyle products. Then, in the late 2000s and 2010s, social media came to China. Within a few years, in a way that would have been unimaginable in the controlled world of Mao Zedong, the Chinese internet burst into life as debates, gossip, arguments, and scandal were passed from phone to phone. Even the arrival of Xi Jinping as leader in 2012, which inserted a new authoritarian chill into China's public sphere, did not shut down this trend.

The new media opportunities, and the techno-authoritarianism that accompanied them, have shaped perceptions of China's experience during the Second World War. Celebrity culture has sometimes interacted with public memory in unexpected ways, not least in 2018 when one major television personality, Cui Yongyuan, made a complaint that helped to destroy the marketing efforts for a Second World War–themed project featuring China's most famous female movie star, Fan Bingbing. Yet beneath this spicy celebrity tale lies the same theme that has fueled much of the debate over the meaning of the war since the 1980s: what are the building blocks of a new Chinese nationalist identity, at a time when economic concerns seem to outweigh ideas about abstract ideology?

We begin here with Cui Yongyuan's 2010 project, *Wode kang-zhan* (My war of resistance), a documentary on the long-forgotten Nationalist soldiers of the Second World War. We will then examine the complexities of how the war was represented onscreen in the early 2000s, and the contrast between treatment of two different events: the horrors of the Nanjing Massacre and the heroism of the resistance war in Chongqing. We also explore how China has attempted to use film to speak to an international audience and create a wider understanding of China's wartime experience that seeks to generate moral standing and warmth for China. The focus then moves from producers to consumers, the *Guofen* (or "Republican fans") who make revisionist views about China's World War II experience part of their personal identity on the internet. The phenomenon that emerged in the 1990s, through which the war was used to make statements about Chinese identity, is now flourishing onscreen and online.

The Television Odyssey of Cui Yongyuan

During the years between the Beijing Olympics of 2008 and Xi Jinping's rise to power in 2012, some limited space became available for relatively liberal views to appear in Chinese politics. This opening was partial at best; after all, the dissident thinker Liu Xiaobo was arrested in 2008 and would die as a prisoner of the state in 2017. Yet ideas were being voiced in that era that would seem daring in the light of the media clampdown that marked the 2010s. One phenomenon that emerged during this period was a remarkable television program hosted by one of China's best-known broadcasters, Cui Yongyuan.

Cui Yongyuan has been a media phenomenon in China for decades. His show *Shihua shishuo* (Tell it like it is) aired on CCTV from 1996 to 2002 and proved a huge hit because of its host's natural and authentic-seeming personal style, which was very different from the staid and stilted sort of presentation that dominated Chinese broadcasting at the time. He then achieved a different kind of fame when he took time off to be treated for depression in 2001. Mental health issues are rarely discussed in public in China, and Cui's openness on this issue broke long-standing taboos. He then returned to the screen in a succession of popular programs, before giving up most of his broadcasting presence for an academic career in 2013. He continues to be a controversial figure. In the early 2010s, he campaigned strongly against genetically modified foods, even opening himself up to a lawsuit, and in 2018, he was embroiled in a public spat with the movie star Fan Bingbing, a confrontation whose effects we will revisit later in the chapter. In 2019, he made a high-profile intervention in a row over the record of a Chinese Supreme Court judge.[1]

Back in 2010, Cui launched a project in a rather different area from his previous work: an online film series titled *Wode kangzhan* (My War of Resistance), which celebrated the lives of former Nationalist wartime soldiers.[2] This was an important moment: one of China's best-known media figures was taking up hidden aspects of the war as a personal theme. In an interview with the liberal paper *Nanfang zhoumo* (Southern weekend) on 7 October 2010, Cui was asked when he had become interested in wartime history. He picked up on the phrase *quanmin kangzhan* (the war of resistance of the whole people), remarking that those using this term are "hoping to imply that we're bringing you along with us when we are relating this part of history." It was only quite late in life, he said, that he understood the implications of widening the interpretation of the war. When he was young, movies had hinted that the Nationalists had collaborated with Japan. He realized that this idea was wrong when he visited Songshan in Yunnan, the scene of a major campaign in 1944. The guide, a former Nationalist soldier who didn't recognize Cui, escorted him to the site of the battlefield where his comrades had been killed and "suddenly yelled out the names of his comrades." "I felt very sad at this," Cui said. "This was perhaps the first time that I had met a Nationalist soldier, and I really began to feel respect for them."[3]

While making a documentary on the politically acceptable topic of the Long March, Cui used the opportunity to interview over one hundred former Nationalist soldiers in Yunnan. These interviews became the basis for his documentary, and he then expanded to around 3500 interviews conducted between 2002 and 2010. He had been motivated in part by seeing Japanese documentaries that, while impressive in their professionalism, seemed misleading. In one of them, "in narrating the Nanjing battle [of 1937], you couldn't see a single corpse." Asked why he had made a documentary, Cui remarked that "individual stories" were better at raising consciousness than textbooks.[4] Cui could not find any mainstream television outlet to show the interviews, but the new media environment of the 2010s came to his rescue, as he was able to place them online. "It wasn't like deciding to make kung pao chicken," said one of Cui's collaborators, meaning that instead of deciding to make the program and then finding the ingredients, the material came to them and they had to work out how to use it. The stories of the Nationalist veterans they met were very raw. One soldier, Li Hebing, who had served with the Nationalist 29th Army, declared that he wanted to kill himself, that he had been left with no pension, and that his life was of no value. Another veteran pleaded, "Don't interview me—if you do, I don't think my brain can take it."[5]

Perhaps one reason it was difficult to find a platform for his videos was that the stories Cui told did not fit into the standard mold of official interpretation. One episode on the Eighth Route Army does not show the army blending in with the people, in line with Mao's dictum that the army should be fish swimming in the sea of the people; rather, it documents how locals in one community pointed out to the enemy exactly who the Communist army members were. Another episode deals with the sensitive topic of collaboration with the enemy. Some might have collaborated because they had to make a living, noted Cui; although some were real traitors, "there were some collaborators with a conscience" who did the people no harm and just wore a uniform. Their oral histories give "a variety of self-justifications," he said, "but it's not as simple as just betraying one's country."[6] Pushing ever further, Cui added, "There were even some traitors who used collaboration as a form of the War of Resistance, trading space for time." Exactly such a justification—referring to the strategy of gaining time by giving up territory to be recovered at a later date—had been used by the most prominent wartime collaborator, Wang

Jingwei, and indeed by Chiang Kai-shek himself. In a separate interview in the *Zhongguo zhoukan* (*China Weekly*), Cui told stories of the former soldiers who felt that they had been abandoned by society.[7]

The series was a great success online. It was then shown by a range of local television stations and eventually on a national station and gave rise to a second season. In the book accompanying *Wode kangzhan II*, Cui aimed his knife at another sacred cow, casting doubt on the idea that memory of the war could successfully support an unthinking nationalism via the internet. He claimed that the often-debated question, "What if there were another Sino-Japanese War?" was in fact a "pseudo-topic." Today's "angry youth" (*fenqing*) may claim that they are going to "leap from the trenches," but in fact they may not be so reliable. He also dismissed the idea that the Japanese invasion, beginning in 1931, was particularly distinctive: in the past, there had been Japanese attacks during the Ming dynasty and then again in 1894–1895 during the Jiawu War (First Sino-Japanese War). Finally, he dismissed another myth that was growing in popularity, the idea of China as the key battleground in Asia during World War II. "Without the Pacific War, the Soviet Red Army, and American nuclear bombs on Nagasaki and Hiroshima, when would the Chinese have had a decent victory?" he asked. "Not in 1945, that's for sure."[8] Cui's sardonic approach shows how far the most daring could go in putting a new gloss on orthodox history.

As a celebrated media figure, Cui is no more "typical" than the prominent authors Fang Jun and Fan Jianchuan. But all of their works sit on an ever more clearly defined spectrum on the meaning of the Communist-Nationalist divisions in the war, from the idea of the CCP as the leading actor in a nationalistic conflict against

Japan, to the idea of the CCP and Nationalists as both playing a significant role, to the acknowledgment that much of China was controlled by collaborationist governments.

Cui's take on the war with Japan was by no means the only one to appear on Chinese television screens. For most viewers, the most obvious cultural manifestation of the war would have been the constant stream of nationalistic and often violent dramas that were being aired. In 2014, the writer Murong Xuecun observed that some seventy dramas set during the war against Japan had been broadcast in China in 2012, and in the following year, one studio alone was filming forty-eight such productions.[9] By 2015, even the official *China Daily* admitted that many such series were being pulled offscreen because the ludicrous plots (for instance, Chinese soldiers beating back Japanese with one blow of a fist) were making the war into a laughing-stock.[10] Yet there was undoubtedly a market in China for such dramas, whether on the small or the large screen.

Films and the Power of Victimhood

The phenomena we have examined so far—museums, memoirs, and television series—are primarily oriented toward a domestic audience. In the 2000s, the Chinese began to make an effort to reach an international audience in one area: the cinema. Chinese producers and audiences have been impressed by the Western ability to use images from World War II to shape views of the war, as in the 2017 movie *Dunkirk,* directed by Christopher Nolan, which told the story of the massive evacuation of British and other Allied forces from Dunkirk in 1940. Some Chinese commentators panned the movie because it told the story of a retreat—a topic that they claimed did not accord with "Chinese values." One publication argued that *Wolf Warrior 2,* a violent Chinese action film with Chinese heroes, Western villains, and a contemporary setting, better reflected these values because it depicted a "complete victory," a phrasing that brings to mind Xi Jinping's praise for the War of Resistance as China's first "complete victory" against foreign invaders. Yet *Dunkirk* topped the Chinese box office on release.[11]

Chinese filmmakers have attempted to emulate American film successes to tell a different story. To date, however, Chinese movies about their own wartime experience have had little success in the West. For that matter, Western films on the war in China have also ignored the Chinese perspective. Several Western pictures set in wartime China have achieved prominence; these movies, however, are about Europeans in China, rather than the war experience through Chinese eyes. The 1958 movie *Inn of the Sixth Happiness,* based on the life of a British missionary in China, was the second-highest-grossing film in the United Kingdom in 1959; in 1987, Steven Spielberg's *Empire of the Sun,* based on J. G. Ballard's semi-autobiographical novel about his experience in Shanghai during the war, won a slew of awards and did moderately well at the US box office.

In the 2000s, the cinema was an important location for a conflict that lies within Chinese attempts to reimagine the legacy of the war: the desire to create a discourse supportive of the official propaganda about the war domestically, while projecting the idea of China as a contributor to the antifascist struggle in the wider world. This dual agenda has become more urgent in the past decade, as China's growing economic power has been met by increasing caution and hostility in the liberal world. But the internal and external goals of the project frequently come into conflict. As China's domestic politics has become more authoritarian, the message purveyed by films (as well as television programs) reflects an often rather unthinking nationalism. While cinematic patriotism has some appeal in the United States, non-Americans and non-Chinese tend to find jingoistic productions, whether promoting American or Chinese values, unattractive.

The most prominent cinematic appearances of the war on-screen in the 2000s related to the Nanjing Massacre. This likely had something to do with the growing Sino-Japanese tensions of the period, which included an incident in 2005 when Chinese youths threw bottles at the Japanese consulate in Shanghai, yet no law enforcement officers stepped in to stop them.[12] The theme of the massacre gave these films a particular moral freight, as well as burnishing China's status as a victim during the war. The massacre is also one of the rare events from China's wartime experience that is familiar to people in the Western world. Two of the films, Lu Chuan's *Nanjing! Nanjing!* (2009) (released as *City of Life and Death* in the West) and Zhang Yimou's *Flowers of War* (2011), based on a novel by Yan Geling, achieved significant international review attention.

Lu's film was a major box office success in China, making some RMB 150 million in less than three weeks.[13] The lead character, Lieutenant Lu Jianxiong, was played by Ye Liu, one of China's most famous actors. Lu is shown trying to escape as the Japanese take the city. Meanwhile, a Japanese soldier, Kadokawa Masao (played by Nakaizumi Hideo), makes his way through the city, becoming increasingly distressed at the scenes of rape and murder that he sees around him. Eventually, after allowing two Chinese prisoners to escape, Kadokawa takes his own life.

The film was controversial even before its release. Chinese censors were uncertain about whether to allow it to be distributed, and it came close to being banned.[14] When it was released, there were criticisms of its sympathetic portrayal of Kadokawa. Yet its power lies precisely in its ambiguity and nuance. The film does not in any way condone or soft-pedal the horror of what happened in Nanjing. However, by showing the protagonists as human beings, rather than monsters or heroes, Lu succeeded in making a film of great power. The film also places the clash between Chinese and Japanese at its center; when Western characters, such as the historical figure John Rabe, played by John Paisley, do appear, they remain at the margins.

Unlike Lu's film, Zhang Yimou's *Flowers of War* places a Westerner at the center. Christian Bale plays an undertaker who has to take the place of a dead priest (a fictionalized event). The film received respectable reviews and did well at the box office in China. Yet it suffers from a central weakness: despite being made in China, by a renowned Chinese director, it tells the story of the redemption of a white American rather than the dilemmas or difficulties of the Chinese. The film's gender politics are also deeply problematic; a group of prostitutes cooped up in the safety zone "see the light" and substitute themselves for schoolgirls whom the Japanese aim to capture and rape. The film did very badly at the US box office: its production costs were over $90 million, but it made a negligible $48,558 on its first weekend.[15]

In contrast to the spate of films representing China as a victim, there were essentially no films released outside China that gave any positive account of the country's efforts to fight the Japanese. Thus in 2015, there was some excitement in the Western movie world when it was announced that Bruce Willis was signing up to star in *The Bombing,* a blockbuster movie set during the air raids on Chongqing. The director was to be a Chinese first-timer, Xiao Feng, with Mel Gibson contributing as art director. The budget was set at a respectable $53 million. Tantalizing posters appeared on the internet. But within a year, trouble had clearly struck on set. The film did not make its scheduled appearance at the Cannes Film Festival in 2016, and one US showbiz website suggested in May 2016 that the production problems were fundamental:

> Remember "The Bombing"? This was a Chinese movie starring Bruce Willis as the only American among an Asian cast. At some point, Mel Gibson invested money in it and became the Art Director.
> Now sources tell me we may never see "The Bombing." It's a bomb, alright.
> Willis, who worked hard on it, has to be completely dubbed into Chinese since the rest of the movie is in that language. No one speaks a word of English.
> Can you imagine that film being released in the Western world? . . .
> There are other problems, too. "It's about the Chinese fighting back against the Japanese in World War II," a source told me. "It's not like a lot of people around the world care about that. And the Japanese won't be seeing it."
> Sharp eyed observers will be looking to see if "The Bombing" turns up in the Cannes Film Market next week. But the word is it won't.[16]

The article clarifies why international dissemination of the Chinese story continues to be a problem. "It's not like a lot of people in the world care about that" rather sums up why the Chinese story of World War II continues to resist globalization.

However, things were clearly moving under the surface, and the project did not sink completely. In 2018, filming on *The Bombing* was completed, with a bonus: China's most famous film star, Fan Bingbing, would appear in a small role, giving the film some extra glamor for a domestic audience.

Then in May 2018, Cui Yongyuan made an accusation that disrupted the schedule. Cui had left China Central Television in 2013 but was still prominent in public life. He accused Fan of having used a "yin-yang" scheme for her earnings on *The Bombing,* referring to a common tax avoidance strategy that involves having two contracts.[17] (It was rumored that Cui's denunciation was fuelled by a film in which Fan had satirized a chat show host who seemed remarkably similar to Cui.) Shortly afterward, Fan disappeared, leaving the public, including her millions of followers on Chinese social media, unsure what had happened to her. Meanwhile, the producers of *The Bombing* tried to remove her name from the publicity for the film and edit out her role in it. The film's release date, which was supposed to be in August 2018, to coincide with the anniversary of the end of the war, was moved to October. Fan finally reappeared in October 2018, with RMB 884 million in back taxes to pay. The producers cancelled the Chinese release, and the saga of *The Bombing* finally ended. "It is time to let it go," said the director, Xiao Feng. "My sincere apologies to my crew, the distribution team, and all audiences who had high expectations of the film." Unwilling to drop his campaign, Cui alleged that the film's finances were based in part on the laundering of funds from Shanghai pension funds and urged a boycott should it ever be released.[18] The film received a straight-to-download US release in December 2018 under two different titles (*Air Strike* and

Unbreakable Spirit, the latter an attempt to make a connection with Willis's hit 2000 movie *Unbreakable*).

In the excitement over the scandal surrounding Fan Bingbing, the content of the film itself was less discussed. The plot features a US Army colonel, played by Bruce Willis, who trains rookie Chinese pilots to take on the Japanese airforce and bears some resemblance to Claire Chennault, leader of the wartime Flying Tigers. The computer-generated dogfights have a clunky feel (in contrast to the aerial battles in the politically ambiguous but technically brilliant 2013 Japanese film *The Eternal Zero*). A Chinese pilot (played by Chinese megastar Liu Ye, in a rather less impressive role than his triumph in Lu Chuan's *City of Life and Death*) drives a truck with a mystery piece of military equipment across southwest China while avoiding Japanese air raids and picking up a motley crew of men, women, and children along the way. The trip seems to nod to the "journey to the west," the traditional Chinese folk tale of the Monkey King and his pilgrim friends. In a reference to the Nationalist government's wartime agricultural improvement program, one character is a scientist transporting piglets bred to provide better nutrition for a hungry population. The narrative strands do not marry together well, as Dennis Harvey's review in *Variety* noted: "All this results in a film that is loud and busy, yet lacks any tonal consistency or narrative center—we're never quite sure where whatever's going on at present fits into an ill-defined bigger picture." Harvey did allow, however, that "certain aspects are polished and impressively scaled enough to suggest a movie that was perhaps never going to be inspired, but at least once had a coherent, ambitious scope."[19] Online reviewers of the US version were, to put it mildly, unimpressed: one viewer declared that "Bruce Willis has gone from Unbreakable to Unwatchable," and another declared, "This movie is about the fight of the Chinese against the evil Japanese. The true crime though is the terrible acting, direction and script."[20] It would be hard to argue that this film is worth watching for its artistic quality. If World War II films such as *Ashes and Diamonds* or *Au Revoir les Enfants* sit at one end of the spectrum, then *The Bombing* is very much at the other. Yet the fact that it was attempted at all shows that there is still a hunger in China to create a work that will appeal to the wider world in the way that those other films have done.

The inability of Chinese film depictions of the war to project soft power is part of a larger problem. Films produced by citizens of China and other former Allied powers have tended to succeed when they are part of a broader, often mythic, narrative that speaks to current events. The liberation of Europe by the United States and Britain provides a powerful conventional narrative in many commercially successful films. There is much more ambivalence in the former Axis countries, for obvious reasons. In Japan, the most successful films have tried to combine skepticism about the war aims with empathy for the suffering of Japanese civilians and soldiers, who found themselves in situations supposedly outside of their own control; examples include *The Eternal Zero* and Sunao Katabuchi's sleeper hit manga *In This Corner of the World* (2016). These films tend to have limited impact outside the domestic box office, but Japan is not seeking to project wartime accounts of itself to the outside world through cinema. Notably, few Japanese films on the wartime period engage with the war in China; the vast majority focus on the war in the Pacific.[21] The Pacific war seems to be regarded as the "real" war against a worthy (i.e., technologically and civilizationally "advanced") opponent, who becomes a friend after the war is over. The years between the Marco

Polo Bridge incident and Pearl Harbor are seen as merely a prelude to that narrative and, as a result, are poison at the box office. There is no market in Japan for films about the China war.

The Chinese, in contrast, very much want to create a market for films about "their" World War II in the rest of the world. Part of the reason they have failed has to do with limitations and indeed prejudices in the Western world. Few films relating to purely Asian topics gain widespread attention in a Western-oriented, Anglophone cinematic market, with the partial exception of martial arts productions. There is also a further problem: China's role in the war effort has almost no visibility in the Western understanding of the wartime period. China's goal of rehabilitating that memory, in order to strengthen the legitimacy of the present-day Chinese regime, is not one that attracts widespread support elsewhere, not just because of rivalry between the West and China, but also because China's authoritarian system is not considered internationally attractive; this makes empathy with the goals of China's wartime resistance harder. Keeping the world safe for consumerist authoritarianism is hardly a very attractive offer in the twenty-first century, any more than fighting for the maintenance of European empires was in the mid-twentieth. Of course, there are acclaimed Russian war films that do not promote the values of liberal democracy. But such films—such as Elem Klimov's *Come and See* (1985), with its titular reference to the Apocalypse of St. John—are frequently bleak, nihilistic works that do not endorse Soviet values either. A film like Lu Chuan's *City of Life and Death* comes closest to this sort of ambiguity—another reason that it was nearly banned before release.

The struggle to interpret Chinese realities for an American audience is not new. During the war years themselves, there was an intriguing and very literal example of narratives being changed to accommodate political needs. Lao She's novel *Rickshaw (Luotuo Xiangzi,* 1937) is regarded as one of the finest long works in modern Chinese fiction. Its story of the slow destruction of a young Chinese worker by the pressures of contemporary society is unremittingly bleak; the main character loses his rickshaw business, his girlfriend dies working in a brothel, and he eventually dies in a nameless back street. In 1945, in the pro-China atmosphere of wartime America, the book was translated and distributed by the Book of the Month Club. Lao She was dismayed to find that much of the last third of the book had been fundamentally altered: in the translation, the protagonist rescues his girlfriend from the brothel. The ending had clearly been changed to accommodate American desires for a happy outcome; in addition, the publisher may have felt that one of the United States' wartime allies should not be portrayed, even by one of its own citizens, as a place of death and hopelessness.[22] A similar sentiment led to a rash of pro-Soviet Hollywood films (such as director Michael Curtiz's 1943 *Mission to Moscow*), which portrayed the Soviet Union as essentially an American-style democracy in embryo. In the 2020s, no political or cultural imperatives exist that might encourage anyone to produce a film commemorating Chongqing or Yan'an for a Western audience. Indeed, at a time of growing hostility toward China in the United States, the market for such a film is probably shrinking.

The *Guofen* Phenomenon

The skeptical viewpoint expressed by Cui Yongyuan is easier to find online than onscreen. One particular manifestation is the phenomenon known as the *Guofen,* or "Guomindang [Nationalist

Party] fans" (the character *fen* 粉 is meant to be an approximation of the English word "fan"). Guofen are online, somewhat gonzo, supporters of the former Nationalist government. In 2015, Radio Free Asia interviewed one such figure, a woman named Wang Xueli, whose online name was Air (*Kongqi*) and who styled herself the leader of the Chinese mainland "Republican constitution faction." Wang was one example of a phenomenon of the *Minguo re* (Republican craze), which had become fashionable particularly among well-educated urban types who wanted to find an expressive way to communicate their skepticism of the government.[23] Air (a pseudonym she chose because she believed that air is the freest material that exists) was clearly at the more active end of this phenomenon, much of which was played out on social media. She claimed to be an advocate not only of Sun Yat-sen's Three People's Principles but also of the 1946 constitution—the troubled, only partially democratic constitution instituted by the Nationalists in the midst of China's civil war—arguing that "'the Republican Chinese constitution' means the constitutional government of the Republic of China," which she regarded as "democratic" in contrast with that of the CCP. Wang's group had emerged in 2003 after online clashes with a rival group, whom they called "Maofen" (i.e., "Mao fans"). Wang claimed that her group had been boosted by a visit to the mainland in 2005 by Lien Chan, who at the time was chairman of the Nationalist Party based on Taiwan. During that visit, Wang said, Guofen came to Nanjing from all around China to visit Zijinshan, the site of the tomb of Sun Yat-sen, the founder of the Republic, as well as the Republican-era presidential palace, and "there was a second high tide in 2006, when we rethought the history of the War of Resistance." "At the same time," she noted, "we found more and more smart folks to propagandize for Republican history, even including more and more sympathizers within the system joining us."[24] Their main "battlefield" was on the QQ SMS system, but in 2011–2012 more material went up on the Chinese weblog system Weibo.

The Guofen did not emerge from thin air, so to speak. In the early 2000s there was increasing attention to the *fenqing* ("angry youth"; the *fen* is a different character from that in *Guofen*), young Chinese nationalists who spoke out strongly on patriotic issues and even criticized their own government for being overly soft on Japan.[25] One such youth, Guo Quan, began his activism by investigating the Nanjing Massacre and obtained an academic position to pursue this work. Within a few years, he had become a full-blown critic of the government, and in 2008 he was arrested for advocating multi-party democracy.[26]

The Guofen exist in uneasy opposition to the government. While gauging overall numbers is impossible in the restrictive environment of the Chinese internet, it is apparent that the phenomenon has never been more than a specialist pursuit. Still, it attracted enough adherents that in October 2014, the nationalistic *Global Times* issued a warning that people should not be nostalgic for the Nationalist period or the Republic within which it sat:

> Nowadays, a morbid nostalgia for the Republic of China has emerged among a few Internet communities and a small number of intellectuals.
>
> "Republic of China fervor" is fixated on beautifying that historical period, claiming it was a time of "democracy, freedom and respect for wisdom."
>
> However, supporters merely base their views on the states of a minority of senior intellectuals during that time, who belonged to the upper class and were respected due to their academic performances. . . .

Nostalgia is a basic emotion of human beings. Great masters Wang Guowei and Gu Hongming preserved their pigtails even after the overthrow of the Qing Dynasty (1644–1911), and the Cultural Revolution (1966–76) is still being remembered with nostalgia by some. There are complicated reasons for nostalgia and a mature society should give it a wide tolerance.

However, we should make no bones about exposing their tricks when fanatics make use of nostalgia for the Republic of China as an ideological, and even a political tool, to challenge mainstream historical and political views in the Chinese mainland. Chinese people abandoned the Republic of China 65 years ago.

If the Kuomintang (KMT) [i.e., Nationalist] regime hadn't been rotten at the core and alienated the sympathies of the people, the Communist Party of China wouldn't have been able to mobilize the whole country to defeat it.

KMT rule in the mainland was a mess. Its national governance failed to reach the grass roots and smash the separatist warlord regimes. Moreover, KMT was subject to Western powers. British warships were still sailing in the rivers of the Chinese mainland in the 1940s. China as a gigantic country was unable to resist the aggression of a small island nation like Japan. The KMT regime is held responsible for the humiliation that China suffered from the Japanese invasion.

The Republic of China cannot be compared to present-day China, be it national comprehensive strength, international status, level of livelihood, and social security.

We could miss the songs, sceneries or figures of that period, but praising the then state system and its influence is a humiliation to the whole Chinese history.[27]

A few months later, despite this warning, Air declared, "We have above all persuaded the youth, and the youth are more and more putting their faith in the blue sky, white sun, red background flag [of the Nationalist government]. . . . Most of the youth's families have no connection with the Nationalist Government or the Party; they are purely logically considering the Republic of China."[28]

The Guofen phenomenon continues to appear online, as do other manifestations of nostalgia for the Republican period, expressed in cosplay and tourism revivals. Between the uncritical enthusiasm of people such as Air and the state-backed critique of the *Global Times,* there are a range of views that draw on different understandings of the war period. One self-declared Guofen, with the web name Qiuba Shiji, wrote a nuanced critique of the phenomenon in 2017, in an article titled "How I see the Guofen."[29] Qiuba identifies "three types of Guofen," whose characteristics he describes:

> First, the changeable Guofen. This sort of Guofen is at one stage of loving history, and that's all. It comes from a dissatisfaction with reality, and comes from having a contrarian [*nifan*] mindset, having taken on board official history for a long time. . . . When they first begin independently to seek out historical traces, for many people it's a process of . . . running in the opposite direction from officialdom. . . . I myself was this first type of Guofen after Reform and Opening.

Most Guofen, he claims, are of the second type:

> Second are the fake Guofen. This sort of Guofen is on web forums. . . . When eating at the side of the road, or riding public transport, . . . or chatting at home, you can hear their voices putting out things like "the War of Resistance was dependent most of all on the Nationalist armies," or "The Nationalist armies' contribution during the War of Resistance has been neglected."

These fake Guofen don't read proper books but just gather "historical splinters and shards" from the internet: "They easily accept some voice that is at odds with the official version of history, and like to spread those voices."

The third type—"Iron Guofen"—are political actors with their own agenda, and they comprise less than 5 percent of the total. Qiuba does not name Air, but presumably she would be part of this group. "Each of the type of Guofen . . . has a loud voice, but loudness of voice does not mean correctness."

Qiuba does not accept the idea that the Nationalist armies made the major difference in the war, pointing out that in significant battles, such as Nanning in 1939, they were defeated by the Japanese (who are referred to throughout his post as "Japanese devils"). He concludes:

> During the War of Resistance, the Nationalist armies maintained the major battlefields, and many Nationalist generals and soldiers did not surrender. On the battlefields at the beginning of the war, the resistance of the Nationalist armies to the Japanese army was particularly fierce, and their sacrifice particularly great. All of these, we have to confirm, have contributed to the record of names of the countless heroes of the nation. . . . But many Guofen . . . have to say that the War of Resistance had only the Nationalists at its core, and have to rate the Nationalists' contribution as high as possible—this is unreliable and in fact is nonsense.[30]

The Guofen are surely not a terribly large category, and figures like Air, with her wholehearted endorsement of Nationalist governance, are most likely rare. Nevertheless, the issues that concern them reflect larger cultural trends. Qiuba's first group overlaps in some respects with the scholarly phenomenon of revisionist history about the war examined in Chapter 2. The second group echoes a more widespread sense of dissatisfaction with contemporary life. The "fake Guofen" are not really interested in a forensic dissection of the Nationalist performance on battlefields some eight decades distant. They are representative of those who are unhappy, to some extent, with the Communist Party, but also with everyday life as a whole. It does not take too much imagination to see a middle-aged commuter on the Beijing metro ignoring his stressful surroundings by texting away on his phone about what really happened in the first phase of the battle of Changsha in 1939.

The Guofen phenomenon bears some resemblance to the nostalgia over the Confederate legacy in the United States. Defenders of Confederate flags and statues often argue that they are seeking to preserve "history not hatred." Opponents argue that it is not possible to separate the historical epiphenomena from the political system that created the Confederacy. Many advocates of the Confederacy put forward dubious historical interpretations, for instance, that the South could have won the Civil War, or that Jefferson Davis would have abolished slavery. Such theories usually say more about the speaker's view on contemporary America than about the events of the 1860s. The new discourse about the Nationalists' wartime role in the China of the 2010s surely plays a similar role. It is not surprising that it might become important to alienated netizens in a consumerist China with no clear sense of ideological direction.

Concerns about the Guofen phenomenon may have been behind a recent instance of pushback against the attempt to acknowledge the Nationalist war record in public culture. In June 2019, the film *The Eight Hundred* (*Babai*) was scheduled to open the Shanghai International Film Festival. The film depicts one of the most famous events of desperate heroism in the early part of the War of

Resistance: the last stand by some eight hundred Chinese Nationalist soldiers in a waterside warehouse in Shanghai as they fought against the approaching Japanese. The film's budget was over $80 million, and it was the first Chinese film to be shot entirely in the IMAX widescreen format. Late in June, there was a sudden announcement that the film would no longer be shown as the opener at the festival, and just a few days later, the film's general release in China was cancelled.

In early June, the Chinese Red Culture Association, linked to the Chinese Academy of Social Sciences, had condemned the film, arguing that it gave far too rosy a view of the Nationalist government's contribution to the war. The group was outraged over scenes such as one in which Chinese soldiers defend the Chinese Nationalist flag, with its distinctive white star and blue background. While a link between the criticism and the film's withdrawal cannot be proven, it seems likely. One of the comments on Weibo from a disappointed would-be viewer got straight to the point: "Why was this? Because the eight hundred brave fellows who fought the Japanese were from the Nationalist armies, not the Communists?" *South China Morning Post* reporter Elaine Yau gathered critical views about the cancellation from Chinese social media, which seemed to echo the Guofen agenda. "Nationalist soldiers constituted the main forces fighting the Japanese. This is fact," declared one user. Another complained, "I feel sad for the soldiers who died [during the warehouse siege]. They sacrificed for their country and get attacked by such people [now]. Please remember forever the soldiers who laid down their lives for an independent China."[31]

The critic Lan Lin gives a thoughtful analysis of the way in which parastatal organizations in China, such as the Red Culture

Association, have started to influence cultural production and censorship, complicating our understanding of how top-down state intervention on individual artists works: "The fate of *The Eight Hundred* also offers a glimpse into some systematic and administrative changes inside China's movie censorship apparatus: SAPPRFT [State Administration of Press, Publicity, Radio, Film and Television] still stands at the center, but there are other forces coming into play, and they are politically motivated."[32] China's public sphere does not just allow (very limited) space for liberal pushback against the state; it also allows organizations with their own more politically conservative agendas to pressure cultural producers, even when particular products, such as films, have already been officially approved, as was the case with *The Eight Hundred*. The uneasy balance between allowing a more inclusive history and trying not to damage the mythos of the CCP's history, which Hu Qiaomu and others had articulated as long ago as the 1980s, continues.

The interaction between the different vectors of memory in China is complex, and not unidirectional. Academic studies like those of Yang Tianshi and Zhang Xianwen on Chiang and the Nationalists can be found in regular bookshops. Fan Jianchuan's subversive take on the Sichuanese contribution to the war is not a huge distance away from the investment made in Chongqing in glorifying the war years. Cui Yongyuan's difficulties in promoting the cause of the Nationalist soldiers were addressed through new social media, which then pressured the mainstream broadcasting authorities in China to rehabilitate them further; by 2015, figures such as Luo Yuan, a hardline CCP commentator and officer in the People's Liberation Army, were talking about the need to acknowledge the Nationalist contribution to the war effort.[33]

A culminating point to these efforts came on 3 September 2015, at the parade in Tiananmen Square. While much of the world noticed the extravagant military hardware and the guest list (Vladimir Putin of Russia, Park Geun-hye of South Korea, and Ban Ki-moon of the UN all present; Kim Jong-un, Barack Obama of the United States, and David Cameron of the United Kingdom absent), less attention was paid to the moment midway through when various elderly men were presented to the president. These men, all over ninety years old, had fought in the war against Japan in both the Communist and Nationalist armies. Finally, in front of China's president and secretary-general of the party, and with all of China watching on television, the contribution of the Nationalists to winning the war was acknowledged in the most prominent manner possible. The acknowledgment was not unequivocal—the Chinese Communist Party was still presented as the "leading" actor in prosecuting the war. But in just five years, from Cui Yongyuan's boundary-pushing documentary in 2010 to this 2015 parade in Tiananmen Square, the Nationalists had been raised to a greater level of official acceptance.

The ideas that underpin the new discourse of the war derive in significant part from the academic studies discussed earlier, but refracted through more public forums. There is now a solid, discernible discourse around the Second World War in China. What was protean and in formation in the late 1990s is now clearly defined, and—although subject to pushback—is clearly here to stay, thanks to the social media and public culture of the 2010s and 2020s.

5

From Chongqing to Yan'an

Regional Memory and Wartime Identity

In 1946, Theodore White, an American journalist who was perhaps the most famous foreigner to report from China during the Second World War, described the period when Chongqing was the temporary wartime capital. It was "a point in time, a temporal bivouac with an extrageographical meaning, like Munich or Versailles," he wrote. "It was an episode shared by hundreds of thousands of people who had gathered in the shadow of its walls out of a faith in China's greatness and an overwhelming passion to hold the land against the Japanese."[1]

Zhou Yong, a scholar who is associated with the revival of interest in Chongqing's wartime history within the city itself, talked about the significance of the city's period as temporary capital. "I recognize that this period of history is a very precious resource for a country, and for a city," he told me in 2018. "War is a human tragedy, but the memory of war becomes a resource for humankind."[2]

Eighty years apart, the American reporter who had lived through the war and the Chinese historian who has made it part of his life's work agreed on one thing. The war years in Chongqing created a new moral universe for China, both at the time and in retrospect. The same is also true of war stories from other parts of China. After all, the war involved multiple sites of resistance and collaboration. Yet those regional memories remained hidden or neglected for decades. For many years, collective memory concentrated on one particular site and set of images: the cave dwellings of the wartime Communist capital at Yan'an, in the Shaanxi-Gansu-Ningxia region of northwestern China. For Westerners, the story of the 1944 "Dixie Mission," when American diplomats visited Mao and his followers in Yan'an, became one of the defining images of the wartime period in China. After 1949, the narrative of guerrilla resistance led from the base areas became a central part of the founding myth of the People's Republic. The center of gravity of that particular historical myth was located in the harsh loess soil of the Northwest, and a whole narrative with ideological and moral freight concerning the ultimate victory of the Chinese Communist Party emerged from it.[3]

Since the 1980s, though, there has been a shift in the way that different regions and localities in China have created collective memories of the war years. Parts of China whose history had mostly been ignored during the Mao years began to revive, mourn, and celebrate their own experiences, above all in southwestern China. In remembering the war, that region does not stand in open opposition to the narratives built at a national level. Yet a new emphasis on the Southwest's resistance to Japan has inevitably drawn attention to the role of the Nationalist government, which dominated the region during the war. Additionally, the new collective memory in the region commemorates the sacrifice of individuals. In the far Southwest, at Songshan, near the border with Burma, a privately built museum showcases the record of the Chinese Expeditionary Force that fought there.[4] Outside Chengdu, Fan Jianchuan's private museum, one of the biggest in China, highlights the Southwest's role in resisting Japan.

Even in parts of China where memory of the war years never faded, such as in Yan'an, there are new visions of the period. "Red tourism," the commercialization of sites related to the founding and rise of the Communist Party, brings streams of pilgrims to Yan'an and a range of other places associated with Mao's wartime years. Yet even in this most officially venerated of narratives, there are unorthodoxies; authors such as the historian Zhu Hongzhao have appropriated the Yan'an myth as a way of reassessing their own lives in a China that is postsocialist in reality if not in name.

Requiem for a Forgotten City

Much of the renewed mythology of the war that started in the 1990s came out of Chongqing, China's temporary wartime capital between 1937 and 1946. Chongqing would be nobody's first choice as a capital city. Had China known peace during the twentieth century, the city would likely have grown and industrialized but would probably have been little different from a mid-size city such as Zhengzhou or Shijiazhuang. The decision to shift the government from Nanjing to Chongqing during the war made the city's reputation. "Because the War of Resistance created the Chongqing people's basic character," Zhou Yong said, "it also created the city's core culture."[5]

To move a capital city is no small business. When the British moved India's capital from Calcutta to Delhi, the announcement was made at the Delhi Durbar of 1911, a parade of pomp and magnificence attended by King George V himself. The announcement to move China's capital to Chongqing in 1937 was not accompanied by the same level of splendor, though there were some similarities. The move to New Delhi had been made at a time of crisis, with increasing pressure from Bengali politicians leading the imperial authorities to feel that that province could no longer house the capital. The move to Chongqing was also made during a time of crisis, but a much more serious one: an imminent war between China and Japan. Although the decision came quickly, plans to move the capital to the interior had been underway for some years.

The city of Chongqing experienced major changes during the course of the twentieth century. Liu Xiang, the militarist leader who controlled Sichuan province, where Chongqing sat (until it was granted autonomy in 1997), ruled from the traditional provincial capital at Chengdu. After the occupation of Manchuria in 1931, to which Chiang Kai-shek's government could offer no military resistance, plans were put into place to provide a means of opposition to Japan in the event of a war. On 29 December 1932, the National Defense Planning Council was established, and it carried out detailed surveys of China's needs for chemicals, fuel, and other resources. It concluded that much more preparation was needed in China's interior.[6]

The plan for a wartime capital to be established at Chongqing was part of a wider set of changes in China's political geography, as the Nationalists sought to consolidate what was still only partial control of the country. Chongqing has geographical advantages as a last redoubt: it sits on two rivers, the Yangtze and the Jialing, making river transport convenient, but because of its clifftop location, it is extremely difficult to attack by land. (Indeed,

Chongqing would be one of the harder places for the Communists to conquer in the Civil War.) However, the area had never been a natural area of Nationalist strength, even after 1927. Liu Xiang was a wary partner at best of Chiang, whom he—rightly—suspected of wanting to bring Sichuan under central control.

In March 1935, Chiang made his first visit to Chongqing to scope out its potential as a base for an anti-Japanese war. He declared on 4 March, "Sichuan is not only an important revolutionary place for us, but it's the base where our Chinese nation established itself."[7] This statement was followed by the establishment of the Military Affairs Commission at Chongqing. The insertion of Nationalist Central Army structures in the provinces was the beginning of the process to bring Sichuan warlords under control.

On 7 July 1937, fighting broke out between local Chinese and Japanese troops at Wanping. Within weeks, China and Japan were in the midst of an as-yet-undeclared war. After the fall of Beiping and Tianjin, Nanjing began to look more vulnerable, and the Nationalist high command felt a greater urgency to move the capital.[8] On 7 August, Chiang held a meeting of China's top leaders, including He Yingqin, Wang Jingwei, and Yan Xishan, in which all present were made to declare their support for the expansion of the war (which would then be extended to Shanghai). Liu Xiang, who was at the meeting, made a pledge of five million troops to the effort. On 13 August, as the attack on Shanghai began, Chiang wrote to Liu, "Suggesting the central government moves to Sichuan, with the idea of a long war of resistance." Officials began to put the move into action.[9]

By this time it was clear that the Nationalists could not hold Shanghai. The city was torn apart by brutal hand-to-hand combat, and the best Nationalist Central Army troops were being over-whelmed by huge numbers of Japanese reinforcements, who ben-efited from the technological superiority of the Japanese army. On 15 November, the Central Political Committee of the Nationalist Party declared, "The National Government and the Central Party department will move to Chongqing."[10] As eastern China fell and Shanghai and Nanjing both collapsed, there were some hurried journeys to safety, including that of the president of the republic, Lin Sen, who flew to Wuhan on 11 November and then trans-ferred to the steamer *Minfeng* to continue on to Chongqing, where he arrived on 26 November. By the end of 1938, all major insti-tutions of government had moved to the new capital.

The task that the authorities faced in Chongqing was very dif-ferent from that in any other major World War II capital. (Had the Nazis taken Moscow in 1941–1942, Stalin might have had to move to the planned temporary capital at Kuibyshev, but the plans to do so were never implemented.) For a start, the move had to be accomplished at great speed. Although preparation had been going on for some two years, there was still much work to do to create a solid base for resistance. The city had poor roads, little transport infrastructure, and few buildings that were suitable for the estab-lishment of a solid regime. The very qualities that made Chongqing a plausible center for sustained resistance also made it difficult to supply and defend. Access came through a variety of routes, in-cluding the Burma Road via Yunnan, the sea route via the Guang-dong coast, and the northern route via Qinghai. The Japanese invasion made the east coast of China much less accessible, al-though routes through Hong Kong were open until 1941.

The difficulties of the journey to Chongqing prompted a wry observation from the writer Xu Wancheng, who, in his impressions of life in the wartime capital, wrote about the ironic juxtaposition of two signs he saw on a street corner:

> At the headquarters of the Dazhong steamer company in Baixiang street in Chongqing, there are two advertisements. One says: This company's boat . . . is safe and swift from Nanjing to Shanghai. The second says: Traveling by boat is pretty dangerous; be quick to get insurance from this company.[11]

Nor did the dangers and difficulties end when one arrived in town. A huge influx of refugees were flooding into Chongqing and Sichuan province; the city's population more than doubled from under half a million in 1937 to 1.05 million by the end of the war.[12] However, the factor that affected the city's security perhaps more than any other was the destruction wrought by bombs. By the early 1930s, Chinese political thinkers were already regularly speaking of being in an "exceptional period" (*feichang shiqi*), and the chaos caused by the war certainly increased the sense of being in a period that stood somehow outside normality.[13]

In the midst of the horrors of war, there was a clear desire to make something new from the constant turbulence and violence. Nationalist politicians often used the need for order as a central reason for prosecuting the war. In that context, construction was a powerful analogy. In Chongqing, construction was more than a metaphor. It was a literal statement of need, particularly during the period from February 1938 to August 1943 when the city was being frequently bombarded from the air. According to incomplete statistics, during this five and a half year period, 9,518 Japanese aircraft sortied during 218 raids, killing 11,889 and wounding 14,100, and destroying some 17,608 houses.[14] Reconstruction was vital to maintain Chongqing at the center of the wartime resistance. Yet the air raids made it difficult to plan for the rebuilding in any sort of orderly way. In 1939, the "Capital City planning law" established a variety of regulations on residences, shops, factories, and government, as well as calling for the improvement of the road system, water supply, and drains; the dividing up of land; and the setting up of hygiene, education, airraid, and other public provisions. By 1940, it had become a "wartime three-year reconstruction plan." There were also educational and cultural improvements, such as the establishment of thirty new high schools.[15]

The reconstruction of the city was a top-down project, as the authorities sought to respond to an increasingly chaotic war. There was also a less controllable element shaping the city's atmosphere: heightened emotions among the populace. Graham Greene wrote about this aspect of warfare in reference to the bombing of London: "The nightly routine of sirens, barrage, the probing raider, the unmistakable engine (Where are you? Where are you? Where are you?), the bomb-bursts moving nearer and then moving away, hold one like a love-charm."[16] That sense of emotional heightening of Theodore White's "point in time" was also important for rebuilding a sense of identity among the many Chinese and foreigners streaming toward the temporary capital. Yet the heroic often gave way to the elegiac and even the cynical.

On 3 August 1944, Xu Wancheng noted, the Sichuan government gazette carried a warning "against licentiousness," noting that "it is not appropriate to record or publish announcements about living together." The authorities regularly publicized official collective wedding ceremonies. But, according to Xu, newspapers had apparently been publishing notices of men and women living together openly:

It was as if they were making formal engagement and wedding announcements. But men and women cohabiting couldn't be regarded as a formal marriage. The open announcements are really a stimulation for a wind of licentiousness. . . . Therefore the day before yesterday, an order went out to the whole country, according to article 22 of the Law on Correction of Publications, announcing the repression of notices of men and women living together, because it harmed virtuous customs.[17]

Xu's parting reflection was that the new regulation was, in effect, an acknowledgment of what had been widely rumored: that there were many "temporary husbands and wives" in the "interior" (the Nationalist zone).[18]

Xu's story highlights the fear behind the Nationalist authorities' attempts to create a new moral core: that sexual freedom was destructive of social norms.[19] Chongqing was supposed to become a crucible of national renewal, and this image was seriously compromised by the reality of a dirty city full of desperate refugees and illicit sex. Still, whatever the authorities may have wanted, by the end of the war, corruption, disease, and the continued fear of invasion made conditions in Chongqing unbearable for much of the population. Then the war ended suddenly in August 1945, and the city's inhabitants prepared for an uncertain peace.

Forgetting and Remembering

During the years of Mao's rule, the authorities gave Chongqing little space to remember or mourn its suffering during the war. The cold fact was that the narrative of Nationalist resistance provided no ideological ballast for the new socialist state.

Yet in private, the wartime years were not forgotten. When I asked Zhou Yong, director of the Chongqing Research Center for the War of Resistance against Japanese Aggression in the Unoccupied Area, whether his family had discussed this aspect of history when he was a child, he replied, "We couldn't *not* talk about it. But in the 1950s and 1960s, this topic was mostly discussed face to face, at home."[20] At that time, he said, "older folk were still alive and their memories were clear," so while they did not discuss the War of Resistance in public, they remembered it privately. Among the stories that older people would tell were memories of how everyday life had changed during the war. During air raids, they recalled, people would have a small bag ready, in case they were stuck for hours in the shelters. Police officers would come around ahead of a raid, ringing a bell to urge people to take cover. Zhou's family would also tell stories of eating low-quality rice full of pebbles and wearing cheap clothes made out of rough, domestically produced cloth. Their clearest memory was of the Japanese surrender. "On 10 August 1945," he told me, "when the news got to Chongqing, the whole of the city went wild." People set off endless firecrackers and started drinking in celebration. "Even my granny, who was a country girl, went many miles to Chongqing to see the parade, and to see the wild celebrations." "Their memories were very vivid," he added.[21]

During the Cold War years, while they may have been vivid, these memories remained private. Other issues occupied Chongqing under Mao. During the Cultural Revolution, Chongqing was the scene of some of the most vicious fighting between Red Guards, with ammunition from local arsenals being used in the city streets.[22] The combatants were the children of those who had lived in Chongqing during the war; the arsenals were also in some sense legacies of those years.

The fortieth anniversary of the end of the war in 1985 was a major turning point for Chongqing's collective memory of the war. As early as the 1950s, some sites of memory had already been preserved, though they related to the more politically acceptable parts of Chongqing's history: these included the CCP headquarters in the suburb of Hongyancun and the prisons operated by SACO (the Sino-American Cooperative Organization), in which the Nationalist security chief, Dai Li, and his American partners had arrested, tortured, and killed political dissidents. The majority of Chongqing's wartime history had not been publicly discussed for much of the Mao era.

In the 1980s, the factors which changed China's public sphere more broadly also affected Chongqing. Local identity became stronger, particularly as cities sought to attract foreign investment. Chongqing's identity was further shaped by political changes that culminated in its establishment, in 1997, as China's fourth autonomous municipality (after Beijing, Shanghai, and Tianjin). Much effort began to go into collecting local histories, such as the oral histories contained in the *Wenshi ziliao* series of historical records compiled under a government program.[23]

Over the next two decades, the urban topography of Chongqing was reimagined to incorporate the elements of wartime history that had been elided in public memory after 1949. The air raids that had been remembered only in family histories were now restored to the city's public narrative. The Three Gorges Museum, opened in 2005, contains a section that commemorates the history of the War of Resistance. Its most striking element is a diorama of the bombing of Chongqing, complete with a fiery orange glow re-creating the incendiary bombings, and mournful violin music to accompany the destruction at the end.[24] Some of the restaurants in central Chongqing have unusually long, narrow rooms because they are converted air-raid shelters, and this feature is used to bring in diners to try the local hotpot being served there. Huangshan, the old wartime house of Chiang Kai-shek, outside Chongqing, has now been restored as a tourist site; it showcases Chiang's decisions and features an actor who plays the generalissimo and shows visitors around.[25] In the 2010s, the artistic and historical memorials to China's wartime experience steadily increased in number all around the city. There are memorials and statues all over town commemorating various events and personalities, including the house occupied by Chiang's chief of staff, General Stilwell. Private enterprise is also represented, as Fan Jianchuan opened a new Chongqing museum in 2018.

The revival of wartime memory in Chongqing does not, however, merely echo the earlier shift in memory at the national level. The crucial difference is that the central actors in the revived social memory of Chongqing are the Communists' great opponents, the Nationalists. The national-level suppression of their story after 1949 (other than as stage villains) meant that the local history of all those who had been in their area of influence was also ignored or reviled. This had been a double blow to those living in Chongqing during the war: not only did they suffer much worse air raids and their effects than anywhere else in China, but their contribution to victory was then sidelined by history. The opening up of space at the national level to discuss aspects of the war other than Mao's contribution allowed local memory in Chongqing to revive in a way that was not in direct opposition to the national-level story, where the CCP was still dominant, but rather at right angles to it, a subversion by omission.[26] Today, Chongqing clearly commemorates and celebrates the period when the city was the temporary capital of a regime deeply opposed to the Communists. It also lays stress on the Nationalist war record, giving relatively less emphasis to the activities of the CCP, as well as giving new attention to a local history that was long disregarded.

This shift became possible because of the distinctive confluence of factors that shaped Chongqing's history. After all, Chongqing was not the only city in China to be bombed during the war—far from it. Some of the most devastating air strikes on Chinese territory were carried out by the United States; General Curtis LeMay coordinated the bombing of Japanese-occupied Wuhan in 1944 and went on to bomb other cities, including Taipei.[27] However, the bombing of cities in occupied territory or in a Japanese colony, run with Chinese collaborators, did not fit in with either of the most important narratives that emerged during the war years and would reemerge after the Cold War: China as victim (as in Nanjing) or as brave resister (as in Chongqing).

The revision of local history was welcomed in Chongqing. "At that time, Chongqingers were really very happy that this historical memory had returned to the city," Zhou Yong told me.[28] Yet it had come very late in the day. In 1985, when local historians and authorities had started to revive the idea of Theodore White's "point in time" in earnest, there were still many older people who had been alive during the war. Two decades later, on the occasion of the sixtieth anniversary, those survivors were far fewer in number.

This loss of people with direct memories of the war led to an emphasis on finding ways to propagate the new collective memory to those who might have little knowledge of or connection to the events. Local newspapers covered the sixtieth anniversary of the war's end extensively in the summer of 2005, with articles on local heroes, artistic and cultural figures, and commanders associated with Chongqing. The authorities also took note of the fact that the sixtieth anniversary would almost certainly be the last major commemoration when more than a few survivors would still be alive. Therefore, the participants' stories were made part of the narrative, both in newspaper interviews and in public art projects; for example, a sculpture depicting air-raid victims was displayed in July 2005 alongside a survivor of the raid itself, ninety-one-year-old Yuan Yongzhen.[29] Public artworks like this were just one part of a wider political agenda to give China a global role by stressing its participation in a wartime antifascist alliance; in the words of one study that exemplifies this trend, "China was one of the four Allied powers that opposed fascism, and . . . the battle-fields of China were among the most important battlefields of the antifascist war."[30]

The local media also publicized the idea of Chongqing's importance. In 2005, Chongqing Television released the documentary *Wartime Temporary Capital (Kangzhan Peidu)*. The artwork on the cover of the DVD epitomizes the message of the documentary. On the left side are the US Capitol in Washington, DC; the Kremlin in Moscow's Red Square; and the clock tower of the Houses of Parliament in London. On the right side, larger than any of the other buildings, is the Monument to Victory in the War of Resistance to Japan, which was erected in 1944 in the center of Chongqing and has since been reimagined as the Liberation Monument. In short, in the Second World War, there were not three great Allied capitals, but four. Even though the "meaning" of the wartime alliance was very different in each country—liberty, empire, communism, nationalism—the moral agenda was shared.

The further implication of the image is that even in the present day, when values seem ostensibly very different among the main actors in the international order, cooperation across ideological boundaries is still possible.[31] The suggestion is that China plays a similarly cooperative role in today's international community, in unstated but clear contrast with the revolutionary confrontation of Mao's China.

The Southwest and Beyond: Unofficial Memories of the Nationalist Zone

The opening up of space for a new, officially sanctioned public memory of the war in museums and television documentaries also made room for unofficial memories to reemerge. This phenomenon was not exclusive to the Southwest, but it did find particular purchase there because of the heavy weight of officially repressed memory since 1949. Fan Jianchuan was a pioneer in retrieving previously unheard voices in his book *One Person's War of Resistance* (2000). In contrast to his fellow writer and friend Fang Jun, Fan Jianchuan stresses the record of the Nationalists and spends very little time on the CCP and the Eighth Route Army in this book. Although Fan's nationalist (in the wider sense) credentials are strong, his account is strongly flavored by a particular regional issue: the exclusion of the Nationalists from Chinese historiography until very recently meant that Sichuanese contributions to the war, few of which related to the CCP, were also underreported.

This regional focus explains why the white sun on the blue sky of the Nationalist flag recurs over and over again among the photographs of prized objects in Fan's collection, such as enamel badges from Sichuan militias and regular troops.[32] Fan recounts heroic tales of people who served in the Nationalist army: one tells of seven Sichuan heroes on the frontline, and another of a woman medical orderly named Zhang Shufen.[33] Fan observes that in Zhang Shufen's picture on her ID card, now in his collection, she looks determined. Did she survive? he wonders. Did she have children? If she were alive now (in the year 2000), he muses, she would probably be about eighty years old. And then, the leap from the personal to the general: "If we fought a just war, isn't it correct that we relied on the contributions and sacrifices of millions of soldiers such as Zhang Shufen?"[34] The "just war" was not solely about leaders but about ordinary people, regardless of their party affiliation. Studs Terkel would have little to argue with here. The regional element comes out strongly near the end of the book, where Fan declares, "Sichuan, you are the strongman who held up the War of Resistance!" and goes on to point out that Chongqing was the center of the nation's resistance during the war. Chongqing rather than Yan'an, he implies.[35] Nods toward Chiang Kai-shek become more pronounced as the book progresses. In one section, Fan declares that Chiang's much-mocked New Life Movement of the 1930s, with its aim of moral renewal, was not such a bad idea: suggestions such as not spitting on the street or waiting politely in line for buses rather than pushing on board, he says, are sensible enough.[36] (In the early 2020s, the Chinese government is attempting to regulate personal behavior through a "social credit" system in ways that the developers of the New Life Movement would have found very familiar.)

In his introduction, Fan Jianchuan observes that his friends regard his collections of memorabilia as somewhat eccentric and suggest that he should leave such matters to the government. Yet he declares that he finds himself personally connected to these themes, and it is clear that the way in which he uses his collection to make observations about contemporary China does not exactly match the messages of an official institution such as the Museum of the War of Resistance to Japan in Beijing, even if they are not in direct opposition to it.[37] "I hope that having read this," he writes, "my readers will continue to hold onto reform and opening up, and have determination to enrich the people and strengthen the country."[38] In the years since the publication of *One Person's War,* Fan has built a whole complex of museums outside Chengdu, including one on the Nationalists. In 2018, he opened his first museum in Chongqing, which commemorates the city's experience during the war. For Fan, the recovery of China's non-Communist wartime experience has been part of a wider experiment in pushing the boundaries of what can and cannot be said about the recent past in contemporary China. Another memorial sponsored by a local farmer and amateur historian, Yang Guogang, was established in 2013 at Songshan, in Yunnan province in southwestern China, to commemorate the China Expeditionary Force that served on the Burma-China border in 1944–1945. Its most striking feature is a field filled with statues of soldiers, recalling the Terracotta Army in Xi'an. One of the figures depicts General Joseph Stilwell.[39]

Another recent project addressed one of the major gaps in memory of the war in Chongqing and the Nationalist zone in the Southwest: the experience of the millions of refugees who had fled the Japanese invasion. In 2005, the historian Su Zhiliang led a team that published the oral history collection *Going to the Interior (Qu da houfang)*. It was actually produced in Shanghai, but it was a reminder of the link between the people of that city and those in the "downriver" city of Chongqing, who had been forced into a relationship during the war years. The book was an offshoot of a film documentary about the wartime refugee experience made by Shanghai television in 2002–2004, which sparked the idea that a book ought to be published as a permanent reminder of the war generation's experience. The older people interviewed for the project expressed concern that their experiences would not be remembered. One of them said despondently, "Today's generation knows very little about the Second World War. We don't fear dying; we fear being forgotten."[40]

For those who grew up in Britain in the postwar decades, evacuation stories were one of the most powerful tropes in the construction of the narrative of the Second World War. Children's novels on this theme, such as Nina Bawden's *Carrie's War* and Jill Paton Walsh's *Fireweed,* were staples of school libraries. The circumstances were less favorable for such literature to emerge in China. Fleeing to Yan'an would have been a politically acceptable theme in the post-1949 era, but only a minority of refugees undertook that journey. Far more people made their way to Chongqing, yet their stories could not be easily told in the Mao years. In Su's words, "In a time of unprecedented disaster, sixty million boys and girls, government officials, university professors, factory and shop bosses, and workers . . . came to the far southwest. With no differentiation of age, sex, faith, or party or faction [*dangpai*], for survival, . . . to resist the invaders. . . . They had just one aspiration: go west, go west, again go west!" Su marveled at the massive relocation effort: "Where in the world is there a country that undertook such a strategic move during a war of resistance? Where in the world is there a country that could bear this sort of difficulty?"[41] He emphasized that "this book's story is of the ordinary people [*xiao renwu*] of that great time," uncovering the "traces of what you can sing about and what you can weep about."[42] The book was a restoration of the patriotic honor of the ordinary people who fled to Chongqing and whose stories were not only repressed in the postwar decades, but even considered shameful. Su realized that relatively few of the survivors of the war would still be alive in 2005, and those who were would be in their eighties and nineties. The project editors traveled all across China and to North America to interview over a hundred survivors of the war. *Going to the Interior* is highly patriotic in tone, but very far from being a propaganda version of the war. One interviewee, Yan Yangchu, refers to the transfer of China's government and factories to the interior as "Chinese industry's Dunkirk." Xu Ying, former reporter for the newspaper *Da gongbao,* declares that "there was no difference between our Dunkirk and the British one. Ours may have been worse." Another interviewee notes that when under bombardment, "we were very patriotic."[43] Yet the overall theme is of a war that is messy, not sanitized, and marked by the heroism of the everyday rather than grand nationalistic gestures. It reflects the Chongqing found in Xu Wancheng's account from the 1940s: grimy, unromantic, but holding on regardless.

Among the memories preserved are those of young men rescuing goods lost in sunken boats (the "water-rats"), poor food and nonexistent transport, and the sight of corpses, some whole, some partial.[44] One telling moment comes when an interviewee, asked about what it was like to be caught in an air raid, describes it not as terrifying or thrilling, but tiring, waiting for the all-clear signal day after day.[45] The sense of constant fatigue and boredom as a civilian in war is not exclusive to China; there is an old saying that war is 99 percent boredom and 1 percent sheer terror. Taking note of this aspect of war adds one more element to understanding the emotional palimpsest that formed the politics and society of the time, when heightened sexual tension existed underneath lassitude and lack of purpose as life became harder and more unpredictable.[46] These stories of terrible dysfunction do not bolster a narrative of uncomplicated or bombastic patriotism, but they add texture to social memory. Rather than the state-defined tropes of memory and mourning that are featured in museums, the stories in *Going to the Interior* provide what Su calls the "ordinary person's" (*xiao renwu*) approach to the wartime experience. The documentary and book create a three-dimensional memory of war in which the chance to recover and commemorate experience, whether in celebration or mourning, is most important, not the value of the story for state propaganda. Su Zhiliang told me that he had received letters from veterans who said they had seen the film and wept.[47]

There have been other cultural products that capture the popular mood on the memory of war. A memoir by Qi Bangyuan (Chi Pang-yuan), *The Great Flowing River* (*Juliuhe*), tells Qi's story of being forced to flee her hometown in the face of the Japanese invasion, and the breakdown of her romance with a young man, Zhang Dafei, who was eventually killed in an aerial battle above central China. The brilliance with which Qi combined romance, despair, and determination in her story made it a hit not just in Taiwan (where she had moved after 1949), but in mainland China, too.[48] In 2017, in an interview with Qi, the mainland Xinhua news agency reported that "on her bookshelf were gifts and toys with which she had been presented by mainland readers." Qi admitted that "the reaction of mainland readers surprised me—that they could feel my sadness and frustration." She noted that an old lady from Beijing about her age often wrote her "long, long" letters, saying that although she grew up in a red revolutionary family, she still became emotional and cried while reading Qi's story.[49] This cross-strait wartime memoir was an unexpected success, but many other, untold stories remain buried. The accounts of women forced into sex slavery ("comfort women") by the Japanese seem to have been too sensitive to cover broadly, both in terms of their sexual politics and the always delicate question of diplomatic relations with Japan; Su Zhiliang's display on them at his university in Shanghai is one of the rare manifestations of this issue in a public forum in China.[50]

War Memory, Insider Politics, and the Bo Xilai Affair

The revival of memory about wartime Chongqing became entangled with one of the strangest, most high-profile moments in the city, and for that matter in China's post-Mao history: the rise and fall of the senior Communist leader Bo Xilai. After postings in several other parts of China, the charismatic Bo served as party secretary for the municipality of Chongqing from 2007 to 2012. His predecessor, Wang Yang, had used the position to rise to national prominence, and Bo hoped to follow in his footsteps. A local scholar hoped that he would help promote remembrance of the city's history. But in 2013, Bo Xilai's career came to a sudden end.

During his tenure in Chongqing, Bo became famous for what was known as the "Chongqing model." The model involved promoting a more socialist local economy (a dig at the Chinese Communist Party, which was inclined toward neoliberal solutions to the country's economic problems) and cracking down on organized crime (exponents of which were often, conveniently, political foes of Bo). "Sing red, smash black" (*changhong dahei*) was the shorthand for Bo's policies, referring to the "red" songs of the Mao era, which Bo encouraged people to revive, and the "black" gangs who ran large parts of the city.[51]

Bo held power during a relatively liberal time in China as a whole. In the years running up to the Beijing Olympics in 2008, and for a time afterward, China was concerned to show a more open face to the world. This not only allowed foreign reporters to access stories that were not normally available, but also opened up a wider conversation about sensitive areas of history. On 15 November 2009, Wang Kang, a local scholar and Chongqing booster, spoke to the *Yazhou zhoukan* news magazine (based in Hong Kong) about Chongqing's wartime past. Wang Kang himself is a rather unusual figure. Having first come to prominence as a liberal protestor during the 1989 democracy movement, he then became known not only for his pronouncements on Chongqing's history and culture but also for his seeming inside knowledge of the twists and turns of the Bo Xilai affair, which he communicated to reporters.[52]

In the interview with *Yazhou zhoukan,* Wang argued that for Chongqing to "build up its cultural memory, it has to extend its historical memory." He vigorously advanced the idea that Chongqing's romantic, desperate wartime years could serve as a source of inspiration for the city and the country.

Wang specified what made the Chongqing wartime moment "a special era" (*teyou de niandai*): the combination of the international antifascist Pacific War, the Nationalist-CCP United Front, and the resistance in the interior. The period brought together a remarkable range of talents, he argued, as well as a blending of cultures between East and West. Without Chongqing, he suggested, China could not have resisted for eight years, yet the government based there did not make any sort of accommodation with the Japanese. Chiang Kai-shek, Wang pointed out, regarded the period as one when China made use of its "spirit, traditions, culture, ethics, and morality."[53]

Yet the remains of that period, Wang Kang pointed out, are remarkably few, and the history of that time has left almost no traces: "Chongqingers ought to reflect on this." Of this historical amnesia, he said, "The War of Resistance was a crucial time in Chinese development—but it has been covered over for ideological reasons." He declared that the National Political Consultative Council of the Nationalist Party was the first modern Chinese organization to include aspects of the popular will: "In 1945, it would not have been impossible for China to establish a two-party system." Returning to the present, he claimed that "the slogans of the Chongqing talks [between Chiang and Mao in 1945]—nationalization of the army, democratization of politics, equal legal status for political parties—still have validity today."[54] In the China of Xi Jinping, a decade after Wang's interview, such ideas have been fiercely suppressed. Even in 2009, they were daring, to say the least.

Wang Kang concluded the interview in a fervor of local boosterism: "The temperament of Chongqing people was formed by living through fire and coming through—like a phoenix. Without the air raids, the temperament of Chongqing people today would not have formed." In the future, when the CCP and Nationalists shake hands again, "It can't be in Beijing or Taipei, it can only be in Chongqing."[55] (In fact, the first meeting since 1945 took place even further south: on 7 November 2015, Xi Jinping and recently retired Nationalist president of Taiwan Ma Ying-jeou met and shook hands in Singapore.) Wang was keen that Bo Xilai take note of his suggestions, urging him to stress Chongqing's time as "a capital that defended the nation during the war, at a time when China was in grave peril from inside and outside."[56]

Bo would not be in a position to take such advice much longer. His rise had clearly unnerved his political rivals, and it led to the biggest shock in the leadership since CCP secretary-general Zhao Ziyang's fall in 1989, or perhaps the arrest of the Gang of Four in 1976. In a stunning coup, Bo was charged with corruption and political indiscipline in July 2013. Even more sensationally, his wife, Gu Kailai, was convicted of the murder of a British businessman in a hotel in a Chongqing suburb. The leadership of Chongqing was taken over by the less high-profile Zhang Dejiang, who steadied the ship before handing it over to Sun Zhengcai. Sun's rule in Chongqing was decidedly more low key than that of Bo, particularly as it coincided with the rise to power of Xi Jinping, the most centralizing leader in recent Chinese history, yet even he was abruptly ousted from office in July 2017. It became apparent that Chongqing was a posting that could lead either to glory or to disgrace. Yet the development of Chongqing's memory of wartime has continued, regardless of changes in the city's leadership; it is a project that goes beyond the interests of any specific political leader.

The Other Side: Memories of Yan'an

The anomalies surrounding the rise in Chongqing's status have to be understood in the context of the other pole of political magnetism in wartime China: the town of Yan'an, in Shaanxi province, which became the crucible of Mao's leadership and the training ground for the generation that would eventually rule China. A sense of near-religious sacredness around "red sites" is not new in China. During the Cultural Revolution, trainloads of pilgrims would make their way to Shaoshan in Hunan province, Mao's birthplace, crowding the place so much that the authorities had to construct a replica version of Mao's old house to accommodate twice as many visitors.[57] The town of Yan'an is significant as the former capital of the most important Communist base area. It was here that Mao and other leaders considered how the Communist Party would respond to the Japanese invasion. It was in Yan'an, in effect, that the Chinese communist revolution was made. There is still considerable "red tourism" to Yan'an, and the tourist sites there faithfully reflect the official version of the CCP's rise to power.

Just as understandings of Chongqing's history have shifted, the official, hagiographical interpretation of the wartime leadership of the CCP has also become open to question. This more broadminded attitude toward Yan'an is apparent in a remarkable book that appeared in 2007, a period of relative freedom in Chinese publishing, by the academic Zhu Hongzhao. Zhu had taught in Yan'an and had written for *Liberation Daily* (*Jiefang ribao*), which began its life as the CCP's newspaper in Yan'an. Zhu's book is titled *Yan'an richang shenghuo de lishi* (A history of everyday life in Yan'an), with the subtitle *Zhanshi yi ge ni bu zhidao de Yan'an* (Showing you the Yan'an you never knew). It is a narrative history of Yan'an in the wartime years, with extensive citations from a wide range of documents from those years, as well as from memoirs and oral histories compiled in the reform era after 1978. Its account of Mao's time in Yan'an is in many ways highly sympathetic, but it provides a distinctly rough-edged and not remotely sanitized account of life in this sacred site for Chinese communism.

One of the most prominent elements of the experience of living in Chongqing during wartime was the construction of a wider moral universe in which the individual's role was reflected in the changing nature of a society in flux. In Yan'an, too, the construction of such a moral universe is evident in the articles, interviews, and memoirs that Zhu draws upon.[58]

Compared with the impression of both lassitude and wild abandon that characterized Chongqing, descriptions of Yan'an focus on the disciplining of time. Eating according to a fixed schedule is a recurring theme along those lines. The journalist Chen Xuezhao wrote, "We ate three meals within six or seven hours, so I felt that eating was a task that took up most of the day. Space between meals was too small, so we often had to interrupt our work. The meals were all millet, and the vegetable was always pumpkin."[59] Another memoirist remembered that as a band played, "the whistle signaling food time drowned out the instruments, and they ran and the cook brought a big container of noodles . . . people fought for food and noodles spilled on them."[60]

These stories are quite different from the ones Xu Wancheng told of deprivation and hunger in Chongqing. In one dry anecdote, Xu claimed that a university canteen in that city had put up a notice reading, "Don't try to eat enough to be full."[61] Zhu's Yan'an, in contrast, is not a place of radical unfairness in food distribution, or a lack of nutrition overall. His book describes many acts of generosity; Chen Xuezhao, for example, was given eggs and spring onions by locals who took pity on her as an outsider, and special provisions were made for students (who were thought to need nourishing food) at the Lu Xun College. But there was a distinct hierarchy of how food was distributed. An account from the famous poet Ai Qing tells of being given "middle-tier" food, whereas his wife and child were given lesser "regular-tier" provisions. Discipline was enforced: young soldiers would bring food to the party members' doors, and if they did not eat it, it would be taken away untouched. It was not permitted to give away food to someone else.[62] These stories about food supply must be understood in the context of other, darker stories relating to lack of food; later in this chapter, we will see how the erased memory of the Henan famine of 1942 has reentered public discourse in China.

Zhu's book helps to blurs a narrative that has taken hold since 1949: that to be committed to Chongqing or Yan'an was a purely binary choice. For devotees of the "Yan'an Way," the evils of Chongqing and the "feudal" Nationalists supposedly provided a clear contrast. But individuals were sometimes torn between the two.

From the sources that Zhu cites in his book, we see some of the overlap between work in Chongqing and in Yan'an. Retrospectively, the divisions between those who worked in Yan'an for the CCP and in Chongqing for the Nationalists seem stark. Because of the economic blockade on Yan'an from 1942 to 1943, it became increasingly difficult to leave or enter the Shaanxi–Gansu–Ningxia region, and the ability to move between the two cities was limited. Early in the war it was much easier. After the founder of the Yan'an hospital, He Mu (who was married to Chen Xuezhao), became angry at what he regarded as disrespectful treatment by colleagues, he left for Chongqing. Once he got there he found it difficult to work because he was associated with the CCP, and so he returned to Yan'an. The CCP was keen to have him return because the clinic was doing badly without him. He's experience in Yan'an left him feeling ambivalent. His work was valued, but he found the self-criticism and struggle sessions difficult to deal with, and he became a subject of mockery because of his unwillingness fully to go along with the new political demands in Yan'an. His professional status entitled him to a horse, but the groom gave him a sick one, a contemptuous gesture that suggested that people were laughing at him behind his back.[63] This mixture of emotions—a sense of mission, but an everyday experience of spite and resentment—is very human. But it does not fit into a simple categorization of heroes and villains.

Zhu Hongzhao's remarkable portrait of Yan'an is neither hostile nor hagiographical. It shows "everyday life" as being rather like that in Chongqing, where cruelty and political pressure vied with attempts at reform in highly constrained wartime circumstances. In Chongqing, the torture chambers of the SACO prisons, built as a joint venture between the United States and Chinese Nationalists, are still preserved as a macabre site of historical memory. Although similar tactics were used in Yan'an, they are not part of official remembering of the era. Zhu breaks with convention by discussing the extensive evidence that the Yan'an regime, like many wartime regimes under pressure, used tactics of immense cruelty. Citing an archival document, Zhu tells a distressing story: "A mother called Zhang Yuanfang and her child, plus a pregnant woman called Lin Fu, were locked up, often with no food or water, and their winter clothes were delivered but not given to them."[64]

One document from October 1945 which Zhu cites describes what happened at the Lu Xun Art Institute of Yan'an University:

"Swearing, beating, tying people up. These methods, I'm afraid, were the same in all units in Yan'an, but specific to the Lu Xun Art Institute was imprisonment in the Industrial and Agricultural Collective Labour Camp."[65] Some observers remarked that "this labour camp was as bad as [that of] the Nationalists." Such torture could shape memories for life. Fifty years after being condemned by the Communist Party, the activist Li Na recalled how terrified she was at being labeled a "problem."[66] Making the connection with later history, she saw these tactics as similar to those used in the reeducation camps that were set up some two decades later during the Cultural Revolution.

Such tactics did, however, sometimes have the desired effect. Zhu quotes one activist as declaring that he had felt "broken apart" in 1942, and that this helped him realize the importance of the collective and of "re-creating" his mind to appreciate phenomena he had previously despised, such as popular culture.[67]

While abuses took place in both Chongqing and Yan'an, there was one significant difference. In Yan'an, these tactics were being used on people who were (supposedly) on the same side: the intellectuals who had come to the city voluntarily. In Chongqing, the thuggish Nationalist security chief Dai Li tortured his political opponents.[68] In his recovery of Yan'an's wartime history, Zhu does not deny the immense importance of the period for shaping Chinese Communist rule, or seek to denigrate what came out of it. But his work does show that the dark side of Yan'an was integral to that history, not a minor issue that can be swept aside.

One abiding theme that emerges in memories of both Yan'an and Chongqing is the persistence of dirt. There is nothing surprising about this; wartime conditions are rarely hygienic, and indeed much of the Nationalist government's social policy during the war centered on trying to improve hygiene. History that ignores dirt is literally "sanitized" history. Memories of Yan'an that are recounted in Zhu's book repeatedly mention filthy conditions. A party member recalled a location where political meetings were held: "What I remember most was how many lice there were on the ground, and when we held a meeting, myriads of insects would clamber up your trouser leg."[69] Wang Huide, an intellectual, recalled working in the fields and becoming covered in dung: "on my body, my feet, my hands—after half a day, no matter how you wash, when you hold your rice bowl, you still smell." Unhygienic conditions could breed disease; one woman recalled that at Yan'an Women's University, "we shared *kang* [bed], towels, and toothbrushes."[70]

Zhu's book also reveals another aspect of life in Yan'an that does not appear in official accounts: the importance of gender and sexuality in shaping the revolution. Male Chinese revolutionaries, both Nationalist and Communist, had always had an ambivalent attitude toward women, at best. The Nationalists had a prurient, often misogynistic view of women at the heart of their interpretation of modern society.[71] But there were progressive strands in the party. As early as 1936, at a time when France and Switzerland, to name two liberal Western societies, did not allow women to vote, the Nationalists pledged that men and women would be given equal voting rights (although this was not implemented until the postwar constitution was promulgated in 1947.)[72] The Communists made more explicit claims to gender equality early on, but in practice were deeply patriarchal. In March 1942 the writer Ding Ling, who had made an arduous journey to reach Yan'an, made a plea for the importance of feminism and individual rights in the revolution, only to have Mao rebuff her harshly.[73]

The difficult lives of women are described in memoirs of wartime Yan'an; they were also a subject of fascination, from afar, in Chongqing. A story told by Xu Wancheng gives a flavor of the cynical way in which many in Chongqing thought about the remote communist base area, bringing together favorite Chongqing themes of hunger and prurience. Xu tells of "a certain female student" who suddenly played a "clever trick." She fled to Yan'an with an "empty belly" and returned after half a year. "However," he noted, "her belly had grown larger now."[74] Memoirs from Yan'an also mention pregnancy and childbirth, but they do not use Xu's sardonic tone. The "four fears" of women in the town were pregnancy, childbirth, childcare, and having to abandon their children. Women who had been there recalled that unexpected pregnancy was commonplace, that medical conditions and facilities to bring up children were severely lacking, and that women could only carry on their revolutionary careers if they gave their children away to peasant families to bring up.[75]

The accounts of senior men who would later rise to power in Mao's China are quite different, focusing on their dedication. The memoir of Yu Ruomu, wife of Chen Yun (who would become one of the most senior leaders of the People's Republic), which Zhu draws from, focuses on Chen's conscientiousness. She notes that he "worked so hard that his nose started to bleed," and that they rarely saw each other except on Saturdays. The phenomenon of "Saturday living together" apparently became well known in the town.[76]

The senior leaders in Yan'an were able to live their lives according to a narrative that not only showed revolutionary heroism but also enabled them to mold themselves into traditional patriarchs. The proportion of men to women in Yan'an varied from thirty to one in 1938 to eight to one in 1944. Despite the shortage of women, the senior party members managed to find partners. Zhu cites a volume on Yan'an edited by Mei Jian which declared:

> Dance parties were very lively; not just for reasons of recreation and health, but also because there were so many younger-aged girls. Many officials and generals were compensating for their lost youth, and this encouraged and helped them to get married. . . . Of all the high leaders and officers above the level of divisional commander, about 80 per cent of them fell in love, got married, had children in Yan'an—so for them it was a warm and sweet memory.[77]

One of those future leaders who retained sweet memories was Hu Qiaomu, who would be so instrumental in addressing memory of war in the academy some four decades later.

Not all the leaders succeeded in their quest for love, however. Lin Biao, who would later be condemned as a traitor to the revolution after a coup attempt in 1971, was rebuffed when he asked for a bride, according to one report: "A female cadre was brought in to be his bride, but nobody told her! When Lin Biao said, 'Shall we get married?' she ran off yelling, 'I won't! I won't!'"[78]

For women, their sexuality hindered them from participating in the revolution, whereas for men, exercising it in a traditional way was crucial to consolidating their power. The war exacerbated this contrast.[79]

Zhu's book is one of the most powerful and nuanced accounts of what life in Yan'an was really like during the war. He introduces the work with an account of why the topic was of such importance to him, even though he was born long after the war was over. In doing so, he makes it clear that his project, for all its honesty about Yan'an, is celebratory, not critical:

> At the start of a new century, . . . when remembering the twen-
> tieth century social history made . . . by our parents and forefa-
> thers, there are only two periods that have real value and signifi-
> cance when it comes to social and cultural history: May Fourth
> and Yan'an. May Fourth discovered the human, and Yan'an cre-
> ated it.[80]

"May Fourth" refers to the liberal cultural movement of the
early twentieth century that sought to bring "science and democracy" to China. But, he continues,

> The ten years of the history of Yan'an, in its richness, complexity,
> and contemporaneity, far exceed May Fourth. I believe that . . .
> in constructing a society and civilization for the twenty-first
> century . . . nothing is greater than Yan'an. I hope that each of us
> who loves life and seeks prosperity will pay attention to Yan'an,
> think over Yan'an, to find [points] for contemporary life and
> existence.[81]

Zhu's idea of Yan'an seems to be in sharp contrast with many
of the values of contemporary China. On Nanjing Road in
Shanghai, Zhu laments the consumerism that seems to have taken
over China's youth in the present day.[82] He says that he is looking
not for the Yan'an that is to be found in library books, but the one
that is present in written materials that have not yet been discovered and in people's memories—in other words, for a Yan'an that,
he implies, is quite unlike the one in official, hagiographic, CCP
accounts.[83]

Zhu contends that the Yan'an years were crucial for the formation of a coherent political, social, and cultural identity for all
Chinese. He does not shy away from the cruelty and horror of
Yan'an, but neither does he condemn it—rather, he uses it as part
of an argument that adversity and even cruelty might be justifiable

in the drive to create a new society. It is an argument not so far removed from that of Wang Kang and others who claimed that the adversity found in the other wartime capital, Chongqing, also helped to forge a more robust modern China.

Hunger and Memory

Social histories of wartime frequently combine narratives of deprivation and discipline. Generations of British schoolchildren have been brought up on stories of rationing and the need to go without luxury goods and foods in the service of the war effort. Chinese narratives center on similar themes; Zhu Hongzhao's reconstruction of the Yan'an experience, for example, draws heavily on the idea of food distribution as a way of creating hierarchies and a sense of obligation to the communist system of redistribution. The Chongqing narratives concentrate more on the inequities that people saw around them, such as both workers and professionals being unable to feed their families because of soaring prices, while black marketeers cashed in illicitly.

One regional Chinese wartime narrative that emerged in the 2010s was specifically tied to hunger: the rediscovery of the horrific famine that ravaged Henan province in 1942. During that year, and continuing into 1943, some three million people starved to death because of a combination of natural factors, including adverse weather, and human-made ones, such as the seizure of grain by the government to feed the military. In one sense, acknowledging the 1942 famine should have been politically unproblematic for the CCP, since it was partly caused by Nationalist policies of taxation by grain seizure. Yet it is only in recent years that the event has reentered the wider public culture.

The recovery of this story centered on the seventieth anniversary of the famine in 2012 and a film that appeared that year: *Back to 1942 (1942 nian)*, directed by Feng Xiaogang, based on a novella by Liu Zhenyun. This exercise in memory combines a variety of elements: a long-forgotten and politically sensitive topic, the use of celebrity culture to expose it, the existence of accounts by foreigners to add weight to Chinese ones, and the rediscovery of historical materials.

The writer Liu Zhenyun, winner of the 2011 Mao Dun literature prize, has become one of China's best-regarded authors. In 1990, at the age of thirty-two, Liu was approached by a friend who wanted to write a history of several Chinese disasters, including the 1942 famine. Liu had never heard of the famine and was shocked when he found out about the huge death toll. In 2012, he recalled the time when he first realized that his family had lived through that calamity:

> Overwhelmed, I return to my home province determined to travel back to that awful period, determined to salvage three million souls from the sands of time.
>
> Soon I make a strange discovery: The surviving famine victims and their descendants have relegated all their memories of 1942 to oblivion. This is the reason I know nothing about this tragic period.
>
> My grandmother lived through the famine. When I ask her about 1942 she responds: "1942? What about it?" I tell her it was the year many people died of starvation. "People died of starvation all the time," she replies. "What's so special about that year?"[84]

Rather like Cui Yongyuan, Fang Jun, and Fan Jianchuan, Liu's discovery of an unknown part of the history of the Second World

War became part of a process of understanding his own identity. Liu began to ask why forgetting major historical events seemed to be such a common phenomenon:

> Why do we Chinese have such a black sense of humor? And why are we so forgetful? The answer my grandmother gave when I asked about 1942 provides a clue: There are innumerable instances of starvation and cannibalism throughout Chinese history, and when a people are constantly confronted with death through starvation, how else can they deal with it other than by forgetting? . . . Humor and a large helping of amnesia are the secrets to facing tragedy.[85]

Liu Zhenyun persevered with the task of recovering his own family's stories, and those memories informed a novella titled *Remembering 1942* (*Mangu 1942 nian*), first published in 1990. About a decade later, the Henanese historian Song Zhixin also began investigating the famine, and she discovered that the historical record was not a complete blank. In 2005, after five years of work, Song published a large volume of news reports, memoirs, and documents from the famine years in a volume titled *1942: The Great Henan Famine* (*1942: Da Henan jihuang*). Song was born in Kaifeng, Henan, in 1949, and her mother, born in 1913, had been a witness to the famine.[86] Song's work was part of the *Wenshi ziliao* project, a nationwide project to collect historical memories and materials at a local level, some of a more reliable nature than others. Her book is unusual in that it gave extensive credit to the work of a foreigner, the American journalist Theodore White, as a key source for understanding the effects of the famine.[87] The volume contains many poignant, detailed, and deeply moving contemporary accounts by Chinese journalists such as Zhang Gaoli of *Da Gongbao*, along with material giving historical context and biographical accounts of the writers who recorded what they saw.[88]

During the same period, in the 1990s and 2000s, Liu Zhenyun had been working with his longtime collaborator, the film director Feng Xiaogang, one of China's most critically and commercially successful directors, to obtain permission from the authorities to make a movie about such a sensitive topic. The film was eventually authorized and was released in 2012. It was a hit at the Chinese box office, earning some ¥364 million on a budget of ¥210 million. It was not well received by Western critics, however, who complained that it favored loud spectacle and cheap sentiment over genuine emotion (as was also said of Zhang Yimou's *The Flowers of War* and Xiao Feng's *Unbreakable Spirit*). Jay Weissberg of *Variety* said that it displayed its "budget but not its heart," and Xan Brooks of the *Guardian* called it "an ongoing marriage of bombast and sentiment."[89]

But what was important about the film was not its quality. Rather, it provided an opportunity for the hitherto forgotten history of the famine to enter the Chinese public sphere. It also brought greater publicity to Song Zhixin's book. An updated edition was issued in 2012 with a still from the film on the cover; a shorter version, marketed as a reader with materials from the film, was also issued.

In the same year, a group of journalists (Meng Lei, Guan Guofeng, and Guo Xiaoyang) published a book titled *1942: Starving China* (*1942: Jihuang Zhongguo*), a work of reportage that incorporated interviews with elderly survivors of the famine, along with contemporaneous sources.[90] Meng introduces the book by calling the year 1942 a "black hole of history," declaring that he had been inspired by a journalist who told him to go and find out about "a year that was forgotten, intentionally or not, . . . a year that brought about hunger and fear." He adds that "it's hard to find any detailed materials about this year." He discusses the prominence that Liu's novella and Feng's film have brought to the subject, declaring that previously the famine was "almost a historical blank" (*kongbai*) that had been studied by only a few scholars, of whom he acknowledges Song Zhixin as the most significant. The most "frightening" thing, he observes, is that there seemed to be no historical memory of the famine: "When we interviewed people and brought up 1942, even people who managed the archives, the first sentence was 'What *about* 1942?'" Meng details his attempts to find materials in the official Henan provincial archives, running up against claims that the material only began a decade later, in 1952. He did find some other sources, including local gazetteers, that gave an account of a great drought in those years, but he did not see how a drought on its own could kill so many people.[91]

Meng and his collaborators continued to look for materials and survivors. As they did so, Meng developed a strong sense of the significance of the story to his own identity as a Henanese. "The peasants of Henan sent their children to the battlefields to protect the country, gave their last morsels of grain for the country, and themselves ate grassroots and stalks," he observed. "In 1942, three million of them died in the drought, part of which was a natural disaster, but the primary cause of which was a human-made disaster. . . . That is to say, the lives and deaths of hundreds and thousands of our fathers and relatives somehow were voicelessly 'buried.'"[92] Meng's coauthor Guan Guofeng likewise declared that "as a Henan man, as someone who had been in news media since the 1970s, I had never heard of [the famine]." He engaged in the project for three reasons: "as a Henanese, to find out about our own history; to record material of historical value; and to carry out my 'responsibility' as a journalist."[93] The three authors regarded the rediscovery of their own province's history as a way of affirming their own identity, and by implication, as in Chongqing, of reassessing a top-down version of modern history that had erased their parents' and grandparents' experience.

This motivation also had implications for collective memory at the national level. The team of authors concluded their account by declaring, "We await more people to do accurate searches, and historical investigations," and adding, as their final words:

So as to awaken the present
So as to make clear the future.[94]

What, precisely, are Guo and his coauthors seeking to warn the present and future about? After all, while contemporary China faces many perils, mass starvation seems relatively unlikely. Yet the cover of the book warns that "If we forget, the next famine may bury us!" The message hints, but with no specifics mentioned, that a worse famine than the one in 1942 is possible. Of course, such an event did happen, less than two decades later—the famine that occurred during the Great Leap Forward, which killed more than twenty million people. The authors of *1942: Starving China* may not have mentioned the Mao-era disaster by name, but others were not so circumspect.

One of the effects of the release of the film *1942* was to provide a vehicle for discussion of that later famine by analogy. Murong Xuecun (the pen name of the well-regarded novelist and blogger Hao Qun) made an explicit link between the film's topic and the Great Leap Forward famine. Quoted by Voice of America radio, Murong said: "We all know that the famine in 1942 was not the most severe [in recent times], the most severe was the 1959–1962 years," adding, "but I can understand very well why Feng Xiaogang did not portray the famine of the 1960s." He noted, "I believe that if this were a free and open environment he would have definitely chosen to make a movie about 1959–1962."[95] (After a series of controversies, Murong's Weibo blogs were shut down in 2013.) Another blogger of the time, Li Yong, who was reported to have more than two hundred thousand followers on Weibo, wrote, "The nationalist government cannot use the excuse that Henan was situated in a war zone to avoid responsibility for the problems in relief efforts. . . . For the same reason, and even more so, people should look back at the great famine of 1959–1962 that took place in the central plains, as well as in the entire country, during times of peace."[96] One Weibo contributor declared, "I watched the movie and, as a result, I went and downloaded the book about the 1959 famine, *Tombstone*."[97] (This is a reference to the journalist Yang Jisheng's monumental account of the Great Leap Forward famine, which was banned in China.[98])

Feng himself could hardly make such a direct statement about the film's intentions, although he used his status as "China's Spielberg" in 2013 to criticize "ridiculous" film censorship and to declare that there should be more Chinese films analyzing the Cultural Revolution.[99] Feng's film, however, contained many elements that could be seen as allusions to the Great Leap Forward, according to the critic Wendy Qian. In one scene, notes Qian, a bureaucrat declines to report details of the famine to Chiang Kai-shek; similarly, during the Great Leap Forward, one reason that the famine worsened was that lower-level bureaucrats were too frightened to inform their superiors about what was happening in the countryside. In another scene, starving refugees are shown being blocked by police from entering the city of Luoyang; peasants were likewise forbidden from coming to the cities during the Great Leap Forward famine.[100]

The reappearance of the Henan famine in the public sphere is another example of the ambiguous nature of the recovery of wartime memory in China's public and private spheres. Even during the period of official silence about the famine, there were still opportunities for individuals such as Liu Zhenyun and Song Zhixin to draw on family memories and resurrect forbidden or buried memories. For Chongqing families, memories had to be hidden because they related to a period when the Nationalist regime led the wartime effort. For Henan families, the reason for the official discomfort about the famine is harder to define; it seems to result from a combination of a depressing story with little patriotic or nationalist value, along with uncomfortable reminders of the Great Leap Forward famine.

The more tolerant atmosphere about wartime history that began in the 1980s did allow more official discussion of the Henan famine over the next few decades, but it was one particular vehicle, Feng Xiaogang's 2012 film, that thrust discussion of the famine to the forefront of the public sphere, at least during the year of its release. As was the case with other (grudging) relaxations of interpretations of the war, it opened space for much more open criticism of the CCP and its attitude toward history—at least until China's powerful internet censors managed to shut much of that discussion down again. Furthermore, the debate around the film showed that there was an appetite within Henan to engage with the province's historical traumas, whether in 1942 or during the Great Leap Forward.

From the perspective of the Chinese government, the problem with revisionist memory of Chongqing's wartime experience is that it requires viewing the role of the Nationalists during the war against Japan in a positive light, while continuing to regard their role in the civil war that followed almost immediately afterward as illegitimate.

The comprehensive reassessment of the Nationalist record in Chongqing is not the only locally inflected memory that sits at odds with the top-down, heroic narrative promoted by the party-state. Mao's base area in Yan'an is portrayed in Zhu Hongzhao's book as an inspiring place that deserves to be honored by later generations, but at the same time as a place where authoritarian and coercive tactics were used to shape minds into ideological correctness. In Henan, the terrible famine of 1942 disappeared from collective memory for some seventy years. Yet even now, it cannot be easily discussed because of its association with the famines during the Mao era. People in each region of China have their own memories of the war years, and they often have little to do with what Beijing would like them to remember.

Similar conflicts over memory have occurred in other countries that have experienced civil wars and conflicts, such as Spain and Vietnam. As Spain democratized, a pact of silence developed over the legacy of the civil war; yet this pact proved ever more difficult to maintain as it became clear that although the Republican side had lost the war in 1939, it had essentially won the war of clashing mythologies. In Vietnam, the cemeteries of the South Vietnamese army had been neglected after North Vietnam's victory, and they were inaccessible without special permission. But there has been a slow movement to rehabilitate the experiences of the South Vietnamese war dead. The United States restored full diplomatic relations with Vietnam in 1995, which allowed more consideration of the sensibilities of the defeated South. Ten years later, the former South Vietnamese vice president Nguyen Cao Ky visited Vietnam for the first time since the defeat of his regime and declared, "I think the first thing to do for the current government to really erase past hatred . . . is to restore the cemeteries of the former South Vietnamese Army, so we friends or relatives can visit . . . and organize prayer ceremonies for the souls of our friends."[101] Since 2006, families have been permitted to tend individual graves in South Vietnamese army cemeteries, and one major site, the Binh An cemetery, has been maintained for private mourning.[102]

Nationalist civil war dead in China still do not receive much commemoration, and this remains one of the great holes in the country's collective memory; after all, countless families have former Nationalist soldiers from that conflict in their ranks. However, the issue with the Nationalists is more complex than with the South Vietnamese; in China, the task is not only to rehabilitate a former enemy, but actually to praise it for its contributions. In Vietnam, there is no equivalent to the Guofen—the all-out supporters of the former Nationalist regime. In China, people in different regions have taken episodes in the War of Resistance and used them to tell stories that are otherwise hard to articulate. The Chinese like to say that history is a mirror. But sometimes history is a periscope, forcing the viewer to observe at an angle.

6

The Cairo Syndrome

*World War II and China's Contemporary
International Relations*

In 2010, two new productions on World War II hit the screens,
one in the United States and one in China. For US television
viewers, the Hollywood power team of Steven Spielberg and Tom
Hanks presented *The Pacific,* a ten-episode miniseries about a US
Marine division fighting in the Pacific Theater. In China, cinema-
goers could see Liu Yundong's *East Wind Rain* (*Dongfeng Yu*), a
lush drama starring major actors such as Fan Bingbing (whose
career would founder on a fiscal rock nearly ten years later). The
film's plot hung on a (fictional) intelligence discovery by Chinese
Communist agents about the upcoming Japanese attack on Pearl
Harbor; although the information is relayed to President Roosevelt's administration, the Americans simply refuse to believe it.[1]
The movie was a bigger hit in China than the HBO series was in
the United States. Yet both said something important about the
way that their countries of origin thought about the wartime legacy
in international relations.

Bloggers Sima Pingbang, a well-known leftist commentator,
and Mingbo Shalong discussed these two productions in a piece

titled "Why are China and US both rewriting the history of the Pacific War?" Analyzing the two works, they detect an attempt in both countries to claim a political legacy from the wartime years: "If you peel below the surface of the stories of justice and heroism, then there is this hidden tendency toward conspiracy and competition in their own interests." On the Chinese side, they suggest, although *East Wind Rain* is not an overtly nationalistic production, it is still subtly trying to give China the upper rhetorical hand by suggesting that Pearl Harbor was an American failure that could have been solved by heeding Chinese advice. By implication, this is a rejection of the view that China was nothing more than a victim, waiting to be saved by the Americans. The message of *The Pacific,* on the other side, is, "Because the Americans saved people from the claws of the demon Japanese, that's why the US has now got the strongest army in the world." They conclude:

> The release of these two films is not just about their plots or performances: just as the US lets the world know that at a most dangerous time for humanity it bore burdens and made sacrifices, so China has finally dared to propagate in the same way the idea that during the war it also bore burdens and sacrifices. This represents another type of continuity of the competition over politics, economics, and culture of these two countries.[2]

China's international relations have been significantly shaped by its attempt to change the collective memory of the war, particularly in the twenty-first century. The first section of this chapter begins with a discussion of the US–China relationship because there is a common assumption that the significance of World War II in the present day relates almost exclusively to China's relationship with Japan. And indeed, that troubled encounter is immensely important in understanding how China projects its narratives about the conflict. But the relationship with Japan is not the only one that is affected by memories of the Second World War; others include its relationship with the United States and with neighbors such as South Korea. The relationship with Japan is shaped by a sense, both genuine and constructed, that Japan has not done enough to acknowledge its war crimes in China, as well as a desire to limit Japan's international influence. The relationship with America is based on resentment that the United States continues to use its wartime presence in the region, after more than seven decades, to take a hegemonic role. With its Asian neighbors, who also suffered under Japanese rule, China wishes to create a sense of solidarity to facilitate new alliances. However, this attempt regularly falls victim to inconsistent diplomacy: China's solidarity with South Korea on issues such as compensation for wartime sex slaves ("comfort women") fades quickly when South Korea goes along with the United States on security issues.

China's language about the war years is driven in part by the growing enthusiasm in recent decades for justice in international relations.[3] There is a widespread sense that China has been cheated in the international order, and that it deserves to have its status and claims treated with greater seriousness. That quest for status relates largely to China's position as part of the international order, but there is also an impetus to create a moral standing for China that would enable it to persuade other actors to support its aims. In this respect, China's attempts to draw on war memory reflect its desire to modify its international relations strategy, which is almost entirely realist, driven by considerations of power. The attempt to add moral weight to the Chinese presence in the region is one of the purposes of the "memory work" that is in progress.

The idea of China as a creator of a new order after 1945 was evident in the revisionism of the 1980s. Hu Qiaomu's 1987 editorial in the *People's Daily* about the "great significance" of the War of Resistance (discussed in Chapter 2) was in large part concerned with rejecting arguments that the Nationalist contribution to the war ought to be given greater prominence. But Hu also highlighted another aspect of the war:

> Another great significance of the War of Resistance is that it fundamentally changed the international politics of the Far East. Before the conclusion of the eight years of the War of Resistance, Japanese imperialism was [on the rampage].[4]

Hu continued with a teleological historical account leading up to the communist victory. In 1945, he wrote, "the Soviet army eliminated the Kwantung Army and entered Korea." Following the atomic bombings of Japan, the defeated Japanese adopted a "peace constitution," while new powers, including China, sat in judgment on Japan at the International Military Tribunal for the Far East (IMTFE) in 1946–1948. "Just a year later," Hu noted, "the PRC declared its foundation. The old China that was called the Sick Man of East Asia would not return. At the same time, the old structure of the Far East and the old structure of the world would not return."[5]

Several decades on, Hu's statement looks like an incipient version of a new vision of international order waiting to come into being. In 1987, there were many assumptions about that order that would turn out to be false—most notably, that the USSR would remain stable.[6] Another assumption, that the United States and China would continue to be accommodating to one another, was already in abeyance at the time that Hu was writing, less than a decade after the formal reestablishment of diplomatic relations between the two countries in 1979.

Hu's statement that a large part of the war's significance had to do with "international order" was important in that it implied that the end of the war in 1945 was the point of origin for the contemporary international system in Asia, not Mao's revolution in 1949. Choosing this date meant that his summary of the high points of the postwar era included actions undertaken by the Nationalists, even if he did not specify them in those terms; for instance, the Chinese judge at the IMTFE, Mei Ru'ao, had been appointed by the Nationalist government. The foundation of the PRC by the CCP, an act which Hu credited with ending the idea of China as a "sick man," was now blended in with other changes for which the Nationalists, not the CCP, were responsible. Hu's idea that China was, to use Dean Acheson's phrase, "present at the creation" of the postwar international order meant a rehabilitation of the Nationalist role in reality, if not explicitly.

The rehabilitation of the Nationalists' war record at home in the 1990s and 2000s meant that there was also more opportunity to bring their involvement into the Chinese view of international relations. Then, in November 2013, there was widespread Chinese media reporting of the seventieth anniversary of the Cairo Conference, which had taken place on 22–23 November 1943. During this contentious meeting, although China was treated as an ally of the Western powers, it was sidelined because the European theater and the opening of a second front in Europe were given top priority.[7] It was not a sudden interest in the minutiae of Allied war conferences, however, that led to the flurry of reporting on the anniversary of the conference. Rather, attention focused on the communiqué issued at the end of the session:

Until such a new order is established and until there is convincing proof that Japan's war-making power is destroyed, points in Japanese territory to be designated by the Allies shall be occupied to secure the achievement of the basic objectives we are here setting forth.

The terms of the Cairo Declaration shall be carried out and Japanese sovereignty shall be limited to the islands of Honshu, Hokkaido, Kyushu, Shikoku and such minor islands as we determine.[8]

This section of the declaration, some Chinese commentators declared, demonstrated that China's territorial claims on a particular island chain in the middle of the East China Sea, known as the Diaoyu Islands to the Chinese and Senkaku Islands to the Japanese, were entirely justified. This new argumentative tactic on the part of the Chinese is an example of the political shift that had been going on during the previous decades as the historiography of the war had changed. Events relating wholly to the Nationalist government and its conduct of the conflict with Japan were now being incorporated, without explicit acknowledgement, into a new Chinese narrative about the formation of the postwar international order.

As the blogger Sima Pingbang observed, the United States justifies its presence in Asia based on the sacrifices made by US troops in helping to defeat the Japanese during World War II. China has, over time, developed a similar justification for its own desire for greater influence. Up to fourteen million Chinese were killed during the eight years of the war against Japan. Without that sacrifice, the argument goes, China (and the rest of Asia) might have fallen to Japanese imperialism. This idea was not invented in the 2010s; an article by Huang Meizhen and colleagues from 1987 argued that China's war against Japan "delayed the outbreak of the

Pacific War, so that the Western democracies could strengthen their strategies and gain precious time" and that China "provided strong support for the war of the British and Americans in the Pacific."[9] But in 1987, there was little chance of leveraging that viewpoint into an explicit statement of China's strategy in international affairs.

The intervening decades have changed the situation entirely. During this period, China's overall aim has been to promote ideas that change the narrative of World War II in Asia: first, that China made a contribution to the war that has never been acknowledged by the West; second, that China consequently deserves a greater say in the arrangement of the Asia–Pacific region; and third, that Japan is an increasing menace that justifies greater wariness by China. The implication in the 1980s that China had been part of the creation of international order had, by the early twenty-first century, become a much firmer claim.

Cold War and Post-Cold War

The end of the Cold War in 1989–1991 became a turning point for China's sense of its place in Asia. In Europe the situation changed rapidly after 1989, with marked shifts in power, as Moscow's former satellites were welcomed into organizations such as the North Atlantic Treaty Alliance, and, for a brief moment, it appeared that Russia might democratize fully. In contrast, Asia seemed to change relatively little. In retrospect, we can see that the near-collapse of the Chinese Communist Party in 1989, followed by the actual collapse of the USSR, hardened the determination of the Chinese leadership to find a new status for China that would allow it to secure its position in the region.

It was the extraordinary Chinese economic growth of the 1990s and 2000s that ultimately provided the basis for China to raise its status. From the late nineteenth century, Chinese thinkers had used the phrase *fuguo qiangbing* (rich country, strong army) to describe what national security might look like; the 2000s was perhaps the first time since then that China had actually managed to achieve these two goals of wealth and strength.

China's economic success boosted its international position, as did the perception in much of the world in the 2000s that the George W. Bush administration was determined to create a unipolar world—a project that helped support Beijing's case that it could serve as a counterbalance to the world's only remaining superpower.[10] The Cold War in Asia had never formally ended. But by the turn of the new century, it was clear that it was thawing fast.

During the 1980s and 1990s, the rethinking of China's past had largely been oriented toward a domestic, not an international, audience. In addition, the twists and turns of Asian détente meant that in practice, China and the United States did not seek to dispute the overall regional state of affairs; for Beijing and Washington, it was much more important to contain the Soviet Union than to confront each other, as well as being easier, since the Soviet influence in the region was minor by the late Cold War period. At that time, China was also keen to be seen to follow international norms, a tendency which became more urgent after its international isolation in 1989.

By the early 2000s, however, this combination of factors shifted in significant ways. Russia and China became closer, an association marked by the establishment of the Shanghai Cooperation Organization (2001), a security grouping that, although sometimes mocked as an alliance of dictators, had an interest in challenging the "Washington consensus." China also made it clear that it saw the US role in the region as intrusive rather than stabilizing. It perceived the US role as shielding Japan, which China now felt was an obstacle in the way of its growing power and territorial claims in the region.

In contrast, US alliances in the region were becoming more consensual. During much of the Cold War, American claims to be protecting "freedom" rang hollow as the United States sought to protect undemocratic regimes in places such as South Korea, Taiwan, and South Vietnam. In the early 1980s, Japan was the only full democracy allied to the United States in the region, and aside from India, the only stable one. By the start of the 2000s, democratized allies of the United States included not only South Korea and Taiwan but also the Philippines, and (intermittently) Thailand. Since the American alliances were now supported by freely voting electorates, it was harder for China to claim that the American presence in the region was illegitimate.

Yet delegitimizing the US presence remained a top priority for Beijing, and the unfinished nature of the Cold War in East Asia became a first-order issue as a result. The rise of China as a regional and even global power has happened in tandem with the rediscovery of the history of China's war and immediate postwar experience and its use to create a narrative point of origin for China's role in the Asian order. Because there had been no Asian Yalta Conference to carve up spheres of responsibility, there had never been a postwar order that allowed China a secure place. The difficulty in obtaining any sort of stable interpretation of the postwar settlement in Asia is that the present-day actors disagree on fundamental points. However, the lack of an Asian Yalta also opened up new opportunities for China to reinterpret the process, precisely because it had never been completed.

The late 2000s saw further important changes in the nature of the regional order. One was the election of Barack Obama as US president in 2008. Obama advocated a more internationalist approach than George W. Bush had, and he sought to rebuild America's reputation after the disastrous Iraq and Afghanistan wars. At the same time, there was a period in Japan (2009–2012) when the Democratic Party of Japan was governing, during which successive prime ministers edged away from the United States, at least rhetorically, and suggested that they might be more willing to accept a greater Chinese influence in the region. Another important change resulted from the astonishing power struggle within the Chinese leadership between 2011 and 2013. During that time, the leadership ambitions of Bo Xilai, party secretary of Chongqing, led to his downfall and arrest as his political rivals moved to destroy his base of power. Soon afterward came the transition of leadership away from the administration of Hu Jintao and Wen Jiabao, and the confirmation of Xi Jinping as new CCP secretary-general in November 2012.

Xi swiftly showed that he wished to create a much more conformist atmosphere at home alongside a harder line overseas. The Bo Xilai affair, which had been a terrifying experience for the Chinese leadership, contributed to a shift to a more authoritarian approach. China took a harsh tone with its neighbors, especially Japan and the countries in the Association of Southeast Asian Nations. China's resulting diplomacy was inept, alienating countries that had been willing to listen to an alternative narrative involving replacing US influence in the region with Chinese power. The Obama administration in 2011 declared that it would "pivot to

Asia," building up relations with its formal allies, while offering support to unlikely allies (and former foes) such as Vietnam. The return of Shinzo Abe as prime minister of Japan in 2012 marked a more assertive stance by Japan toward China, along with a domestic policy that included an unsettling campaign of wartime revisionism on the Japanese right wing. China was not without partners. Thailand's military dictatorship was in some respects pro-Chinese, although the country remained a US ally; also sympathetic to Beijing were the governments of Laos and Cambodia, and even the newly democratized government of Burma after 2015–2016. But these were not major players, in comparison with the pro-American forces that China had managed to alienate. China had to find new tactics to undermine the US presence in East Asia. One way it did so was to make diplomatic jabs at Japan.

As a consequence, in the mid-2010s, China and Japan drew on clashing interpretations of their World War II experience. Japanese right-wingers spoke in ever-louder tones about a revisionist view of Tokyo's imperial wars in Asia in the 1930s and 1940s. The Japanese revisionist view is only prevalent within one group of the Japanese public, but that group does include prominent politicians in the ruling Liberal Democratic Party. It is almost entirely domestically directed, and is vigorously opposed by liberal elements within Japan itself. There is no significant constituency outside Japan that supports reassessing Japan's aggression in Asia before 1945 in a positive light.[11]

China, in turn, produced a revisionist argument about its role during the war: that it had played a highly significant role in the ultimate defeat of the Japanese empire in 1945 and now deserved to reap the benefits of its sacrifices. As I showed in earlier chapters, there is a significant domestic audience in China for the idea that China should be given more credit for its contribution toward defeating Japan. Unlike the revisionist Japanese discourse, the Chinese rediscovery of its wartime history is intended to have an internationalist element. However, it shares a problematic element with the Japanese discourse: it is based on political rather than historical considerations.

The eruption of this dispute shows how the Cold War in postwar Asia prevented the creation of multilateral organizations and treaties that might have created a stable framework in the region. China notes, correctly, that the 1951 Treaty of San Francisco, which was supposed to mark the final settlement of the war in Asia, excluded the People's Republic. But the blame for this exclusion rests on both actors in the dispute. The United States refused to recognize Mao's regime, excluding an emergent power from a role in defining a regional settlement. And China, with Stalin's support, backed up North Korea in its attack on South Korea, making a swift settlement with the United States close to impossible.

In his address to the study group of the Academy of Military Sciences on 30 July 2015, Xi Jinping observed that "the goal is to reconsider the great path of the Chinese People's War of Resistance, and confirm the great contribution that the War of Resistance made to the victory in the world antifascist war, [and] show our upholding of the results from the victory in the Second World War, and determination for international peace and justice." Yet he warned that "in comparison with the historical position and significance of the War of Resistance, in comparison with the influence of this war on the Chinese nation [*zhonghua minzu*] and the world, our research on the war is still not nearly enough. . . . We must encourage international society accurately to recognize the position and role in the world antifascist war of the Chinese People's War of Resistance."[12]

The emergence of World War II precedents and analogies in China's international relations has not been a linear process. A range of historical examples, many relating to Chinese ideas of "national humiliation," are used to promote the view that China is a state that has been under siege in the modern era and has every right to be defensive about its status.[13] Other historical comparisons have been used in more recent years to suggest a new expansiveness, such as the revival of interest in the voyages of the Ming admiral Zheng He, who visited Southeast Asia and East Africa, among other destinations.[14]

China has used its World War II history for particular purposes in international relations. The revival of claims in 2013 on the disputed Diaoyu / Senkaku Islands, derived from the 1943 Cairo Conference, is specifically aimed at resolving a still-current territorial dispute with Japan. The military parade held in Tiananmen Square in September 2015 was aimed in part at the global community; it stressed China's past contribution to an alliance against fascism and also asserted its ability both to make new friendships and to burnish its credentials as a responsible global actor. China has also been keen to press the legal validity of claims against Japan for war crimes, as well as to pursue maritime claims in the South China Sea that derive in part from Nationalist arguments to secure their position in Asia, taken in the aftermath of victory in 1945.

China is eager to claim that its standing in Asia today derives in part from its participation in the war that gave rise to the order that still dominates the region. It seeks to combine the power it exercises in the region, both economic and military, with the more elusive sense that it has moral standing for its claims. Let us now look at some of the specific ways in which China has used tropes relating to World War II in its recent engagement with international order.

The Second Life of the Cairo Conference

On 8 January 2014, the British television show *Newsnight* featured interviews by the presenter, Jeremy Paxman, with the Japanese and Chinese ambassadors to the United Kingdom on the disputed sovereignty of the Diaoyu / Senkaku Islands, a subject rarely discussed in Western media. At one point, Ambassador Liu Xiaoming of the PRC declared that the origins of the disagreement lay in provisions of the 1943 Cairo Conference. Paxman, generally one of the best-informed interviewers on the BBC, replied that he was unfamiliar with that particular event.[15]

Jeremy Paxman was not alone in his puzzlement. Most of the Western world paid little attention to the seventieth anniversary of the Cairo Conference, which occurred in November 2013. But in China and Taiwan, it was noted with interest. The 1943 Cairo Conference was the only conference of World War II in which China was treated as an equal Allied power with the United States and Britain (the Soviet Union, which was neutral in the war against Japan, was not present). For decades, the conference was discussed only in passing in Chinese history texts because of the unfortunate fact that the leader who represented China there was not Mao Zedong but Chiang Kai-shek. But the new tolerance of Chiang in the mainland meant that it became possible to use Cairo to demonstrate that China was on the side of the Allies at the most crucial moment for civilization in the past century. Rather in the same way that the memory of the Vichy regime has influenced postwar life in France, characterized by the historian Henry Rousso as "the

Vichy syndrome," so the Cairo Conference has preoccupied China's foreign policymakers, creating what we might call a "Cairo syndrome."[16]

The Cairo Conference was not among the most consequential of the summit conferences held during World War II. Some issues discussed there were never fully resolved: plans for an Allied recapture of Burma that would involve naval commitments in Southeast Asia, for example, were canceled just a month or so later.[17] However, Chiang's presence as an equal alongside Roosevelt and Churchill did have strong symbolic significance. In addition, the communiqué issued at the end of the conference on 1 December 1943 affirmed the Allies' intention to put an end to Japan's empire in Asia once the war in Europe was over, without equivocation.

It is this communiqué that has piqued the interest of China's foreign policymakers. The "meaning" that the Chinese draw from the Cairo Declaration is heavily oriented toward their views of the current Asia-Pacific territorial settlement. The Cairo Declaration stated, speaking for the Allies,

> It is their purpose that Japan shall be stripped of all the islands in the Pacific which she has seized or occupied since the beginning of the first World War in 1914, and that all the territories Japan has stolen from the Chinese, such as Manchuria, Formosa, and the Pescadores, shall be restored to the Republic of China.

The declaration also added that Japan should "be expelled from all other territories which she has taken by violence and greed."[18]

Because of the estrangement of the United States and China during the Cold War, the dismantling of the Japanese empire took place under American direction alone. The official ending of the war in Asia, with the Treaties of San Francisco and Taipei in 1951 and 1952, not only excluded the People's Republic but also prevented further development of a postwar settlement in the region because of the fact that Japan was now a Cold War ally of the United States, and China was an opponent.

The Diaoyu / Senkaku dispute lay dormant for decades until the early 2010s, when tensions began to rise over these eight small, uninhabited, rocky islands in the East China Sea. There is a question as to whether the islands may have mineral deposits offshore, but the dispute is primarily a symbolic one over sovereignty. The Chinese interpretation of its claim to these islands shows the fluid way in which China has been using the legacy of World War II. The first part of the Cairo Declaration does not name the Diaoyu Islands explicitly, and since the Japanese took them over in 1895 during the first Sino-Japanese War, they do not fall under the "since 1914" part of the clause.[19] Yet in 2013, on the occasion of the conference anniversary, Chinese news media reported extensively that this formulation in the declaration gave the authority of international law to Chinese claims over the Diaoyu / Senkaku Islands. An article in the *Global Times* explained the reasoning:

> On the eve of the 70th anniversary of the signing of the Cairo declaration, which stated that all the territories Japan had stolen from the Chinese should be restored to China, experts at home and abroad called on the international community to jointly safeguard the established international order.
>
> The Cairo Declaration, issued by Britain, China and the United States in 1943, was of great significance in rebuilding international order after the end of World War II, experts said.
>
> The Chinese Embassy in Egypt marked the anniversary of the declaration.

Chinese Ambassador Song Aiguo said Saturday that the Cairo Declaration cements the legal foundation for the solution to the territorial disputes with Japan over the Diaoyu Islands. . . .

"The Cairo Declaration, together with other World War II documents, provides a legal basis for the Chinese exercise of sovereignty of Taiwan and the Diaoyu Islands. The documents also formulated the basis for international order after the war," Li Li, a research fellow with Chinese Academy of Social Sciences was quoted by China News Agency as saying.

The People's Daily, the Party's flagship newspaper, said Sunday that Japan has been trying to deny historical facts and the spirit that the Cairo Declaration conveys as well as breaking international order.[20]

Chinese official sources, were, of course, undertaking a remarkable historical sleight of hand. The implication was that a straight path led from the declarations of 1943 and the Potsdam Declaration of 1945 (which stated that "the terms of the Cairo Declaration shall be carried out and Japanese sovereignty shall be limited to the islands of Honshu, Hokkaido, Kyushu, Shikoku and such minor islands as we determine") to the present-day Chinese administration—that Chiang Kai-shek had written a check that the CCP was now ready to cash.

To add to the complexity, the Ma Ying-jeou administration on Taiwan (2008–2016) supported return of the islands to "Chinese" sovereignty. Since the Cairo Declaration declared that the islands and other territories should be returned to "the Republic of China," this opened up a new area of confusion in which the government in Taipei, not Beijing, might be considered the rightful inheritor of Chiang Kai-shek's regime.

A more comical (and certainly less dangerous) take on the Cairo Conference occurred in 2015, when the film *Cairo Declaration*

(*Kailuo xuanyan*), directed by Wen Deguang and Hu Minggang, was released in China. A heroic war epic, it was mercilessly mocked by commentators on the Chinese internet for its poster, which featured the faces of Stalin, Roosevelt, Churchill, and Mao. Neither Stalin nor Mao had attended the conference. Chiang, who had, was nowhere to be seen in the publicity for the movie. People made fun of the poster by creating online versions that showed Barack Obama, Saddam Hussein, and even Gollum from *The Lord of the Rings* as conference attendees.[21] In creating the poster, the producers were adapting history to a very specific present-day end—a version of history that accorded with the CCP's revisionist interpretation of the Cairo Conference's significance for territorial sovereignty.[22]

The film itself is not as one sided as the poster controversy might make it appear, with plenty of appearances by Nationalist figures, including Chiang, as well as an intriguing portrayal of Winston Churchill with an American accent. But it does hew to current political orthodoxy in a number of ways. At one point, the actor playing Roosevelt declares, "War has changed China; China's war has changed the world. China is a responsible world power." The phrase "responsible world power" would have been hard to find in 1943 with reference to China, but it has become a mainstay of China's discourse about its "peaceful development" in the 2000s.[23]

The Parade: War History as Geopolitical Spectacle

On 3 September 2015, the Chinese government held a major military parade in the center of Beijing. It commemorated the seventieth anniversary of the end of the Second World War, making it quite distinct from most such pageants. Parades in this high-profile location had previously been restricted to events relating to CCP history. The government was using this parade both for domestic political purposes and also to send signals to the outside world about China's international role.

Yet the outside world reacted cautiously. The only former major Allied power to send a high-level representative was Russia, which sent President Vladimir V. Putin. The United States sent its ambassador, former US senator Max Baucus, and the UK sent former chancellor of the exchequer Kenneth Clarke. Former British prime minister Tony Blair was present, although not as part of the UK delegation. France was represented by the foreign minister, Laurent Fabius. China would likely have preferred to welcome higher-level figures from its wartime allies, the United States and Britain, as a mark of its membership in the alliance. Both countries, however, were no doubt wary about sending senior representatives to an event that centered on a display of China's military hardware and took place in a location associated with the mass killings of protestors in 1989.

Prime Minister Shinzo Abe of Japan was invited but chose not to attend.[24] Another notable absence was that of the relatively new leader of North Korea, Kim Jong-un. Whether he had been invited but refused, or was not invited in the first place, is unclear. But his absence added piquancy to the presence of one of the major figures who did turn up: South Korean president Park Geun-hye. Although the Republic of Korea was a strong ally of the United States, the ability of China to create common cause through shared anger at the Japanese, along with a major trade relationship, encouraged Park to show herself at China's big day. Her attendance suggested a new tactic for the middle powers in the Asia-Pacific—

it might be possible to find a way to navigate between US and Chinese power so as to gain advantages while not becoming tied to one side or the other.

President Putin's presence at the parade suggested more permanence in the relations between China and Russia than had been the case since 1945. The Soviet Union had indeed been a wartime ally, but through much of the war, it was not allied directly with China. (Although its air force provided essential assistance in 1937–1938, the Soviet Union did not formally declare war until the very last days of the war, in August 1945.) Indeed, the very Cairo Conference which was being feted by the Chinese in 2013 had had its conclusions reversed in significant part by Stalin at the Tehran Conference, which took place just a few weeks later. Moreover, Stalin had shown no particular inclination to include China in the Potsdam Conference in 1945, even though the conference dealt with the fate of postwar Asia, and he showed rather less enthusiasm than did Roosevelt for the proposal to raise (Nationalist) China's standing.

Nonetheless, the warming of relations between Russia and China in the 2010s meant that Russia would inevitably take a prominent place at the parade. Aspects of this collaboration were also evident in the academic historiography in China in the 2010s, where historians began to stress Chinese and Soviet achievements in the war over those of the Western powers, as well as to attempt to equalize the number of Chinese and Soviet casualties and to downplay both countries' histories of collaboration. In an example of macabre one-upmanship, Chinese texts have started to mention the figure of thirty-five million casualties in China's War of Resistance; this figure includes both dead and wounded, and not coincidentally overshadows the more familiar figure of twenty million Soviet fatalities.[25]

So the parade featured low-profile appearances from China's actual wartime allies, and a prominent role for the ally who didn't do very much until quite late. It also nodded toward the future by featuring soldiers from seventeen carefully chosen countries in addition to China. Russia was one of those countries, as was Belarus, along with a range of countries from the areas in which China was seeking new security partnerships through its Belt and Road Initiative (BRI): Kazakhstan, Kyrgyzstan, and Tajikistan in central Asia; Laos and Cambodia from ASEAN; Pakistan and Afghanistan in South Asia (but not India, even though many Chinese soldiers were based there in World War II, and it fought with China during the Burma campaigns). Socialist allies such as Cuba and Venezuela also participated. Serbia, Mexico, Mongolia, and Vanuatu were the only full(ish) democracies to join the parade. An occasion commemorating the Second World War was being used, in effect, to create new partnerships, while bolstering myths about the old ones.

The South China Sea Dispute

The South China Sea dispute is probably the single most prominent territorial conflict in which China has been engaged in recent decades. I will not go into the complexities of the dispute here, which continue to be the subject of extensive political as well as academic debate.[26] (In broad outline, the argument concerns China's claim of sovereignty over the majority of the South China Sea and a number of island groups in it, including the Paracel and Spratly Islands, a claim strongly resisted by several Southeast Asian nations.) One particular element of the dispute, however, relates directly to China's postwar circumstances: the Nationalists' drawing up of a line of control in the South China Sea in 1946–1947, sometimes known as the "nine-dash" line because of its original representation as a series of dashes on the map. Discussions about the South China Sea are not generally connected to the history of the Second World War, not least because Japan is not a direct participant in the current controversy. But recent arguments surrounding this dispute have been tied to the territorial claims made by Chiang Kai-shek's government as it sought to reshape the region after 1945.[27]

As in other cases, academic historiography has worked in tandem with the changing atmosphere in international relations. A 2017 article by the distinguished historian Chen Qianping draws on a variety of primary documents to argue for the Chinese case in the South China Sea. "After World War II," argues Chen, "the Republic of China, as one of the Big Four, took back the sovereignty of the islands in the South China Sea in accordance with international law and the new international order in the Asia-Pacific region laid down by the Cairo Declaration and the Potsdam Declaration." By renaming the islands and projecting its naval power, "the Chinese government declared its sovereignty to the world."[28]

Chen's rigorous historical scholarship is what makes this piece so interesting. Chen proposes, of course, that the documentation from the Chinese side should necessarily be accepted as the correct version of events. But more significantly, he elides the breach in sovereignty between the Nationalist and Communist regimes. Much of today's Chinese foreign policy analysis assumes that there was no gap between the Nationalist state of the 1940s and today's CCP.

The Cold War context explains why the Nationalist claims to the South China Sea might have met fewer objections in 1947 than today. A postwar Nationalist China would have been US-oriented, and therefore the United States would have been more tolerant of the Nationalists' bid to assert sovereignty over the islands than of such a bid from Mao's China. Still today, the CCP is in a position where it is making several conflicting arguments simultaneously: that (by implication) the Nationalist state was legitimate and sovereign, presumably up to 1949, even though the civil war was based on the premise that it was not; that the Republic of China had no continuing sovereignty after 1949 and therefore its proposals today (as Taiwan) over the islands have no validity; yet that there is a continuity of sovereign claims stretching from the Nationalists in the 1940s all the way up to the People's Republic today (hence the need for rehabilitation of the Nationalists' former mainland regime).

The state has still not found the right balance to enable it to use but also control the memory of the Nationalists. In 2014, when the *Global Times* attacked the Guofen as having a "morbid nostalgia" for the Nationalist era, it indicted the weakness of the Nationalists in the face of foreign invaders. Yet the CCP's current international strategy is based on the idea that the Nationalists' diplomatic achievements were so significant and legitimate that they should be respected, at least until the crucial date of 1949.

There is one element of genuine continuity between the Nationalist maritime claims in the 1940s and the Communist ones in the 2010s: the drive to end imperialism in Asia. Both Chinese parties made opposition to empire a crucial part of their policies. However, the Nationalist claims in the immediate postwar took place in a world where classic imperialism was still very real. The Japanese empire was being dismantled, but Britain, France, and the Netherlands still sought to control significant parts of East and

Southeast Asia. Until 1943, just two years before the end of the war, China itself had been compromised in its sovereignty. Even in 1945, while technically sovereign, China was extremely weak. It was economically crippled and was riven by an incipient civil war. By asserting its territorial claims in 1946–1947, it was signaling its intent to become an exemplar in a world full of non-European states that had yet to achieve independence.

Today's China is reviving such claims in a world where its own economy and political standing are immeasurably stronger. Yet it continues to deploy a variety of rhetorical devices learned from that earlier period. First, China still portrays itself as a victim of the global order, an image for which memory of the war against Japan, a conflict that China did not seek or provoke, is very useful. Then, it seeks to portray itself as a mentor to other Global South countries, arguing that the Belt and Road Initiative provides a practical means for rejecting Western hegemony, in the form of the "new imperialism" of the Washington consensus.

Justice, Morality, and Diplomacy

One of China's main reasons for looking back to the war and postwar periods is to prove that it deserves justice from international society in terms of its territorial claims. The "Cairo syndrome" is about finding ways to strengthen the argument that China should have sovereignty over the Diaoyu / Senkaku Islands as well as the South China Sea.

Drawing on this history is useful for its moral value. China has been beset by an inability to create a narrative with ethical weight behind it. There has been some attempt to seek that moral basis from the value of Chinese economic development, centering on the claim that Chinese investments through projects such as the BRI have created new infrastructural benefits for developing countries; this is one argument behind the "Community of Common Destiny" promoted under Xi Jinping. But, at least during the 2010s, China has gained little ethical traction in this way, owing to concerns about its practice of "debt diplomacy" and its authoritarian politics.

Instead, China has been using aspects of collective war memory to create a moral narrative with international standing. Among them are the legal issues surrounding Japanese use of sex slaves ("comfort women") during the war, and comparisons of China's experience with the Holocaust. China's quest for justice is not solely for itself; it wishes to be perceived as a virtuous actor, not just a powerful one, in international society. It wants its presence in the region and the world to be regarded as based on more than pure self-interested realism.

Of course, it is possible for a justice claim on one's own behalf to be grounded in a broader moral footing (as was the case with the struggles of Martin Luther King, Jr., for civil rights and Nelson Mandela against apartheid), but China's argument for justice relating to its wartime record has not yet found wide support. That deficiency has stimulated a set of discourses that seek to provide an interpretation of China's experiences during World War II that compares them to the recognized global, largely European, understanding of the war.

Comparing Nazi Germany to Japan

One strategy China has used to craft a morally constituted narrative is to attempt to connect the Chinese wartime experience, in particular the Nanjing Massacre, with that of occupied Europe under the Nazis. The Holocaust has become the most powerful internationally recognized symbol of atrocity, both because of the genocidal ambitions of the Nazi regime and because of the cold, industrialized way in which the crimes were carried out. The steady growth of references to the Holocaust in China reflects a discursive strategy with two major purposes: first, to provide a sense of moral purpose to China's wartime resistance, and second, to provide a basis on which to counter Japanese claims to international status.[29]

In the 1990s, the emphasis on China's status as a wartime ally of the United States had been building domestically, in both the academy and in popular culture, along with the desire to make use of that historical link. Several Chinese leaders who visited the United States in the mid-1990s promoted this idea as the journalist Richard McGregor has noted.[30] McGregor reported that in 1996, the Chinese defense minister, Chi Haotian, arrived for talks in Washington, DC, with pieces of a US Army B-24 bomber that had been shot down over Guangxi province during the war. Chi's discussions with US secretary of defense William Perry included the topic of China's sacrifices during the war years, and in his speech at the National Defense University, Chi referred to the "earnest cooperation" between the two countries during World War II.[31] During the same 1996 visit, the head of Chinese military intelligence, Xiong Guangkai, was taken to the US Holocaust Memorial Museum. He was reported to have said, "Terrible! But there is no comparison to how cruel the Japanese soldiers were," adding, "You know, China should have a Holocaust Museum of its own."[32]

Over the years, the Nanjing Massacre has come to symbolize Chinese suffering in the aftermath of the Japanese invasion of

China. The discourse over Nanjing is, of course, shaped by present-day political considerations. The description of Chinese wartime suffering as a "holocaust" runs the risk of equating it to the Nazi program of genocide, which involved a murderous race war against European Jews and Roma and Sinti people, as well as the murder of other groups of people considered "inferior." The Japanese occupation of China was brutal and involved numerous atrocities in addition to those in Nanjing, but it was not an attempted genocide against the Chinese people. In Japan, meanwhile, although the country's war guilt has been a topic of discussion ever since 1945, involving newspapers, television, social media, and popular fiction, it has focused mostly on the Pacific war; there has been relatively little public discourse about the China War (or "Incident" as it is still sometimes dismissively termed). A frequently heard accusation in China is that Japan has not come to terms with its wartime record. To anyone who looks at Japanese political discourse and popular culture, this is clearly not the case: the *sensō sekinin* (war responsibility) question is embedded in the identity of postwar Japan. However, it is fair to say that the Japanese role in China is the poor relation of the discussions of the post–Pearl Harbor War against the Allies. That is doubly enraging for the Chinese, since, as we have seen, China is not widely recognized or perceived as one of the Allies, even by the other former Allies themselves.

This anomaly has led the Chinese government to try to bring its wartime experience into the moral repertoire of global discourses on World War II, as well as into proposals for restorative justice, such as support for researchers examining Japanese bacteriological warfare against Chinese civilians.[33] The Chinese have not had much success in promoting their plan for such justice, however. One reason is the often clumsy nature of Chinese diplomacy. In 2013, for example, China curried favor with South Korea by supporting the erection of a commemorative statue in Harbin, China, of Ahn Jung-geun, a Korean nationalist who shot the Japanese prime minister, Ito Hirobumi, at that spot in 1909.[34] But only two years later, Beijing was encouraging its people to boycott South Korean pop singers, soap operas, and vacations in retaliation for the Seoul government's acceptance of a US-sponsored anti-missile system. China's willingness to coerce smaller nations in Asia reminds them of one geopolitical reality in which the 2010s are not like the 1940s: while many Asians are keen to gain greater acknowledgment from Japan of the historical injustices they have suffered, if pressed, most would name China, not Japan, as the major source of concern in the region in the 2010s.

China has not yet managed to find any sort of meaningful pan-Asian discourse using the wartime trope of resistance to Japan. The legacy of the Japanese occupation in other parts of Asia is complex. Postwar South Korean society was extremely hostile to Japan; yet its most notable figure, President Park Chung-hee, had served as a senior officer in the Japanese army. In Burma, the independence leader Aung San worked closely with the Japanese military during the war. While most other Asian states acknowledge the ambiguous nature of the Japanese occupation, China has tried to ignore it. The collaborationist regime of Wang Jingwei has produced no significant political genealogy. This is in part because the Wang regime only ruled a limited part of China and left behind relatively little organizational legacy. But it is also possible that the postwar Nationalist regime, despite its opposition to the Wang regime, might have co-opted some of that regime's junior officials (just as many lower-level Nazi officials moved into positions in West and East Germany). Little is yet known about how many former Wang regime officials stayed on at a local level after 1949; if any did, it seems unlikely that they would ever openly admit their connection with the collaborationist government.

Even countries that still resent or mourn the Japanese presence do not find that their war memories provide a pathway to greater acceptance of contemporary China's role in the region. One rhetorical direction that might have provided this narrative framework—the description of the BRI as a successor to the Marshall Plan—has, as I describe in the next section, been rejected as an analogy.

This leads us back to the Holocaust connection that China has increasingly focused on in recent years. In 2000, Fang Jun contrasted what he saw as Japan's continued denial of war guilt with widespread education in Germany about the horrors of Nazism.[35] Since then, the discourse linking the European genocide and the Chinese war experience has grown. The Museum of the War of Resistance in Beijing contains, as of 2018, descriptions of Chinese who helped to rescue Jewish refugees from Europe.[36] In the 2000s, there was a revival of interest in the Jewish refugees who had migrated to Shanghai during the war. A museum was opened in the former Moishe Synagogue in 2008, and it was further expanded in 2019.[37] Chinese scholars are now encouraged to travel to Israel to learn about the Holocaust.[38]

Many Europeans are uneasy about this comparison of China's suffering with the Holocaust, however, particularly when it is used for geopolitical aims. In February 2014, there was a diplomatic imbroglio when Xi Jinping's advance team suggested that his state visit to Germany include a visit to the Memorial to the Murdered Jews of Europe in Berlin. German officials were concerned that Xi's intention was not to honor the victims of the Nazis so much as to make pointed comments about Japan's supposed inability to admit to its war crimes, and in the end, the visit was not scheduled.[39]

The competition over war memory continued a few months later. In June 2014, in response to attempts by Prime Minister Shinzo Abe to enact constitutional change allowing an expansion of the role of Japan's military, the Chinese authorities publicly and pointedly released a series of archival photographs of Japanese war atrocities. China also applied to register documents relating to the Nanjing Massacre as part of the Memory of the World register maintained by Unesco. Japan protested vehemently at the Chinese application in 2015, and it was not until 2019 that the materials were officially accepted. The Japanese Foreign Ministry declared that "it is extremely regrettable that a global organisation that should be neutral and fair entered the documents in the Memory of the World register, despite the repeated pleas made by the Japanese government."[40] The Japanese government further hinted that it might seek to reform Unesco to prevent such applications in future; China in turn hinted at increasing its own contributions to the organization.

China's quest to raise its moral standing in the world, along with its quest for "justice" for itself, continues to run up against snags. For one thing, there is little global enthusiasm for the idea that a country that has become immensely powerful is in need of justice. The China that emerged from war in 1945 was a country that had essentially destroyed itself in the service of keeping the war effort going. In the 2010s, the China of those years is simply unknown or unrecognizable to most observers. There is little global support for the idea of "restorative justice" to the world's second biggest economy, particularly since the nature of that justice is still so disputed. (Furthermore, many Japanese politicians would argue that overseas development assistance to China in the 1970s and 1980s was in effect a form of reparations.)

The associated idea of China sharing in the moral agenda of the war effort is also difficult to animate. China's economic growth is cautiously welcomed by many in the region and beyond who see it as a source of future prosperity. It also enjoyed something of a coup in spring 2019, when the secretary-general of the United Nations declared that the organization should support the alignment of the Belt and Road Initiative with the UN's Sustainable Development Goals.[41] However, this is a long way from the idea that the Chinese system is virtuous in its own right. In the Cold War, both the American and Soviet systems generated their own moral discourses, often based on similar-sounding vocabulary (freedom, peace, democracy), but consisting of contrasting worldviews which then generated adherents and dissenters. The legacy of the Second World War was drawn into service to argue for the superiority of liberal capitalism or socialism, opposing discourses which could nonetheless draw on shared assumptions about the war as a transformative event. With the war more than seven decades in the past, and little sense that China provides an attractive model for generating "soft power" (in the strict sense, following Joseph Nye, of being able to influence without coercion), Beijing's discourse about the war has had considerably less purchase than it would wish.[42]

A New Marshall Plan?

China's lack of success in its quest for moral standing makes it puzzling that it should reject one of the few areas where its international strategy has had a positive rhetorical impact: the frequent invocation of the Belt and Road Initiative as being "China's Marshall Plan."

The Marshall Plan is inextricably linked with the aftermath of the Second World War. The decision by the United States, in a project approved by President Harry S. Truman and led by Secretary of State George C. Marshall, supplied US$12 billion (around $100 billion in 2018 prices) to reconstruct Western Europe after it had been devastated by the war. In 2013, Xi Jinping announced what would come to be seen as his strategic vision for rethinking China's role in Eurasia, the "One Belt One Road" policy, which was later retitled the "Belt and Road Initiative" (BRI). Overseas media, taken by the idea of the US$8 trillion for infrastructure spending under the initiative, started to refer to the project as "China's Marshall Plan." In a July 2016 podcast featuring two senior partners from the consultancy firm McKinsey, for example, one of the partners told the interviewer, "Some people have talked about this being the second Marshall Plan. It's worth recalling that the Marshall Plan, which obviously was at the heart of the regeneration of Europe after the Second World War, was one-twelfth the size of what is being contemplated in the One Belt, One Road initiative. . . . The ambition is enormous, and the sums of money are equally enormous."[43]

The idea of the BRI as comparable to the Marshall Plan might seem like a gift for Chinese official discourse, particularly coming from a prestigious international consultancy such as McKinsey.

Although some doubts were expressed about the practicalities, the comparison was almost entirely positive. China had managed to portray its geopolitical ambitions in a way that the Western world saw as similar to one of the twentieth century's greatest acts of development, both being viewed as projects in which the sponsoring power would "do well by doing good."[44]

It is therefore ironic that China had already begun to edge away very fast from any comparison with the Marshall Plan. The year before the McKinsey podcast, an editorial titled "'Belt and Road Initiatives' No Marshall Plan of China" had appeared in the official English-language *China Daily*. It began by disputing the comparison:

> Commentators have found certain parallels between China's "Silk Road Economic Belt" and "21st Century Maritime Silk Road" initiatives and the Marshall Plan, indicating that China would use them to spread its influence across Asia and other regions as the United States did in post–World War II Europe.
>
> While a good knowledge of history can help us understand current politics, inadequate comparisons of concepts based on their superficial similarities can distort information and mislead politicians to make the wrong decisions.
>
> China has said it is establishing a fund for the "Belt and Road Initiatives" to promote regional integration, cooperation and common development. The initiatives may be similar to the Marshall Plan in terms of the commitments of China and the US to help other countries' economic development. But a deeper analysis will show the fundamental differences in the historical context, motivation and potential impact between China's approach and the US' postwar plan to provide economic and military assistance to its allies in Western Europe.
>
> The Marshall Plan was part of the US' attempt to contain the expansion of the Soviet Union, and excluded all Communist

countries. The Cold War mentality and bipolar structure, however, have no place in China's Silk Road initiatives, which are open to all countries and aim to achieve win-win results rather than regional hegemony. China has no intention of establishing alliances to confront any country.

Unlike the Marshall Plan, the "Belt and Road Initiatives" impose no political conditions on the participants, as China has always advocated that countries should respect each other's rights to choose their own social systems and development paths.[45]

This description of the Marshall Plan is factually wrong in part.[46] The communist states were excluded from the Marshall Plan because the Soviet Union refused to accept the plan's funding for the Eastern Bloc, instead implementing an alternative Molotov Plan in 1947, which eventually became the Comecon group (Council for Mutual Economic Assistance). The idea that the Marshall Plan was part of the "US' attempt to contain the expansion of the Soviet Union," representing a "Cold War mentality and bipolar structure," is, however, a recognizable position within Western academia. It is also a direct inheritance of an older interpretation of the Second World War, the one which Huang Meizhen characterized critically as a narrative of constant American attempts to subvert China. Chinese reactions to the BRI reflect the Mao-era version of history rather than the version that seeks continuity between the 1940s and the present day. The integration of those two viewpoints remains contradictory, a lingering echo of the conflict between the view of China as a revolutionary challenger and that of China as a state that aims not only to maintain the status quo but also to continue on a trajectory that has lasted over seven decades.

As it happens, a number of cases in 2017–2018 in the BRI backyard began to cast doubt on China's motives, and China may already have lost its opportunity to sell the BRI to the world as an act of generosity, regardless of the analogies used about it. Some observers became nervous about the US$480 million that highly indebted Laos has pledged toward a US$700 million high-speed rail link, with much of the loan financed by the China Export-Import Bank. In Sri Lanka, there was widespread anger when the country took on immense debt to pay for the Hambantota port and could not pay it back; the debt was converted to equity, giving China a ninety-nine-year lease on the port. The specter of countries being lured into long-term indebtedness to China began to create some dissonance that disrupted the harmonious "win-win" scenarios being proposed in China.[47]

The story of China's debt diplomacy over the BRI lays bare additional reasons why China may feel uncomfortable with comparisons with the Marshall Plan. China has less capacity than the United States simply to write off large amounts of loans as, in effect, gifts, although it has done so in a few places, such as Venezuela. Despite the growth in its economy, China is still a much poorer country than the United States. In 1945, even more than now, the United States was essentially in control of the global financial system and could do what it wanted with the dollar; while the dominance of the dollar is less in 2010, hegemonic power for the renminbi, or any other currency, is simply out of the question for years to come.

Just as important as finance is the question of narrative. It is not unreasonable to regard the Marshall Plan as having been a force for American domination in Europe (one major aim was to resist the influence of the communist parties of France and Italy). But the general historical consensus is that the plan is an example of a hegemonic power undertaking a policy that, despite negative short-term effects (for instance, spending without immediate return), creates in the longer term an environment for a relatively benign form of global leadership. It is not immediately evident that China's BRI plans do that.

One other factor deserves to be mentioned: Marshall himself. Marshall was viewed in Europe as one of the men responsible for victory in World War II, and he was recognized by Americans and Europeans alike as one of the greatest public servants that the United States had ever had. In China, Marshall was associated with a more dubious legacy; he was the man who had been sent to mediate the Chinese Civil War in 1945–1947 and failed.[48] One might argue that no Westerner could have done any better, but nonetheless, Mao's denunciation of Marshall is still perhaps better known in China than are his European activities. In his speech "Farewell, Leighton Stuart!" from 18 August 1949, Mao declared that John Leighton Stuart, who had just been recalled as US ambassador to China,

> used to pretend to love both the United States and China and was able to deceive quite a number of Chinese. Hence, he was picked out by George C. Marshall, was made U.S. ambassador to China and became a celebrity in the Marshall group. In the eyes of the Marshall group he had only one fault, namely, that the whole period when he was ambassador to China as an exponent of their policy was the very period in which that policy was utterly defeated by the Chinese people; that was no small responsibility.[49]

Even some Nationalists were suspicious of Marshall because he had been the mentor of General Joseph Stilwell, the general who was recalled as Chiang Kai-shek's chief of staff when the two fell out spectacularly over China's war aims between 1942 and 1944. The rift between Marshall and his supporters and the Chinese Communists was long-lasting, but not permanent. Stuart had expressed the wish to be buried in China, to which he had given decades of his life as an academic and diplomat. More than forty years after his death in 1962, his wish was granted: he is now buried in Hangzhou. Yet the Marshall Plan still remains an analogy too far for today's Beijing; not all war-era comparisons serve the end that China wishes to achieve.

China's relatively weak claim to ownership of the international postwar order was unexpectedly strengthened in 2016 by the election of Donald J. Trump as president of the United States. While Trump's rhetoric, for instance threatening to loosen ties with treaty allies whom he alleged were not paying their way, did not always translate into action, it became clear that the United States no longer regarded its role as that of the "liberal leviathan" (to use John Ikenberry's term) of global order.[50] Trump is the first postwar American leader who has cast doubt on the utility and durability of the post-1945 order. In 2017–2019, the United States pulled out of or threatened to exit agreements on a Trans-Pacific Partnership on trade with Asian allies, the Paris protocol on climate change, and the nuclear nonproliferation agreement with Iran, and it tried to hobble the World Trade Organization by refusing to appoint new judges to its panels. China often claims that it was one of the founders of the post-1945 order, an argument made by Xi Jinping in a range of high-profile venues. At a time when the most important begetter of that order, the United States, no longer seems to seek ownership of it, this has provided an opportunity for China to present itself as the savior of that order, in a bid to strengthen the historical and rhetorical substance behind its quest for international legitimacy.[51]

The jury is still out on how far China really wishes to go to create a strong body of norms that uphold or even adapt the post-1945 order. In regions such as the Indian Ocean, where this order has been rather weak, China shows more enthusiasm for promoting its own economic and military power than for creating a new system of international governance. Yet where there is an existing legacy from World War II, China has been adept at finding ways to tie its own narrative to one of international order. As the bloggers discussing *East Wind Rain* and *The Pacific* put it, competing uses of war memory in the United States and China are part of "the continuity of the competition over politics, economics, and culture of these two countries."[52]

Conclusion

China's Long Postwar

Most of the countries that took part in World War II had a very recognizable postwar—a period during which they rebuilt their infrastructure and reimagined their societies. The historian Tony Judt's landmark work *Postwar,* which stimulated significant debate in the field of European history, argued that the social democratic consensus in Western Europe developed as a direct result of the continent's wartime experience.[1] Japan has been grappling with the idea of *sengo* (a direct translation of "postwar") for decades, even though there have been attempts ever since the Treaty of San Francisco in 1951 to argue that the postwar is over and that the country is surely, finally, in a post-postwar. In both cases, the immense legacy of the years of conflict, whether in Europe or Asia, has made it impossible to simply slough off the memory and impact of the war years. Perhaps only when the last survivor has died will change be possible, although the powerful afterlife of the First World War in Europe suggests that even that may not be enough.

China never had a comparable postwar. The term *zhanhou,* which is the same as *sengo* when written in characters, has never been commonly used to describe the post-1945 phase of Chinese history. Historians typically characterize the period from 1945 to 1949 as being dominated by the devastating Civil War, which serves as a coda to the era of Nationalist rule; contemporary Chinese history does not begin until 1949, with the establishment of the People's Republic of China (PRC). The Cold War and Mao's China dominate from 1949 to the 1970s. In a chronology where the development of China was seen as looking forward to a "New China" from 1949, rather than back to the violent conflicts of the 1930s and 1940s, there was not much point focusing on the "post" to a war that few chose to remember. Throughout the Mao years, as we have seen, memory of the immensely destructive war against Japan was reduced to official commemorations or stylized presentations as part of performances honoring the Communist victory.

The Chinese Communist Party (CCP) did not need to draw much on the legacy of the war years, since it had a founding myth and ideology of its own: the Chinese Communist revolution. From the founding of the party in 1921 through the Long March, the "leading" role in the war against Japan, and then final "liberation" of the country in 1949, the powerful genealogy of CCP power excluded all the non-Communist elements of the war—Nationalists, Americans, and collaborators, in particular. Mao's China had a prime ideological touchstone: the pursuit of class struggle by all means necessary, including violent ones. The early years of the PRC were ones of land reform, struggle sessions, the persecution of landlords, and the creation of an essentially hereditary class system.[2] By the time of the Cultural Revolution, class had become a shibboleth rather than a means of analysis.[3] The Cultural Revolution was also a xenophobic and nationalistic time, but that nationalism was not primarily based on historical events other than a stylized discourse about "imperialism" and "foreign enemies," although one of the Eight Model Operas of the era, *The Legend of the Red Lantern* (*Hongdengji*), was set during the war years.

A turning point for the CCP came with the death of Mao in 1976, the end of the Cultural Revolution, and the rejection of that era's policies with the "Resolution on Certain Questions in our Party's History" in 1981. The Cultural Revolution had deeply disillusioned the population with the idea of class struggle and terrified those leaders who survived. The new era would demand a new ideological thrust. And now, everything that had made China's experience during the Second World War unsuitable for political discussion under Mao suddenly made it a potent source of ideological ballast. Mao's China was isolated from the West; in contrast, during the war, China had turned to the West for an alliance. Mao's China was economically autarkic; the war had revealed China's interdependence with the world economy. Mao's China was concerned with creating a class-based revolution at home and exporting it to the outside world; during the war, China was part of an "antifascist alliance" to preserve a stable order in which nations, not classes, would dominate. Soon, moves to create a new nationalistic discourse around a shared Chinese experience of the war were under way, led by figures such as Hu Qiaomu.

The political circumstances of the early 1980s made this a good time to create such a shift in discourse. Violent class struggle was out of fashion, making a new cross-class nationalism more attractive. In Taiwan, political reform was under way. The prospect of two liberalizing authoritarian states, Beijing and Taipei, coming together seemed perfectly plausible. (In the 2020s, the chances of reconciliation between a PRC becoming more hardline and a fully liberal and pluralist Taiwan seem less likely.) Changing relations with Japan also came into play. In the early Mao years there had been no formal relations with Japan, but informal contacts led to a close economic relationship.[4] It seemed tactless to the PRC to stress the legacy of Japanese war crimes too strongly when trying to detach Japan from the Cold War embrace of the US. However, after formal diplomatic relations with Japan were restarted in 1972 (for the first time as two sovereign nations since 1938), and relations with the United States were restored, there was less reason to soft-pedal Japanese war crimes. The 1982 controversy over the revision of Japanese textbooks provided a pretext to ramp up a new sense of nationalism, with Japan's invasion of China at the center.

What happened after that, and is happening now, and will go on into the 2020s, has been the subject of this book. The process of bringing China's World War II back into its idea of nationhood can be seen everywhere from the academic seminar room to the movie screen, from the V-day parade in Tiananmen Square to Fan Jianchuan's museum outside Chengdu, from Cui Yongyuan's television documentaries to the phones of Guofen bloggers.

China's wartime experience has always been acknowledged, but it was a relative afterthought under Mao; the new discourse of the war has brought it to the forefront. However, that stress on the War of Resistance (as opposed to the Civil War or the Cultural Revolution) has also created something that hardly existed before: the idea of the Chinese postwar. Not only the war years themselves, but that unloved coda from 1945 to 1949 have now come back to haunt contemporary Chinese conceptions of their modern history. Historians in the West should also become accustomed to the idea of the "Chinese postwar," just as we speak of the American, British, European, or Japanese postwar, meaning the years or decades after 1945 that shaped our societies in the aftermath of wartime conflict. For the Chinese postwar matters greatly to understanding both Chinese nationalism at home and Chinese ideas about international order. Reading China's most recent phase of history as if it began in 1945 and not 1949 creates new postwar trajectories of historical continuity for a whole range of questions that were less relevant under Mao but are crucial today, both internationally and domestically.

The revised memory of the war, and the Nationalist role in it, is connected to a new focus on China's role as an international actor. One can see references to this in the new stress on China as a founding member of the United Nations in the War of Resistance museum, as well as the line uttered by the Franklin D. Roosevelt character in the movie *Cairo Declaration* that China is a "responsible world power." Xi Jinping has amplified this discourse with his statement that China was the first signatory to the UN charter, along with repeated references to the "rules-based" order that seems under threat in the 2020s, essentially defining China as the heir to, and protector of, the post–1945 order. China claims joint ownership of the system because of Chinese wartime sacrifices, putting an emphasis on China's desire to be seen as "present at the creation." This presence then gives weight, in Chinese eyes, to their new interest in maritime and territorial claims made by the Nationalist government during the war, for instance at the 1943 Cairo Conference, and in the immediate postwar, such as the 1946–1947 claims on the South China Sea.

China's current self-definition as an anti-hegemonic power committed to "peaceful development" is also boosted by looking back to the wartime years; during the war, Chiang Kai-shek was unequivocal in his support for the independence of India and other Asian states, and the ending of Western dominance in the region. In rather different circumstances, China today can point to its Belt and Road Initiative as a new means of creating peaceful development and removing the last vestiges of Western (i.e., US) hegemony in the region. This argument presents a Schrödinger-like interpretation of Chiang Kai-shek's historical status in the postwar: China has to maintain that the Nationalist wartime and postwar claims between 1945 and 1949 are legitimate, but that the Communist defeat of the Nationalist regime in 1949 was also justified.

Divergent collective memory of the war shapes a remaining fracture from the Civil War: the status of Taiwan. In the summer of 2015, the seventieth anniversary of the end of the war, I attended two academic gatherings on the history of China's role in the Second World War. The first was in Taipei, where the keynote speech was given by the president of the Republic of China on Taiwan, Ma Ying-jeou. Ma made it clear that his Nationalist Party saw a strong connection between the idea of the Second World War as a formative moment for modern China and contemporary cross-straits relations. The second conference was in Beijing. A larger number of Russians were present, compared with the many Americans in Taipei, yet the overall message was very similar—that the war against Japan was central to the formation of modern China. There was even a brief acknowledgment of the Nationalists' role. Just a year later, in 2016, Taiwan's Democratic People's Party (DPP) won the presidency on the island. That party's vision of Taiwan's historical trajectory is of a separate nation-state in formation, and it sees little relevance in the idea that Taiwan draws any legitimacy from the war on the mainland. Taiwan's academy continues to nurture many scholars who work on the history of the war. But the political significance of the conflict's legacy is diminishing in significance on the island even as it grows on the mainland.

Overall it is at the domestic level, as China seeks to reshape its identity, that the war and postwar have had their strongest impact. At its most basic, the decision from the 1980s onward to rehabilitate the Nationalist wartime record was about creating a point of common conversation with Taiwan. But in a process that the state had not foreseen, this loosening of historical interpretation allowed a whole variety of actors to advance their own agendas. For the older generation in the Southwest, who had been forced to repress their memories as young soldiers, refugees, or children living in terror of air raids in the non–Communist parts of China, the past three decades have finally provided space for them to tell their stories. Some tell of heroic acts, but many simply recount the deadly banality of civilian life in the conditions of modern war. For others, being able to write or make films about the war has been a source of analogy or veiled critique: the 1942 Henan famine stands in for the Great Leap Forward in Feng Xiaogang's film *Back to 1942*, and Cui Yongyuan introduces interviews with Nationalist veterans by asking whether today's youth would jump out of the trenches to defend their country. And as with everything else in China, social media has transformed collective memory of the war too, with Guofen (Guomindang / Nationalist fans) battling Maofen (Mao fans) online with ill-remembered scraps of wartime history. This new remembering acts as a kind of safety valve. The state is perfectly aware that China's different regions mark the war in ways that may be at odds with the version told in Beijing. But this form of ideological healing is effective and unlikely to create any fundamental destabilizing of the CCP's power, despite conflicts over films such as the Nationalist-friendly *The Eight Hundred,* whose release was ultimately canceled.

One unstated but discernible purpose of creating a new collective memory of the war has been to try to heal wounds created during the Chinese Civil War. During the Mao era, the only stories that could be told about the Civil War were ones of heroic Communist conquest of a reactionary Nationalist foe. Even in the twenty-first century, too much of the legitimacy of the Communist Party is tied up with its victory in 1949 to allow any serious reconsideration of the role of its enemy. In Vietnam, the Communist authorities have gradually been allowing a limited memorialization of soldiers who fought for the defeated South. In China, at least as long as reunification with Taiwan remains a live issue, memorials on the mainland to the Nationalist civil war dead seem very unlikely to appear. The rehabilitation of Nationalist veterans of the war against Japan serves as something of a substitute—an oblique way of referring to a fissure that is still visible after more than seven decades.

The American, European, and Japanese postwars are historically unusual, because they have been long periods of peace defined by the ending of a war. China's postwar, taken as a whole from 1945, was anything but peaceful: it was followed by a civil war, class-based warfare, the Korean War, and then the Cultural Revolution. Even the period of relative peace that has persisted since 1978 was marked by huge turmoil and horrific killings in 1989. Yet this latter period, coinciding with the era of "reform and opening," constitutes the nearest equivalent to the Western and Japanese postwars. The language that Chinese writers, academics, and filmmakers, as well as politicians, have been using since the

1980s suggests multiple reasons why World War II still has such ideological power. At least when seen through a haze of nostalgia, the war was a time of commonality, of sacrifice, of collective values overcoming consumerism. It was the one time in that era when China had a clearly defined external enemy; in all the other conflicts, Chinese were fighting other Chinese. In fact, this rose-tinted vision of the war against Japan is highly misleading: millions of people died during the war, and it destroyed more social and economic bonds than it created. Similar nostalgia can sometimes be heard for the Cultural Revolution in China today. That nostalgia, too, is highly misleading, but no less powerful.

One of the most powerful claims about the war in the West and Japan was that it established a liberal postwar. This claim lay behind one of the most important circuits of wartime memory. In this version of the story, the Soviet Union and Eastern Europe were anomalous, and the solidifying of a pluralist, welfare-oriented democracy in both victor (the West) and vanquished (Japan) was one of the most important legacies of the war. China did not fit into this story in any meaningful way. It is a moot point as to what would have happened to a postwar Nationalist Chinese state, which would have taken part in the American-derived order in Asia but maintained a version of Chiang Kai-shek's authoritarian state at home (although, judging from the 1946 Chinese constitution, a slow liberalization might have occurred). The Communist victory in 1949 removed any prospect of Nationalist China becoming a powerful state in postwar Asia. There was never much discussion in China or in the West as to whether China was a worthy *postwar* state within the existing order; instead, the discussion was about whether it was a successful *revolutionary* state, and whether it was seeking to overturn the existing order. The assumptions about a postwar world moving toward democracy did not seem to pertain to China.

Developments in the 2010s have changed at least some of those assumptions. After the democratic dawn of the 1990s, when it looked as if dictatorships around the world might fall, the 2000s saw a retrenchment by authoritarian states. Following the financial crisis of 2008, it became clear that a system of technical democracy cannot protect liberal values from elected populist leaders. Jair Bolsonaro in Brazil, Rodrigo Duterte in the Philippines, Recep Erdogan in Turkey, and Narendra Modi in India are just four examples of such leaders. Most notable in this sequence is Donald J. Trump, who was elected president of the United States in 2016. Trump not only disdained liberal values at home, but from his first days in office has been ambivalent, at best, about the post–World War II order in Europe and Asia. In his first two years in office, Trump did not destroy as much of the infrastructure of that order, particularly in Asia, as his rhetoric suggested he might. But his language and attitudes made it clear that he saw little intrinsic value in the order that Roosevelt, Truman, and Churchill, as well as Stalin and Chiang, had made. Nor did the Rooseveltian language of the United States as "the arsenal of democracy" seem to strike much of a chord with him. The fear that prevailed during World War II, that democracies could become dictatorships, has changed to a different fear—that liberal states can become illiberal without much change in form. Liberal values seem to have little valence at present, in the early 2020s.

This antiliberal discourse is helpful for China, since it makes it easier to suggest that there is no fundamental difference between an authoritarian state and a democratic one—that it is a question of degree, not type. This idea bolsters China's arguments about the significance of the Second World War. Rather than portraying China's wartime sacrifices as being made for democracy, which would only be marginally true, Chinese leaders can present the price that their country paid as laying the groundwork for political stances that China chooses to take: as a guarantor of international order, with a strong sense of pride in its achievement of nationhood, and as guardian of an authoritarian domestic social contract that stresses collective economic wellbeing over individual rights.[5] Claims from the liberal world that the Second World War was fought for individual rights as well as collective ones ring more hollow today. This gives weight to China's efforts to obtain justice for itself in international society. That justice would take the form of a greater role for China in Asia, a role that it believes it was robbed of in 1949. China also sees its wartime narrative as useful for persuading other countries that China's regional and global role has a moral standing earned through its wartime sacrifices some three-quarters of a century ago.

In the future, we will hear more about China's claims to a greater role in the construction of order in Asia and globally. Some of those claims will undoubtedly be coercive. China is unafraid to wield its power in profoundly nonliberal, noncooperative ways, as in its militarization of the South China Sea and use of economic boycotts to damage Taiwan's economy. But it will also use its economic power through financing the Belt and Road Initiative and contributing to institutions such as Unesco, the World Trade Organization, and the Asian Infrastructure Investment Bank. Underpinning all of these initiatives will be the story of China's role in World War II. Beijing now argues that China was a creator of the order that emerged in 1945, and that the threat to that order comes from the United States, not China. China is creating a circuit of memory to enhance its standing and authority domestically and internationally, as well as to compete with the long-established circuit of memory that nurtures the narrative of the United States liberating the Asia–Pacific.[6]

In March 2020, as the globe was swept by the COVID-19 pandemic, China declared that it had overcome the virus first in the world, and most effectively. The language Xi Jinping used to describe this event was "Victory for China" in a "people's war," a term that referenced the narrative of the "people's war" of guerrilla warfare led by Mao Zedong during World War II.[7] As China becomes more powerful, the world will have to pay more attention to the stories that it wants to tell. Whether we realize it or not, we are all living in China's long postwar.

Notes

Introduction: War, Memory, and Nationalism in China

1. On war and memory in Europe and Asia, see Rana Mitter, "War and Memory since 1945," in Roger Chickering, Dennis Showalter, and Hans van de Ven, eds., *Cambridge History of Warfare* (Cambridge, 2012), 542–565.

2. Rana Mitter, *China's War with Japan, 1937–1945: The Struggle for Survival* (London, 2013), published in North America as *Forgotten Ally: China's World War II, 1937–1945* (Boston, 2013). The documentary *China's Forgotten War* is available through streaming services; the IMDB reference is here: https://www.imdb.com/title/tt8292600/.

3. Joseph S. Nye Jr., *Soft Power: The Means to Success in World Politics* (New York, 2004).

4. Rogers Smith, *Stories of Peoplehood: The Politics and Morals of Political Membership* (Cambridge, 2003), ch. 2.

5. On ancient (pre-Qin) Chinese ideas of morality in international relations, see Yan Xuetong, *Ancient Chinese Thought, Modern Chinese Power* (Princeton, NJ, 2011).

6. On the importance of the discourse of "national humiliation" in shaping contemporary Chinese nationalism, see William A.

Callahan, *China: The Pessoptimist Nation* (Oxford, 2010) and Zheng Wang, *Never Forget National Humiliation: Historical Memory in Chinese Politics and Foreign Relations* (New York, 2012). On the connections between history and politics in China more broadly, see Howard French, *Everything under the Heavens: How the Past Helps Shape China's Push for Global Power* (New York, 2017); Xi Jinping cited in Chen Hongmin, "Shishi qiushi yu kaituo chuangxin: weiwu shiguan yu kangRi zhanzheng shi yanjiu" [Seek truth from facts, open up and innovate: a material historical viewpoint and historical research on the War of Resistance], *Guangming ribao,* 14 Aug. 2019.

7. John Ikenberry, *Liberal Leviathan: The Origins, Crisis, and Transformation of the American World Order* (Princeton, NJ, 2011); Alastair Iain Johnston, *Social States: China in International Institutions, 1980–2000* (Princeton, NJ, 2008); John J. Mearsheimer, *Great Delusion: Liberal Dreams and International Realities* (New Haven, CT, 2018); Graham Allison, *Destined for War: Can America and China Escape Thucydides's Trap?* (Boston MA, 2017). For a measured, realist view from China, see Yan Xuetong, *Leadership and the Rise of Great Powers* (Princeton, NJ, 2019). Johnston gives a subtle reinterpretation of international order, and Beijing's relationship with it, in "China in a World of Orders: Rethinking Challenge and Compliance in Beijing's International Relations," *International Security* 44, no. 2 (2019), 9–60.

8. Xi Jinping's report at 19th Congress of the Chinese Communist Party, Chinadaily.com, 4 Nov. 2017, http://www.chinadaily.com.cn /china/19thcpcnationalcongress/2017-11/04/content_34115212.htm.

9. For the background, see the groundbreaking study by Julian Gewirtz, *Unlikely Partners: Chinese Reformers, Western Economists, and the Making of Global China* (Cambridge, MA, 2017).

10. Niall Ferguson, *The Ascent of Money* (London, 2008).

11. For contrasting views on China's economy, see two excellent studies: George Magnus, *Red Flags: Why Xi's China is in Jeopardy* (New Haven, CT, 2018) is more cautious about prospects, whereas Yukon Huang, *Cracking the China Conundrum: Why Conventional Wisdom Is Wrong* (New York, 2017) is more bullish.

12. Meia Nouwens, "China's Defence Spending: A Question of Perspective?" IISS Military Balance blog (24 May 2019), https://www.iiss.org/blogs/military-balance/2019/05/china -defence-spending.

13. Rosemary Foot, "China's Rise and US Hegemony· Renegotiating Hegemonic Order in East Asia?" *International Politics* 57 (2020): 150–165.

14. Tom Mitchell, "China Struggles to Win Friends over South China Sea," *Financial Times*, 13 July 2016.

15. For a revisionist global turn on Pearl Harbor, see Beth Bailey and David Farber, eds., *Beyond Pearl Harbor: A Pacific History* (Lawrence, KS, 2019).

16. Eric Helleiner, *Forgotten Foundations of Bretton Woods: International Development and the Making of the Postwar Order* (Ithaca, NY, 2014).

17. On the way in which historical ideas of victimhood have been used in Chinese nationalism, see Wang, *Never Forget National Humiliation;* Callahan, *China.* On the connections between history and politics in China, see Howard French, *Everything under the Heavens: How the Past Helps Shape China's Push for Global Power* (New York, 2017); Peter Hays Gries, *China's New Nationalism: Pride, Politics, and Diplomacy* (Berkeley, CA, 2004), ch. 3.

18. Catherine Merridale, *Night of Stone: Death and Memory in Russia* (London, 2012); Robert Gildea, *Fighters in the Shadows: A New History of the French Resistance* (London, 2015).

19. Chan Yang, *World War II Legacies in East Asia: China Remembers the War* (London, 2017); on the ideological bases of Mao's thought, see Julia Lovell, *Maoism: A Global History* (London, 2019).

20. Arthur Waldron and Parks Coble have written with great insight about this phenomenon. See Waldron, "China's New Remembering of World War II: The Case of Zhang Zizhong," *Modern Asian Studies,* 30, no. 4 (1996): 945–978; Coble, "China's 'New Remembering' of the Anti-Japanese War of Resistance, 1937–1945," *China Quarterly,* 190 (2007): 394–410.

21. Maurice Halbwachs, *On Collective Memory* (Chicago, 1992, from the 1925, 1952 French originals, trans. L. Coser); Pierre Nora and

David P. Jordan, eds., *Rethinking France* (Les Lieux de Mémoire), vol. 1. (trans. M. Trouille) (Chicago, 2001); Paul Fussell, *The Great War and Modern Memory* (Oxford, 1975).

22. See, for example, Peter Novick, *The Holocaust in American Life* (Boston, 1999); Hasia R. Diner, *We Remember with Reverence and Love: American Jews and the Myth of Silence after the Holocaust, 1945–1962* (New York, 2009).

23. Jan-Werner Müller, "Introduction," in *Memory and Power in Post-War Europe: Studies in the Presence of the Past,* ed. Jan-Werner Müller, (Cambridge, 2001), 35.

24. Carol Gluck, "The Idea of Showa," *Daedalus* 119, no. 3, in *Showa: The Japan of Hirohito* (Summer, 1990), pp. 1–26; Ian Buruma, *The Wages of Guilt: Memories of War in Germany and Japan* (London, 1994); Franziska Seraphim, *War Memory and Social Politics in Japan, 1945–2005* (Cambridge, MA, 2016); Yoshikuni Igarashi, *Bodies of Memory: Narratives of War in Postwar Japanese Culture, 1945–1970* (Princeton, NJ, 2000).

25. Viet Thanh Nguyen, *Nothing Ever Dies: Vietnam and the Memory of War* (Cambridge, MA, 2016).

26. This necessarily simplifies a complex issue. For a comprehensive discussion, see Waldron, "China's New Remembering." See also Rana Mitter, "Old Ghosts, New Memories: China's Changing War History in the Era of Post-Mao Politics," *Journal of Contemporary History* 38, no. 1 (2003): 117–131, and "Behind the Scenes at the Museum: Nationalism, History and Memory in the Beijing War of Resistance Museum, 1987–1997," *China Quarterly* 161 (2000): 279–293.

27. On Soviet war memory, see Nina Tumarkin, *The Living and the Dead: The Rise and Fall of the Cult of World War II in Russia* (New York, 1994). Some non-Russian Soviet republics, for instance Ukraine and the Baltics, had a more complicated relationship with the German occupation, with some prominent cases of collaboration.

28. Hans van de Ven, *China at War: Triumph and Tragedy in the Emergence of the New China* (London, 2017), 4.

29. China did take part in World War I, supplying over one hundred thousand workers to the Western Front; see Guoqi Xu, *China and the Great War: China's Pursuit of a New National Identity and Internationalization* (Cambridge, 2005). For a classic analysis of the effects of that war in Europe, see Jay Winter, *Sites of Memory, Sites of Mourning: The Great War in European Cultural History* (Cambridge, 1995); on World War I analogies for current Sino-Japanese tensions, see Alexis Dudden and Jeffrey Wasserstrom, "History as Weaponry," *Guernica,* 13 Feb. 2014, https://www.guernicamag.com/alexis-dudden-and-jeffrey-wasserstrom-history-as-weaponry/.

30. For the Genron NPO annual surveys of Japanese-Chinese public opinion, see http://www.genron-npo.net/en/archives/181011.pdf. The 2018 survey showed over 42 percent of Chinese respondents had a favorable impression of Japan (although only 13.1 percent of Japanese had a positive view of China). On the relationship between conflict and culture between Japan and the United States, Akira Iriye, *Power and Culture: The Japanese-American War* (Cambridge, MA, 1981) remains a classic; on the relationship with China, an incisive account of the long-range history between the two states is Ezra F. Vogel, *China and Japan: Facing History* (Cambridge, MA, 2019).

31. See Melissa Nobles, *The Politics of Official Apologies* (Cambridge, 2008); Hiro Saito, *The History Problem: The Politics of War Commemoration in East Asia* (Honolulu, 2016); Todd H. Hall, *Emotional Diplomacy: Official Emotion on the International Stage* (Ithaca, NY, 2015); Barry Buzan and Evelyn Goh, *Rethinking Sino-Japanese Alienation* (Oxford, 2020).

32. Nicholas Shakespeare, "The Hinge of Fate," *New Statesman,* 19–25 Jan. 2018, 24–29.

1. Hot War, Cold War: China's Conflicts, 1937-1978

1. "Why We fight: The Battle of China," YouTube, https://www.youtube.com/watch?v=m4Ebv-FzP60.

2. Hans van de Ven, *War and Nationalism in China, 1925–1945* (London, 2003), 3.

3. Recent texts include van de Ven, *War and Nationalism*; Diana Lary, *The Chinese People at War: Human Suffering and Social Transformation, 1937–1945* (Cambridge, 2010); Rana Mitter, *China's War with Japan, 1937–1945: The Struggle for Survival* [US title: *Forgotten Ally*] (London, 2013); Hans van de Ven, *China at War: Triumph and Tragedy in the Emergence of the New China* (London, 2017).

4. See Eri Hotta, *Pan-Asianism and Japan's War, 1931–1945* (London, 2007); Robert Bickers, *Out of China: How the Chinese Ended the Era of Western Domination* (London, 2017).

5. Sadako Ogata, *Defiance in Manchuria: The Making of Japanese Foreign Policy, 1931–1932* (Berkeley, 1964); Rana Mitter, *The Manchurian Myth: Nationalism, Resistance and Collaboration in Modern China* (Berkeley, 2000).

6. Parks M. Coble, *Facing Japan: Chinese Politics and Japanese Imperialism, 1931–1937* (Cambridge, MA, 1991).

7. On the battle, see Peter Harmsen, *Shanghai 1937: Stalingrad on the Yangtze* (London, 2013).

8. On the Wuhan phase of the war, see Stephen Mackinnon, *Wuhan, 1938: War, Refugees, and the Making of Modern China* (Berkeley, 2008).

9. For Wang's motivations, John Hunter Boyle, *China and Japan at War, 1937–1945: The Politics of Collaboration* (Stanford, 1972) remains a landmark work.

10. For new perspectives, see Beth Bailey and David Farber, eds., *Beyond Pearl Harbor: A Pacific History* (Lawrence, KS, 2019).

11. Van de Ven, *War and Nationalism*, ch.1.

12. Erez Manela, "The Fourth Policeman: Franklin Roosevelt's Vision for China's Global Role," in Wu Sihua et al., eds., *Kailuo xuanyan de yingxiang yu yiyi* (*The Significance and Impact of the Cairo Declaration*) (Taipei, 2014).

13. See, for example, Henrietta Harrison, "Newspapers and Nationalism in Rural China, 1890–1919," *Past and Present* 166 (2000): 181–204.

14. Mitter, *China's War*, 265.

15. Ruth Rogaski, *Hygienic Modernity: Meanings of Health and Disease in Treaty-Port China* (Berkeley, 2004).

16. Bickers, *Out of China*.

17. Chalmers A. Johnson, *Peasant Nationalism and Communist Power: The Emergence of Revolutionary China, 1937–1945* (Stanford, CA, 1962); Mark Selden, *The Yenan Way in Revolutionary China* (Cambridge, MA, 1971).

18. See, for example, Stephen MacKinnon, Diana Lary, and Ezra F. Vogel, eds., *China at War: Regions of China, 1937–45* (Stanford, CA, 2007).

19. Keith Lowe, *The Fear and the Freedom: How the Second World War Changed Us* (London, 2017).

20. Roosevelt's 1940 "Arsenal of Democracy" speech can be found at American Rhetoric, https://americanrhetoric.com/speeches/fdrarsenalofdemocracy.html.

21. Eugen Weber, *Peasants into Frenchmen: The Modernization of Rural France, 1870–1914* (Stanford, 1976).

22. Klaus Muelhahn, *Making China Modern: From the Great Qing to Xi Jinping* (Cambridge, MA, 2019), 278–282.

23. On the May Fourth Movement, which advocated a more liberal and open culture as a solution to China's political problems, see Rana Mitter, *A Bitter Revolution: China's Struggle with the Modern World* (Oxford, 2004).

24. Jiang Tingfu, "Zhongguo jindaihua de wenti" [The problem of modernization in China] (orig. in *Duli pinglun,* 1937), in Jiang Tingfu, *Jiang Tingfu xuanji* (Taipei, 1978), 638.

25. Jiang, "Zhongguo jindaihua," 640.

26. Jiang Tingfu, "Lun guoli de yuansu" [The factors behind national strength], in Jiang, *Jiang Tingfu xuanji*, 646.

27. Jiang, "Lun guoli," 646.

28. Jiang, "Lun guoli," 650.

29. This idea is reminiscent of the "state of exception" defined by the philosopher Giorgio Agamben, adapting the idea of the legal theorist Carl Schmitt. See Brian Tsui, *China's Conservative Revolution: The Quest for a New Order, 1927–1949* (Cambridge, 2018).

30. Jiang, "Lun guoli," 651, 652.

31. Maggie Clinton has written about the importance of fascist influence on the CC Clique within the Nationalist Party, and Brian Tsui has

examined the party as harbingers of a "conservative revolution." See Clinton, *Revolutionary Nativism: Fascism and Culture in China* (Durham NC, 2017); Tsui, *China's Conservative Revolution*.

32. Hu Qiaomu, "Qing Chongqing kan Luoma" [Chongqing, please look at Rome] (orig. *Jiefang ribao*, 21 Aug. 1943), *Hu Qiaomu wenji*, vol. 1 (Beijing, 2012), 114.

33. On the intertwining of collaboration and nationalism, see Mitter, *China's War*, 206–207.

34. Tehyun Ma, "'The Common Aim of the Allied Powers': Social Policy and International Legitimacy in Wartime China, 1940–47," *Journal of Global History* 9, no. 2 (2014): 254–275.

35. For the Atlantic Charter, see "United Nations, History of the UN Charter, 1941: The Atlantic Charter," https://www.un.org/en /sections/history-united-nations-charter/1941-atlantic-charter /index.html.

36. Joanna Handlin Smith, *The Art of Doing Good: Charity in Late Ming China* (Berkeley, 2009).

37. See essays in *European Journal of East Asian Studies* 11 (2012), special edition on "Relief and Reconstruction in Wartime China," ed. Rana Mitter and Helen M. Schneider.

38. Nicole Elizabeth Barnes, *Intimate Communities: Wartime Healthcare and the Birth of Modern China, 1937–1945* (Berkeley, 2018).

39. Hans van de Ven, *Breaking with the Past: The Maritime Customs Service and the Global Origins of Modernity in China* (New York, 2014).

40. Loren Brandt, "Reflections on China's Late 19th and Early 20th Century Economy," *China Quarterly* 150 (June 1997): 282–308; Felix Boecking, *No Great Wall: Tariffs, Trade and Nationalism in Republican China, 1927–1945* (Cambridge, MA, 2017).

41. Jiang, "Lun guoli," 651.

42. Mitter, *China's War with Japan*, 242–250.

43. According to Wang Jianlang, the 20 December 1941 entry is the first time Chiang mentions China's claims in his diary. Wang Jianlang, "Xinren de liushi: cong Jiang Jieshi riji kan kangzhanhouqi de ZhongMei guanxi," [Loss of confidence: Looking at China-US

relations through Chiang Kai-shek's diary], *Jindaishi yanjiu* (Mar. 2009), 62.

44. Wang Jianlang, citation of Chiang diary (9 Nov. 1942), in "Daguo yishi yu daguo zuowei," [Great power consciousness and behavior], *Lishi yanjiu* (June 2008), 133.

45. Chiang Kai-shek diary, 4 March 1943, Hoover Institution Library and Archives, Stanford University (hereafter CKSD).

46. Wang Zheng, *Never Forget National Humiliation: Historical Memory in Chinese Politics and Foreign Relations* (New York, 2012), ch. 3.

47. See, for instance, Mary Fulbrook, *Reckonings: Legacies of Nazi Persecution and the Quest for Injustice* (Oxford, 2018), 453–54, on the lack of feelings of war guilt in the former DDR (East Germany).

48. There is a huge literature on memory in postwar Europe; for representative essays, see Jan-Werner Müller, ed., *Memory and Power in Post-War Europe: Studies in the Presence of the Past* (Cambridge, 2002).

49. CKSD, 28 Aug. 1945.

50. CKSD, 2 Oct. 1945.

51. CKSD, 13 Oct. 1945.

52. Eric Helleiner, *Forgotten Foundations of Bretton Woods: International Development and the Making of the Postwar Order* (Ithaca, NY, 2014).

53. Christopher Thorne, *Allies of a Kind: The United States, Britain and the War against Japan, 1941–1945* (Oxford, 1978).

54. On the Chinese Civil War, see Odd Arne Westad, *Decisive Encounters: The Chinese Civil War, 1946–1950* (Stanford, CA, 2003) and Graham Hutchings, *China 1949: Year of Revolution* (London, 2020); on General Marshall's mission, see Daniel Kurtz-Phelan, *The China Mission: George C. Marshall's Unfinished War, 1945–1947* (New York, 2018); on immediate Chinese postwar plans for reconstruction during the Civil War years, see Rana Mitter, "State-Building after Disaster: Jiang Tingfu and the Reconstruction of Post-World War II China, 1943–1949," *Comparative Studies in Society and History* 61, no. 1 (2019): 176–206.

55. On the importance of the Korean War in US-China policy, see, for example, Chen Jian, *Mao's China and the Cold War* (Chapel Hill, NC, 2001).

56. Chan Yang, *World War II Legacies in East Asia: China Remembers the War* (London, 2017), ch. 2; Kirk A. Denton, *Exhibiting the Past: Historical Memory and the Politics of Museums in Postsocialist China* (Honolulu, 2014), chs. 5, 6.

57. For a contemporaneous analysis, see David S. G. Goodman, "The Sixth Plenum of the 11th Central Committee of the CCP: Look Back in Anger?" *China Quarterly* 87 (Sept. 1981): 518–527.

58. Kenneth B. Pyle, "Japan Besieged: The Textbook Controversy," *Journal of Japanese Studies* 9, no. 2 (1983): 297–300.

59. Barak Kushner, *Men to Devils, Devils to Men: Japanese War Crimes and Chinese Justice* (Cambridge, MA, 2015), 174.

60. Certain Eastern European states did have a more ambivalent attitude toward the Nazi period; the Baltic states, for instance, briefly regarded the period of Nazi invasion as a release from Soviet occupation.

61. On Bose, see Sugata Bose, *His Majesty's Opponent: Subhas Chandra Bose and India's Struggle against Empire* (Cambridge, MA, 2014).

2. History Wars: How Historical Research
Shaped China's Politics

1. For a key work in this influential school, see Ranajit Guha, *Elementary Aspects of Peasant Insurgency in Colonial India* (New Delhi, 1983).

2. Chalmers A. Johnson, *Peasant Nationalism and Communist Power: The Emergence of Revolutionary China, 1937–1945* (Stanford, CA, 1962).

3. Paul A. Cohen, *Discovering History in China: American Historical Writing on the Recent Chinese Past,* 2nd paperback ed. (New York, 1984), chs. 3–4.

4. Mark Selden, *The Yenan Way in Revolutionary China* (Cambridge, MA, 1971).

5. Suzanne Pepper, "The Political Odyssey of an Intellectual Construct: Peasant Nationalism and the Study of China's Revolutionary History: A Review Essay," *Journal of Asian Studies,* 63: 1 (2004): 105–125.

6. Barbara Tuchman, *Stilwell and the American Experience in China, 1911–45* (New York, 1971). For the major revisionist analysis of

Stilwell, see Hans van de Ven, *War and Nationalism in China, 1925–1945* (London, 2003), ch. 1.

7. Huang Meizhen, Zhang Jishun, and Jin Guangyue, "Jianguo yilai kangRi zhanzheng yanjiu shuping" [A critical review of the research on the War of Resistance since the founding of the PRC], *Minguo dang'an* 10 (1987), 95.

8. Hu Qiaomu, *Zhongguo gongchandang de sanshinian* [Thirty years of the Chinese Communist Party] (Beijing, 1950). Published in English as Hu Chiao-mu, *Thirty Years of the Communist Party of China: An Outline History* (London, 1951).

9. Huang, Zhang, and Jin, "Jianguo yilai," 95.

10. Huang, Zhang, and Jin, "Jianguo yilai," 96.

11. Huang, Zhang, and Jin, "Jianguo yilai," 96.

12. A recent contribution to the debate is Tim Bouverie, *Appeasing Hitler: Chamberlain, Churchill and the Road to War* (London, 2019).

13. Pete Millwood, "(Mis)Perceptions of Domestic Politics in the U.S.-China Rapprochement, 1969–1978," *Diplomatic History* 43, no. 5 (2019): 890–915.

14. "Hu Qiaomu, a Chinese Hardliner, Is Dead at 81," *New York Times,* 29 Sept. 1992.

15. Interview with senior Chinese historian, July 2018.

16. A short biography of Liu in English can be found at Institute of Modern History, CASS online, http://jds.cssn.cn/english/scholars /201605/t20160506_3332921.shtml.

17. Zhang Haipeng, "Zhanshixing de xuezhe, xuezhexing de zhanshi" [Soldierly scholar, scholarly soldier], in *Liu Danian ji* [Liu Danian collection] (Beijing, 2000), 471, 484–485.

18. Zhou Qiuguang, Huang Renguo, *Liu Danian zhuan* [Biography of Liu Danian] (Changsha, 2009), 522–527.

19. Zhongguo di'er lishi dangan'guan, ed., *KangRi zhanzheng zhengmian zhanchang* (Nanjing, 1987).

20. Geremie Barme, "History for the masses," in Jonathan Unger, ed., *Using the Past to Serve the Present* (Armonk, NY, 1993), 278.

21. Richard Baum, *Burying Mao: Chinese Politics in the Age of Deng Xiaoping* (Princeton, NJ, 1994), 6.

22. Huang, Zhang, and Jin, "Jianguo yilai," 97.
23. Huang, Zhang, and Jin, "Jianguo yilai," 108.
24. Huang, Zhang, and Jin, "Jianguo yilai," 108.
25. Huang, Zhang, and Jin, "Jianguo yilai," 96.
26. Huang, Zhang, and Jin, "Jianguo yilai," 96.
27. Huang, Zhang, and Jin, "Jianguo yilai," 97.
28. Huang, Zhang, and Jin, "Jianguo yilai," 97.
29. Huang, Zhang, and Jin, "Jianguo yilai," 100.
30. Huang, Zhang, and Jin, "Jianguo yilai," 100.
31. Huang, Zhang, and Jin, "Jianguo yilai," 99.
32. Van de Ven, *War and Nationalism*, 7.
33. Huang, Zhang, and Jin, "Jianguo yilai," 99–100.
34. Huang, Zhang, and Jin, "Jianguo yilai," 100.
35. Huang, Zhang, and Jin, "Jianguo yilai," 100.
36. Huang, Zhang, and Jin, "Jianguo yilai," 105.
37. Huang, Zhang, and Jin, "Jianguo yilai," 108.
38. Interview with senior CASS scholar, summer 2018.
39. Huang, Zhang, and Jin, "Jianguo yilai," 97.
40. Hu Qiaomu, "Luetan banian kangzhan de weida yiyi" [An outline discussion of the great significance of the War of Resistance], *Renmin ribao*, 7 Aug. 1987, in *Hu Qiaomu wenji* [Collected works of Hu Qiaomu], vol. 2 (Beijing, 2012), 248.
41. See Chan Yang, *World War II Legacies in East Asia: China Remembers the War* (London, 2017).
42. Hu Qiaomu, "Qing Chongqing kan Luoma" [Chongqing, please look at Rome] (orig. *Jiefang ribao*, 21 Aug. 1943), *Hu Qiaomu wenji*, vol. 1: 113–114. On Chinese fascism, see Maggie Clinton, *Revolutionary Nativism: Fascism and Culture in China* (Durham, NC, 2017).
43. Hu, "Luetan," 248.
44. Hu, "Luetan," 249.
45. Arthur Waldron, "China's New Remembering of World War II: The Case of Zhang Zizhong," *Modern Asian Studies* 30: 4 (1996): 945–978.
46. Hu, "Luetan," 249.

47. Hu, "Luetan," 249.

48. Hu, "Luetan," 249.

49. Interview with senior Chinese historian, July 2018.

50. On economic and political reform in this era, see Julian Gewirtz, *Unlikely Partners: Chinese Reformers, Western Economists, and the Making of Global China* (Cambridge, MA, 2017).

51. Interview with senior Chinese historian, July 2018.

52. Jean-Pierre Cabestan, "Mainland Missiles and the Future of Taiwan . . . and Lee Teng-hui," *China Perspectives* 1 (Sept.–Oct. 1995): 43–47.

53. Liu Danian to Li Peng, 15 Oct. 1990, in Wang Yupu and Zhu Wei, eds., *Liu Danian laiwang shuxin xuan* [Liu Danian's selected correspondence] (Beijing, 2006), 564.

54. Liu Danian to Jiang Zemin, 15 May 1995, in *Liu Danian laiwang,* 623.

55. Choi Chi-yuk, "Outspoken Liberal Magazine *Yanhuang Chunqiu* Stops Publication after Management Purge," *South China Morning Post,* 18 July 2016.

56. KangRi zhanzheng yanjiu, ed., *1945–1995: KangRi zhanzheng shengli wushi zhounian jinianji* [1945–1995: Collection in commemoration of the 50th anniversary of the victory in the War of Resistance] (Beijing, 1995).

57. Mark Tran, "China and Japan Agree to Joint History Study," *Guardian,* 16 Nov. 2006.

58. Shin Kawashima, "The Three Phases of Japan-China Joint-History Research: What Was the Challenge?" *Asian Perspective* 34, no. 4, (2010): 19–43.

59. Eli Friedman, "It's Time to Get Loud about Academic Freedom in China," *Foreign Policy,* 13 Nov. 2018.

60. Xi Jinping, "Rang lishi shuohua yong shishi fayan shenru kaizhan Zhongguo renmin kangRi zhanzheng yanjiu" [Let history speak and use facts to deepen and open research on the Chinese People's War of Resistance], 31 July 2015, CPC News, http://cpc.people.com.cn/n /2015/0731/c64094-27393899.html.

61. Kinling Lo, "Textbooks Change: China's war against Japanese Aggression Lasted 14 Years instead of Eight," *South China Morning Post,* 7 Jan. 2017.

62. Hu, "Luetan."

63. Huang, Zhang, and Jin, "Jianguo yilai," 100.

64. See Sandra Wilson, "Rethinking the 1930s and the '15-Year War' in Japan," *Japanese Studies* 21, no. 2 (2001): 155–164.

65. Hu, "Luetan," 243–244.

66. See, for instance, Robert Gerwarth, *The Vanquished: Why the First World War Failed to End* (London, 2016).

67. A major recent biography of He Yingqin, who engineered these agreements, is Peter Worthing, *General He Yingqin: The Rise and Fall of Nationalist China* (Cambridge, 2016).

68. Rana Mitter, *China's War with Japan, 1937–1945: The Struggle for Survival* [US title: *Forgotten Ally*] (London, 2013), 74–77.

69. Interview with senior Chinese historian, July 2018.

70. Interview with senior Chinese historian, July 2018.

71. Xi Jinping, "Rang lishi shuohua."

72. Interview with senior Chinese historian, July 2018.

73. Robert O. Paxton, *Vichy France: Old Guard and New Order, 1940–1944* (New York, 1972).

74. Interview with senior Chinese historian, July 2018.

75. On the military campaigns, see Mark Peattie, Edward Drea and Hans van de Ven, eds., *The Battle for China: Essays on the Military History of the Sino-Japanese War of 1937–1945* (Stanford, CA, 2011).

76. As discussed earlier in the chapter, Zhongguo di'er lishi dangan'guan, ed., *KangRi zhanzheng zhengmian zhanchang* (Nanjing, 1987), is a key set of documents of this type.

77. Interview with senior Chinese historian, July 2018.

78. Interview with senior Chinese historian, July 2018.

79. Pauline Keating gives a very useful bibliographical account of work in Chinese and English up to 2017 on the Communist wartime base areas in "Yan'an and the Revolutionary Base Areas," Oxford Bibliographies, updated 28 Apr. 2014, http://www.oxfordbibliographies

.com/view/document/obo-9780199920082/obo-9780199920082
-0089.xml.

80. Fang-Shang Lua and Hsiao-ting Lina, "Chiang Kai-Shek's Diaries and Republican China: New Insights on the History of Modern China," *Chinese Historical Review* 15, no. 2 (2008): 331–339.

81. Lu Fangshang, ed., *Jiang Zhongzheng riji yu minguo shi yanjiu* (Chiang Kai-shek's diary and research into Republican-era history), 2 vols. (Taibei, 2011).

82. Millwood, "(Mis)Perceptions of Domestic Politics in the U.S.-China Rapprochement."

83. Zhang Baijia, "KangRi shiqi zhongmei hezuo de lishi jingyan: you Shidiwei zaiHua jingli suo xiangdao de" [The historical experience of China-US relations during the War of Resistance: thoughts on Stilwell's experience while stationed in China], *Xin yuanjian* 1 (2012), 31, 35.

84. Zhang, "KangRi shiqi," 39.

85. Zhang Baijia, "If History Is Any Guide," *China-US Focus* (9 Apr. 2019), https://www.chinausfocus.com/foreign-policy/historical
-lessons-and-future-implications-for-evolving-china-us-relations.

86. See, for instance, Joanna Bourke, *Wounding the World: How Military Violence and War-play Invades Our World* (London, 2014).

87. See, for example, the multivolume collection edited by a senior scholar: Zhang Xianwen, gen. ed., *Nanjing datusha shiliaoji* [Collections of materials on the Nanjing Massacre] (Nanjing, 2005–).

88. Bu Ping, *Riben de Huaxuezhan* [Japan's Chemical Warfare] (Harbin, 1998).

89. See, for example, the multivolume collection by Zhang Kaichen and Zhou Yong, *Zhongguo kangzhan dahoufang lishi wenhua congshu* [Historical and cultural collections from the Great Interior during the Chinese War of Resistance] (Chongqing, 2012–).

90. See, for example, Ma Zhonglian, "Huayuankou jueti de junshi yiyi" [The military significance of the breach of the dikes at Huayuankou], *KangRi zhanzheng yanjiu* 4 (1999).

91. A major English work that cites much of the work on collaboration in French is Julian Jackson, *France: The Dark Years, 1940–1944* (Oxford, 2001).

92. On Manchukuo, see Prasenjit Duara, *Sovereignty and Authenticity: Manchukuo and the East Asian Modern* (Lexington, KY, 2003); Thomas Dubois, *Empire and the Meaning of Religion in Northeast Asia: Manchuria, 1900–1945* (Cambridge, 2017); Rana Mitter, *The Manchurian Myth: Nationalism, Resistance, and Collaboration in Modern China* (Berkeley, 2000). On Liang Hongzhi, see Timothy Brook, "Hesitating before the Judgment of History," *Journal of Asian Studies* 71, no. 1 (2012): 103–114.

93. One early example is by Cai Dejin, *Wang Jingwei pingzhuan* [A critical biography of Wang Jingwei] (Chengdu, 1988); Cai also edited Zhou Fohai's diaries: *Zhou Fohai riji* (Diary of Zhou Fohai), 2 vols. (Beijing, 1987). One of the most important recent works on the Wang regime is David Serfass, "Le gouvernement collaborateur de Wang Jingwei: aspects de l'état d'occupation durant la guerre sino-japonaise, 1940–45" (Ph.D. thesis, Paris, 2017).

3. Memory, Nostalgia, Subversion: How China's Public Sphere Embraced World War II

1. Svetlana Alexievich, *The Unwomanly Face of War: An Oral History of Women in World War II,* trans. Richard Pevear and Larissa Volokhonsky (New York, 2017). Alexievich was awarded the 2015 Nobel Prize in Literature for the body of her work.

2. Henry Rousso, *The Vichy Syndrome: History and Memory in France since 1944,* trans. Arthur Goldhammer (Cambridge, MA, 1991), ch. 6.

3. Tamara Hamlish, "Preserving the Palace: Museums and the Making of Nationalism(s) in Twentieth-Century China," *Museum Anthropology* 19, no. 2 (1995): 20–30.

4. Justin Jacobs, "Preparing the People for Mass Clemency: The 1956 Japanese War Crimes Trials in Shenyang and Taiyuan," *China Quarterly* 205 (2011): 152–172.

5. Kenneth B. Pyle, "Japan Besieged: The Textbook Controversy," *Journal of Japanese Studies* 9, no. 2 (1983): 297–300.

6. Hu Qiaomu, "Bowuguan shiye xuyao zhubu you yi ge da de fazhan" [The museum enterprise needs big step-by-step developments], *Renmin ribao*, 5 Nov. 1983.

7. Zhou Qiuguang and Huang Renguo, *Liu Danian zhuan* [Biography of Liu Danian] (Changsha, 2009), 522–527.

8. "Zhongguo renmin kang-Ri zhanzheng jinianguan: Jiangjieci" [The Memorial Museum of the Chinese People's War of Resistance to Japan: Explanation] (Beijing: Zhongguo renmin kang-Ri zhanzheng jinianguan, 1997), 34.

9. "Zhongguo renmin kang-Ri zhanzheng jinianguan: Jiangjieci," 34.

10. "Zhongguo renmin kang-Ri zhanzheng jinianguan: Jianjie" [The Memorial Museum of the Chinese People's War of Resistance to Japan: Introduction] (Beijing: Zhongguo renmin kang-Ri zhanzheng jinianguan, 1997), 3.

11. Yu Yanjun, "Chongfen liyong bowuguan shehui jiaoyu youshi peiyang aiguozhuyi jingshen, zengqiang gongzhong minzu yishi" [Making full use of social education at the museum effectively to nurture a patriotic spirit and strengthen public national consciousness] in *Zhongguo renmin kang-Ri zhanzheng jinianguan: wencong* [The Memorial Museum to the Chinese People's War of Resistance to Japan: Essays], vol. 5 (1994), 379.

12. On socialist consumerism, see Karl Gerth's pioneering *Unending Capitalism: How Consumerism Negated the Chinese Revolution* (Cambridge, 2020).

13. Yu Yanjun, "Jianhao qidi, bozhong weilai: kangzhanguan qingshaonian jiaoyu jidi gongzuo qingkuang huibao" [Build up the base, sow the seeds of the future: a report on the groundwork on basic youth education at the Memorial Museum of the War of Resistance], in *Zhongguo renmin kang-Ri zhanzheng jinianguan: wencong* (The Memorial Museum to the Chinese People's War of Resistance to Japan: Essays), vol. 4 (1993), 329–330.

14. Yu, "Chongfen liyong bowuguan," 380.
15. Yu, "Chongfen liyong bowuguan," 381.
16. "Zhongguo renmin kang-Ri zhanzheng jinianguan: Jianjie," 9.
17. Personal observation, June 2018.
18. *Weida shengli lishi gongxian* [Great Victory, Historical Contributions], museum leaflet, collected 2018.
19. Xi Jinping, "Work Together to Build a Community of Shared Future for Mankind" (United Nations Office, Geneva, 18 January 2017), http://www.xinhuanet.com//english/2017-01/19/c _135994707.htm; "FM Wang Yi's speech at 56th Munich Security Conference," *China Daily,* 16 Feb. 2020.
20. Personal observation, June 2018.
21. Kirk A. Denton, "Exhibiting the Past: China's Nanjing Massacre Memorial Museum," in *Violence de masse et Résistance—Réseau de recherche,* published 25 Nov. 2014, https://www.sciencespo.fr/mass -violence-war-massacre-resistance/en/document/exhibiting-past -chinas-nanjing-massacre-memorial-museum.html. See also Kirk A. Denton, *Exhibiting the Past: Historical Memory and the Politics of Museums in Postsocialist China* (Honolulu, 2014), with references to Qi Kang's views on p. 138.
22. "Chinese Educators Inspired at Yad Vashem," Yad Vashem blog, 22 Nov. 2011, https://www.yadvashem.org/blog/chinese-educators -inspired-at-yad-vashem.html.
23. Iris Chang, *The Rape of Nanking: China's Hidden Holocaust* (New York, 1997).
24. Joshua Fogel, "The Controversy over Iris Chang's 'The Rape of Nanking,'" *Japan Echo* 27, no. 1 (2000): 55–57.
25. Michael Billington, "*Into the Numbers* Review," *Guardian,* 5 Jan. 2018.
26. Personal observation, July 2015.
27. Studs Terkel, *"The Good War": An American Oral History of World War II* (New York, 1984).
28. Charles A. Laughlin, *Chinese Reportage: The Aesthetics of Historical Experience* (Durham, NC, 2004).

29. On Du Zhongyuan, see Rana Mitter, *A Bitter Revolution: China's Struggle with the Modern World* (Oxford, 2004), chs. 1–3.

30. Liu Binyan, *People or Monsters? And Other Stories and Reportage from China after Mao,* ed. Perry Link (Bloomington: Indiana University Press, 1983).

31. Robin Stummer, "Why Has the Great War Come Back to Haunt Us?" *The Guardian* weekend supplement, 7 Nov. 1998, 12–23.

32. Song Shiqi and Yan Jingzheng, eds., *Jizhe bixia de kang-Ri zhanzheng* [The War of Resistance to Japan through the pens of journalists] (Beijing, 1995).

33. Chang-tai Hung, *War and Popular Culture: Resistance in Modern China, 1937–1945* (Berkeley, 1994), ch. 4.

34. Song and Yan, eds., *Jizhe bixia,* 368.

35. *Dikang* [Resistance] [issue 12], 26 Sept. 1937.

36. Song and Yan, eds., *Jizhe bixia,* 374.

37. Fang Jun, *Wo renshide 'guizihing'* [The 'devil soldiers' I knew] (Beijing: Zhongguo duiwai fanyi chuban gongsi, 1997).

38. Reflections on contemporary identity through investigation into one's community's experience of World War II has been a recurring phenomenon in the West for some years. One girl's experiences researching her own small town in Germany became the basis of Michael Verhoeven's film *Das Schreckliche Mädchen (The Nasty Girl)* (1990). An impressive study on the Netherlands and its myth of tolerance and resistance is Simon Kuper, *Ajax, the Dutch, the War: Football in Europe during the Second World War* (London, 2003).

39. On diary writing during World War II in Asia, see Aaron W. Moore, *Writing War: Soldiers Record the Japanese Empire* (Cambridge, MA, 2013).

40. Pei-yi Wu, *The Confucian's Progress: Autobiographical Writings in Traditional China* (Princeton, NJ, 1990).

41. One such author is the noted journalist Zou Taofen. See Wen-hsin Yeh, "Progressive Journalism and Shanghai's Petty Urbanites: Zou Taofen and the Shenghuo Weekly, 1926–1945," in Frederic

Wakeman Jr. and Wen-hsin Yeh, ed., *Shanghai Sojourners* (Berkeley, CA, 1992).

42. *Xinsheng* 1, no. 1 (1934), 1.

43. Wu, *The Confucian's Progress,* 93.

44. *Xinsheng* 1, no. 1 (1934), 11.

45. Fang, *Wo renshide,* 286.

46. Fang, *Wo renshide,* 267.

47. Fang, *Wo renshide,* 12.

48. Fang, *Wo renshide,* 287.

49. Fang, *Wo renshide,* 3.

50. See, for example, John Gittings, *Real China: From Cannibalism to Karaoke* (London, 1996).

51. On how memory of war and atrocity came together in an earlier period, see Tobie Meyer-Fong, *What Remains: Coming to Terms with Civil War in 19th Century China* (Stanford, CA, 2013), esp. ch. 4.

52. Fang, *Wo renshide,* 24.

53. Zheng Yi, *Scarlet Memorial: Tales of Cannibalism in Modern China,* trans. T. P. Sym (Boulder, CO, 1996).

54. Kathy Gao, "Meet the Chinese Property Tycoon Whose Museum Business Brings Him Joy, Fame," *South China Morning Post,* 27 July 2015.

55. Fan Jianchuan, *Yi ge ren de kangzhan: cong yige ren de cangpin kan yi chang quan minzu de zhanzheng* [One person's war of resistance: looking at a whole nation's war through one person's collection] (Beijing, 2000).

56. Fan, *Yi ge ren,* frontispiece.

57. Fan, *Yi ge ren,* 73.

58. Fan, *Yi ge ren,* 136.

59. Fan, *Yi ge ren,* 75.

60. Fan, *Yi ge ren,* 83.

61. As a comparison, in recent years, scholarship on Holocaust responsibility has moved further away from blaming leaders and toward showing the responsibility of ordinary citizens; see, for example, Robert Gellately, *Backing Hitler: Consent and Coercion in Nazi Germany* (Oxford, 2001).

62. Fan, *Yi ge ren,* 105

63. Fan, *Yi ge ren,* 107.

64. The museum's website is at http://www.jc-museum.cn/en/. On the museum's relationship with the Mao era, see Barclay Bram, "Fan Jianchuan's Museum Industrial Complex," Medium.com, 19 Jan. 2018, https://medium.com/@barclaybram/fan-jianchuans -museum-industrial-complex-534108783b62

65. "Chongqing Jianchuan Museum Opened on June 18," China Travel News, 21 June 2018, http://www.cits.net/china-travel-news /chongqing-jianchuan-museum-opened-on-june-18.html.

66. Fang, *Wo renshide,* 284–285.

67. Fang, *Wo renshide,* 69–87.

68. Arthur Waldron, "China's New Remembering of World War II: The Case of Zhang Zizhong," *Modern Asian Studies,* 30, no. 4 (1996): 945–978.

4. Old Memories, New Media: Wartime History
Online and Onscreen

1. Mimi Lau, "China's Whistle-Blower Blogger Cui Yongyuan Appears," *South China Morning Post,* 1 Mar. 2019.

2. Episodes of *Wode kangzhan* can be found at http://tv.sohu.com /20100816/n274237549.shtml.

3. Cui Yongyuan interview, "Cui Yongyuan tan 'wode kangzhan'" [Cui Yongyuan talks about "My war of resistance"], *Nanfang zhoumo,* 7 Oct. 2010.

4. "Cui Yongyuan tan."

5. "Cui Yongyuan de 'kangzhan'" [Cui Yongyuan's "war of resistance"], *Zhongguo zhoukan,* 8 Sept. 2010.

6. "Cui Yongyuan tan."

7. "Cui Yongyuan de 'kangzhan.'"

8. Cui Yongyuan, introduction to *Wode kangzhan II,* Baidu Baike, https://baike.baidu.com/item/%E6%88%91%E7%9A%84%E6%8A% 97%E6%88%98II/26747.

9. Murong Xuecun, "China's Television War on Japan," *New York Times,* 9 Feb. 2014.

10. "Anti-Japanese War Dramas Pulled from TV due to Ludicrous Plots," *China Daily,* 20 Aug. 2015.

11. Gaochao Zhang, "'Dunkirk' Conquers China's Box Office," *Los Angeles Times,* 6 Sept. 2017; Neil Connor, "A Retreat Has No 'Chinese Values': Dunkirk Movie Comes under Fire in China," *Telegraph,* 4 Sept. 2017.

12. Chris Hawke, "Anti-Japan Rampage in Shanghai," CBS News, 16 Apr. 2005, https://www.cbsnews.com/news/anti-japan-rampage-in -shanghai/.

13. Derek Elley, "*City of Life and Death* Review," *Variety,* 14 May 2009.

14. The critic Shelly Kraicer gives an insightful account of how official approval for Lu Chuan's film turned into disapproval over time. Kraicer, "A Matter of Life and Death: Lu Chuan and Post-Zhuxuanlu Cinema," *Cinema Scope* 41 (Winter 2010), http://cinema -scope.com/features/features-a-matter-of-life-and-death-lu-chuan -and-post-zhuxuanlu-cinema-by-shelly-kraicer/.

15. Kurt Orzeck, "Chinese Blockbuster 'Flowers of War' Leaves Audiences Cold," *The Wrap,* 26 Jan. 2012, https://www.thewrap.com /despite-christian-bale-flowers-war-leaves-us-audiences-cold-34515/.

16. Roger Friedman, "That Movie Bruce Willis Made in China—with Mel Gibson as Art Director—Is MIA," *Showbiz 411,* 4 May 2016, http://www.showbiz411.com/2016/05/04/that-movie-bruce-willis -made-in-china-with-mel-gibson-as-art-director-is-m-i-a.

17. Wang Xiangwei, "Meet Cui Yongyuan," *South China Morning Post,* 26 Jan. 2019.

18. Vivienne Chow, "China Release of Fan Bingbing–Bruce Willis Film 'Unbreakable Spirit' Is Scrapped," *Variety,* 17 Oct. 2018; "Fan Bingbing Movie Co-starring Bruce Willis Cancelled," *The Straits Times,* 18 Oct. 2018, https://www.asiaone.com/entertainment/fan -bingbing-movie-co-starring-bruce-willis-likely-cancelled -following-actress-tax.

19. Dennis Harvey, "Film Review: 'Air Strike,'" *Variety,* 27 Oct. 2018.

20. *Air Strike* user reviews, IMDb, https://www.imdb.com/title /tt4743226/reviews?ref_=tt_urv.

21. I explore this issue in the BBC radio documentary *Japan's Never-Ending War* (2018), https://www.bbc.co.uk/programmes/b0b0wrpk.

22. Jonathan Spence, *The Gate of Heavenly Peace: The Chinese and Their Revolution, 1895 1980* (New York, 1981), 360–361.

23. On this phenomenon, see Robert Weatherley and Qiang Zhang, *History and Nationalist Legitimacy in China: A Double-Edged Sword* (London, 2017).

24. "Minguo fuxing yundong xingqi 'guofen' duiwu zhangda" [Movement for revival of the Republic stimulates growth in "guofen" numbers], Radio Free Asia, 5 Mar. 2015, www.rfa.org/mandarin/yataibaodao/zhengzhi/ck-03052015093356.html.

25. Lijun Yang and Yongnian Zheng, "Fen Qings (Angry Youths) in Contemporary China," in Suisheng Zhao, ed., *Construction of Chinese Nationalism in the Early 21st Century: Domestic and International Aspects* (London, 2014).

26. "China Releases Former Nanjing Professor Jailed for 'Subversion,'" Radio Free Asia, 14 Nov. 2018, https://www.rfa.org/english/news/china/professor-release-11142018162943.html.

27. "Double Ten Day Fervor Humiliates History," *Global Times,* 10 Oct. 2014, http://www.globaltimes.cn/content/885475.shtml.

28. "Minguo fuxing yundong xingqi 'guofen' duiwu zhangda."

29. Qiuba Shiji, "Wo zenyang kan Guofen" [How I see the Guofen], (/u/a9a0a52edc88), 23 Sept. 2017, https://www.jianshu.com/p/e6a00469f1de.

30. Qiuba shiji, "Wo zenyang kan."

31. Elaine Yau, "First Chinese IMAX Film *The Eight Hundred*'s Release Cancelled," *South China Morning Post,* 17 June 2019. The trailer is still online (as of 12 Mar. 2020) at https://www.youtube.com/watch?v=41VkLPcB_Cg.

32. Lan Lin, "Release Delay of War Epic 'The Eight Hundred,'" SupChina, 1 July 2019, https://supchina.com/2019/07/01/release-delay-of-war-epic-the-eight-hundred-a-new-era-of-chinese-movie-censorship/.

33. Rana Mitter, "What Is China's Big Parade All About," *ChinaFile*, 2 Sept. 2015, http://www.chinafile.com/conversation/what-chinas -big-parade-all-about.

5. From Chongqing to Yan'an: Regional Memory and Wartime Identity

1. Theodore H. White and Annalee Jacoby, *Thunder out of China* (New York, 1946), 3.
2. Zhou Yong, interview with the author, 29 April 2018.
3. On Maoist myths, see Julia Lovell, *Maoism: A Global History* (London, 2019).
4. Personal observation, August 2015.
5. Zhou, interview.
6. On the society and politics of Sichuan in the early twentieth century, see Di Wang, *The Teahouse: Small Business, Everyday Culture, and Public Politics in Chengdu, 1900–1950* (Stanford, 2008).
7. Zhou Yong, ed., *Chongqing kangzhan shi, 1931–1945* [Chongqing's history during the War of Resistance, 1931–45] (Chongqing, 2005), 98.
8. Zhou, *Chongqing kangzhan*, 99.
9. Zhou, *Chongqing kangzhan*, 99.
10. Zhou, *Chongqing kangzhan*, 100.
11. Xu Wancheng, *Chongqing Huaxu* [Chongqing gossip] (Shanghai, 1946), 6 (hereafter, CQHX).
12. On refugees, see Stephen Mackinnon, *Wuhan 1938: War, Refugees, and the Making of Modern China* (Berkeley, 2008); Rana Mitter, *China's War with Japan, 1937–1945: The Struggle for Survival* (London, 2013), 173.
13. Brian Tsui, *China's Conservative Revolution: The Quest for a New Order, 1927–1949* (Cambridge, 2018), 117.
14. Fu Xiaolan, "Lun Chongqing da hongzha dui chengshi jianshe de yingxiang" [The influence of the great Chongqing air raids on city construction], *Kangri zhanzheng jinianwang*, http://www.krzzjn.com /html/71920.html.
15. Fu, "Lun Chongqing."

16. Quoted in Lara Feigel, *The Love-Charm of Bombs: Restless Lives in the Second World War* (London, 2013), 26.
17. CQHX, 28.
18. CQHX, 28.
19. Christina Kelley Gilmartin, *Engendering the Chinese Revolution: Radical Women, Communist Politics, and Mass Movements in the 1920s* (Berkeley, 1995) suggestively addresses this issue.
20. Zhou Yong, interview by the author, July 2018.
21. Zhou, interview.
22. Roderick MacFarquhar and Michael Schoenhals, *Mao's Last Revolution* (Cambridge, MA), 217.
23. Zhou, interview.
24. Personal observation, July 2013.
25. Personal observation, August 2015.
26. Both popular and academic histories of this period have flourished in the last few years; one example among many is Zheng Guanglu, *Chuanren da kangzhan* (The great War of resistance of the Sichuan people) (Chengdu, 2005).
27. Hans van de Ven, *China at War: Triumph and Tragedy in the Emergence of the New China* (London, 2017), 195.
28. Zhou, interview.
29. Rana Mitter, "Aesthetics, Modernity, and Trauma: Public Art and the Memory of War in Contemporary China," in Vishakha Desai, ed., *Asian Art History in the Twenty-First Century,* (Williamstown, MA, 2008), xx.
30. Hu Dekun et al., *Zhongguo kangzhan yu shijie fan-faxisi zhanzheng* (China's War of Resistance and the world antifascist war) (Shanghai, 2005), 1.
31. *Kangzhan peidu* [Wartime temporary capital] (Chongqing Television, 2005).
32. Fan Jianchuan, *Yi ge ren de kangzhan: cong yige ren de cangpin kan yi chang quan minzu de zhanzheng* [One person's war of resistance: looking at a whole nation's war through one person's collection] (Beijing: Zhongguo duiwai fanyi chuban gongsi, 2000), 104–105.
33. Fan, *Yi ge ren*, 109, 123.

34. Fan, *Yi ge ren,* 123.
35. Fan, *Yi ge ren,* 159. Regional pride has also affected the way in which northeastern China (formerly Manchuria) has reassessed its history of the war years, noting, for instance, that it endured Japanese occupation beginning in 1931, six years longer than the rest of China.
36. Fan, *Yi ge ren,* 219–220.
37. Fan, *Yi ge ren,* 4.
38. Fan, *Yi ge ren,* 5.
39. Li Yang, "Burma Road Sacrifices Recalled after 80 Years," *China Daily,* 31 Oct., 2018. Personal observation, August 2015.
40. Yang Lin et al., *Qu da houfang: Zhongguo kangzhan neiqian shilu* [Going to the interior: True stories of the journey inland during the War of Resistance] (Shanghai, 2005) (hereafter, QDHF), 459.
41. QDHF, 1–2.
42. QDHF, 2.
43. QDHF, 153, 155.
44. QDHF, 392, 352, 411.
45. QDHF, 411.
46. QDHF, 411.
47. Su Zhiliang, interview by the author, July 2018.
48. Chi Pang-yuan, *Juliuhe* (Taipei, 2014), published in English as *The Great Flowing River,* trans. John Balcom (New York, 2018).
49. Zhang Lixin and Cha Wenhua, "Taiwan writer Qi Bangyuan" [Taiwan zuojia Qi Bangyuan], *Xinhuanet,* 28 June 2017, http://www.xinhuanet.com//tw/2017-06/28/c_1121223819.htm.
50. For more on this work, see Peipei Qiu, Su Zhiliang, and Chen Yifei, *Chinese Comfort Women: Testimonies from Imperial Japan's Sex Slaves* (New York, 2014).
51. John Garnaut, *The Rise and Fall of the House of Bo: How a Murder Exposed the Cracks in China's Leadership,* Penguin digital only publication, 2012.
52. Wang himself did not, however, claim to be an intimate of Bo's or even to have had more than a fleeting encounter with the man. Jaime A. FlorCruz, "Daring to Speak Out about Bo Xilai Thriller," CNN,

http://edition.cnn.com/2012/04/26/world/asia/china-bo-insider
-florcruz/index.html. Gloria Davies, ed., *Voicing Concerns: Contemporary Chinese Critical Enquiry* (Lexington, KY, 2001), 66–67, discusses Wang Kang's political life in connection with the 1989 protests.

53. Ji Shuoming interview with Wang Kang, "Chongqing minjian sixiangjia Wang Kang: huifu Chongqing de lishi jiyi" [Interview with popular thinker Wang Kang: recovering Chongqing's historical memory], *Yazhou zhoukan,* 7 Nov. 2009.

54. "Chongqing minjian."

55. "Chongqing minjian."

56. "Chongqing minjian"; Joseph Cheng, ed. *The Use of Mao and the Chongqing Model* (Hong Kong, 2015), also discusses the role of Wang Kang.

57. On "red tourism" in Yan'an, see Chunfeng Lin, "Red Tourism: Rethinking Propaganda as a Social Space," *Communication and Critical / Cultural Studies* 12, no. 3 (2015): 328–346. See also Lovell, *Maoism.*

58. On Maoist discourse in Yan'an, see David E. Apter and Tony Saich, *Revolutionary Discourse in Mao's Republic* (Cambridge, MA, 1998).

59. Zhu Hongzhao, *Yan'an richang shenghuo de lishi* [A history of everyday life in Yan'an] (Guilin, 2007), 11.

60. Zhu, *Yan'an,* 12.

61. CQHX, 5.

62. Zhu, *Yan'an,* 11, 29.

63. Zhu, *Yan'an,* 96.

64. Zhu, *Yan'an,* 132.

65. Zhu, *Yan'an,* 132.

66. Zhu, *Yan'an,* 132–133.

67. Zhu, *Yan'an,* 134.

68. Frederic Wakeman, Jr., *Spymaster: Dai Li and the Chinese Secret Service* (Berkeley, CA, 2003), 305–306.

69. Zhu, *Yan'an,* 351.

70. Zhu, *Yan'an,* 352.

71. On misogyny in the Nationalist party, see Maggie Clinton, *Revolutionary Nativism: Fascism and Culture in China* (Durham, NC, 2017), 140–158.

72. Louise Edwards, "Women's Suffrage in China: Challenging Scholarly Conventions," *Pacific Historical Review* 69, no. 4 (2000): 625–626.
73. Jonathan D. Spence, *The Gate of Heavenly Peace: The Chinese and Their Revolution, 1895–1980* (London, 1982), 330; Zhu, *Yan'an,* 252.
74. CQHX, 27.
75. Zhu, *Yan'an,* 245–250.
76. Zhu, *Yan'an,* 237–238.
77. Zhu, *Yan'an,* 6, quoting Mei Jian, ed., *Yan'an mishi* [Secret stories of Yan'an] (Beijing 1996), 445–446.
78. Zhu, *Yan'an,* 238.
79. Danke Li, *Echoes of Chongqing: Women in Wartime China* (Urbana, IL, 2010), tackles this topic in detail.
80. Zhu, *Yan'an,* 356.
81. Zhu, *Yan'an,* 356.
82. Zhu, *Yan'an,* 356.
83. Zhu, *Yan'an,* 357.
84. Liu Zhenyun, "Why Won't the Chinese Acknowledge the 1942 Famine?" *New York Times,* 30 Nov. 2012.
85. Liu, "Why Won't the Chinese Acknowledge the 1942 Famine?"
86. Song Zhixin, ed., *1942: Henan da jihuang* (zengdingben) [1942: The Great Henan Famine, expanded version] (Hubei, 2012). This information about Song's family is found on the inside cover flap.
87. Song, *1942,* 4.
88. On the famine, see Mitter, *China's War with Japan,* ch. 14.
89. Jay Weissberg, review of *Back to 1942, Variety,* 13 Nov. 2012; Xan Brooks, review of *Back to 1942, Guardian,* 11 Nov. 2012.
90. Meng Lei, Guan Guofeng, and Guo Xiaoyang, *1942—Ji'e Zhongguo* [1942—Starving China] (Beijing, 2012).
91. Meng, Guan, and Guo, *1942,* 3–4.
92. Meng, Guan, and Guo, *1942,* 8.
93. Meng, Guan, and Guo, *1942,* 8.
94. Meng, Guan, and Guo, *1942,* 275.

95. Voice of America news, "Historic Chinese Drama Sparks Debate about More Recent Past," 5 Dec. 2012, https://www.voanews.com/a /historic-chinese-drama-sparks-debate-about-more-recent-past /1558770.html.

96. Voice of America news, "Historic Chinese Drama."

97. Voice of America news, "Historic Chinese Drama."

98. Yang Jisheng, *Tombstone: The Great Chinese Famine, 1958–1962* (London, 2012).

99. Clifford Coonan, "China Should Have Films on Cultural Revolution," *Irish Times*, 8 Mar. 2013, https://www.irishtimes.com/news/china -should-have-films-on-cultural-revolution-says-feng-1.1319576.

100. Wendy Qian, "In China, the Subversiveness of Historical Films," *Atlantic*, 1 April 2013.

101. "Vietnam Ready to Restore South Vietnamese War Cemeteries," Radio Free Asia news, 26 Jan. 2005, https://www.rfa.org/english /news/politics/vietnam_wardead-20050126.html.

102. Viet Thanh Nguyen, *Nothing Ever Dies: Vietnam and the Memory of War* (Cambridge, MA, 2016), 35–37.

6. The Cairo Syndrome: World War II and China's Contemporary International Relations

1. Derek Elley's generally favorable review of *Dongfeng Yu* was published in Sino-Cinema, 6 Feb. 2017, http://sino-cinema.com /2017/02/06/review-east-wind-rain/.

2. Sima Pingbang and Mingbo Shalong, "Zaiping 'Dongfeng yu': Zhongmei weihe tongshi zhongxie Taipingyang zhanzheng shi?" [Critiquing 'East Wind Rain': Why are China and the US both rewriting the history of the Pacific War?] *Zhongguo wenmingwang*, 9 Apr. 2010, http://www.wyzxwk.com/Article/wenyi/2010/04 /137204.html. On Sima Pingbang, see https://baike.baidu.com/item /%E5%8F%B8%E9%A9%AC%E5%B9%B3%E9%82%A6.

3. See Rosemary Foot, John Lewis Gaddis, and Andrew Hurrell, eds., *Order and Justice in International Relations* (Oxford, 2002).

4. Hu Qiaomu, "Luetan banian kangzhan de weida yiyi" [An outline discussion of the great significance of the War of Resistance], *Renmin ribao,* 7 Aug. 1987, in *Hu Qiaomu wenji* [Collected works of Hu Qiaomu], vol. 2 (Beijing, 2012), 251.

5. Hu, "Luetan," 251–252.

6. An error, to be fair, made also by many Western commentators.

7. On the military significance of Cairo, see Hans van de Ven, *War and Nationalism in China, 1925–1945* (London, 2003), 38–45.

8. For the text of the Cairo Declaration, see "The Cairo Declaration," Nov. 26, 1943, History and Public Policy Program Digital Archive, Foreign Relations of the United States, Diplomatic Papers, The Conferences at Cairo and Tehran, 1943 (Washington, DC: United States Government Printing Office, 1961), 448–449, available online at https://digitalarchive.wilsoncenter.org/document/122101.pdf?v=d 41d8cd98f00b204e9800998ecf8427e.

9. Huang Meizhen, Zhang Jishun, and Jin Guangyue, "Jianguo yilai kangRi zhanzheng yanjiu shuping" [A critical review of the research on the War of Resistance since the founding of the PRC], *Minguo dang'an* 10 (1987), 100.

10. See, for instance, analysis of the Project for the New American Century think tank in Maria Ryan, *Neoliberalism and the New American Century* (New York, 2010), 71–90.

11. On attempts by Japanese semi-governmental institutions under Shinzo Abe to lobby overseas scholarly and political communities on the war memory issue, see Jeff Kingston's disturbing piece, "Japanese revisionists' meddling backfires," *Critical Asian Studies* 51, no. 3 (2019): 435–450.

12. Xi Jinping, "Rang lishi shuohua yong shishi fayan shenru kaizhan Zhongguo renmin kangRi zhanzheng yanjiu" [Let history speak and use facts to deepen and open research on the Chinese People's War of Resistance], CPC News, 31 July 2015, http://cpc.people.com.cn/n/2015/0731/c64094-27393899.html.

13. William Callahan, *China: The Pessoptimist Nation* (Oxford, 2012), chs. 2–4.

14. On Zheng He, see for instance, Liao Danlin, "An Animated Struggle," *Global Times,* 5 Dec. 2013, http://www.globaltimes.cn /content/830115.shtml.

15. "Chinese, Japanese Ambassadors Appear on BBC after Voldemort Accusations," *China Digital Times,* https://chinadigitaltimes.net /2014/01/chinese-japanese-ambassadors-appear-bbc-voldemort -accusations/; "Japanese and Chinese Ambassadors on Island Dispute," BBC Newsnight, https://www.youtube.com/watch?v =sbLaPRh71Tc.

16. Henry Rousso, *The Vichy Syndrome: History and Memory in France since 1944,* trans. Arthur Goldhammer (Cambridge MA, 1991).

17. Rana Mitter, *China's War with Japan, 1937–1945: The Struggle for Survival* (London, 2013) [published in North America as *Forgotten Ally: China's World War II* (Boston, 2013)], 312–314.

18. For the text of the Cairo Communiqué, see "The Cairo Declaration," Nov. 26, 1943, Wilson Center Digital Archive, https://digitalarchive .wilsoncenter.org/document/122101.pdf?v=d41d8cd98f00b204e980 0998ecf8427e.

19. The official Chinese Foreign Ministry position is available on the website of the Ministry of Foreign Affairs of the People's Republic of China, http://www.fmprc.gov.cn/mfa_eng/topics_665678 /diaodao_665718/t973774.shtml. The official Japanese Ministry of Foreign Affairs position is available on the website of the Ministry of Foreign Affairs of Japan, https://www.mofa.go.jp/region/asia-paci /senkaku/qa_1010.html#q10.

20. "70 Years of Cairo Declaration," *Global Times,* 2 Dec. 2013, http://www.globaltimes.cn/content/829107.shtml; see also "China Urges Japan for Introspection on 70th Anniversary of Cairo Declaration," *Global Times,* 3 Dec. 2013, www.globaltimes.cn /content/829433.shtml.

21. Tom Phillips, "Bloggers Ridicule Chinese Film Placing Mao Zedong at Key Wartime Conference," *Guardian,* 17 Aug. 2015.

22. See Rana Mitter, "Presentism and China's Changing Wartime Past," *Past and Present* 234, no. 1 (2017): 263–274.

23. The phrase can be found in the trailer for the film *Cairo Declaration,* https://www.youtube.com/watch?v=9N6d9hCBv5E.

24. "China to Invite Foreign Forces to Join Military Parade for War Anniversary," *Guardian,* 26 Mar. 2015.

25. He Na, "New Figures Reveal Chinese Casualties," *China Daily,* 15 July 2015, makes the case for thirty-five million casualties (dead and wounded) over a fourteen-year war.

26. See Bill Hayton, *The South China Sea: The Struggle for Power in Asia* (New Haven, CT, 2014), for an insightful account of the disputes.

27. Stephen Chen, "China's Claims in South China Sea 'Proposed by Continuous Boundary for the First Time,'" *South China Morning Post,* 22 Apr. 2018.

28. Chen Qianping, "The Nationalist Government's Efforts to Recover Chinese Sovereignty over the Islands in the South China Sea after the End of World War Two," *Journal of Modern Chinese History*, 11, no. 1 (2017), 73.

29. China's resistance was, in some ways, similar to that of France, although Nationalist and Communist China resisted rather longer than the equivalent French states did.

30. Richard McGregor, *Asia's Reckoning: China, Japan, and the Fate of U.S. Power in the Pacific Century* (New York, 2017), 196.

31. For the speech, see U.S.–China Relations, C-Span, 10 Dec. 1996, https://www.c-span.org/video/?77263-1/us-china-relations.

32. McGregor, *Asia's Reckoning,* 196.

33. See Catherine Lu, *Justice and Reconciliation in World Politics* (Cambridge, 2017). An example of research on bacteriological warfare leading to a legal case is Zhao Xu, "The Long Fight for Justice," *China Daily,* 7 July 2016.

34. Julian Ryall, "China, Korea Reject Complaint from Japan over Statue of Assassin," *South China Morning Post,* 20 Nov. 2013.

35. Fang Jun, *Wo renshide "guizibing"* (Beijing, 1997), 267.

36. Personal observation, June 2018.

37. Zhang Kun, "Jewish museum in Shanghai to Be Expanded," *China Daily,* 20 Feb. 2019, http://www.chinadaily.com.cn/a/201902/20/WS5c6cf89ca3106c65c34ea5fa.html.

38. Gil Stern Shefler, "Yad Vashem Program Aims to Teach Chinese about Shoah," *Jerusalem Post,* 21 Oct. 2010.

39. Adam Taylor, "This Is Why Germany Doesn't Want China Anywhere near Berlin's Holocaust Memorial," *Washington Post,* 28 Mar. 2014.

40. "Japan Hits Out as Unesco Archives Nanjing Massacre Documents," *South China Morning Post,* 10 Oct. 2015.

41. "UN Poised to Support Alignment of China's Belt and Road Initiative with Sustainable Development Goals, Secretary-General Says at Opening Ceremony," United Nations, press release, 26 Apr. 2019, https://www.un.org/press/en/2019/sgsm19556.doc.htm.

42. Joseph S. Nye Jr., *Soft Power: The Means to Success in World Politics* (New York, 2004).

43. "China's One Belt One Road; Will It Reshape Global Trade?" McKinsey and Company, podcast transcript, July 2016, https://www.mckinsey.com/featured-insights/china/chinas-one-belt-one-road-will-it-reshape-global-trade.

44. Simon Shen and Wilson Chan, "A Comparative Study of the Belt and Road Initiative and the Marshall Plan," *Palgrave Communications* 4 (27 Mar. 2018): article no. 32 (2018), https://www.nature.com/articles/s41599-018-0077-9.

45. "'Belt and Road Initiatives' No Marshall Plan of China," *China Daily,* 31 Jan. 2015.

46. Benn Steil, *The Marshall Plan: Dawn of the Cold War* (London, 2018).

47. Lucy Hornby and Archie Zhang, "Belt and Road Debt Trap Accusations Hounds China as It Hosts Forum," *Financial Times,* 23 April 2019. On the BRI, see Eyck Freymann, *One Belt One Road: Chinese Power Meets the World* (Cambridge, MA, 2020).

48. For an important reassessment of the Marshall Mission, see Daniel Kurtz-Phelan, *The China Mission: George Marshall's Unfinished War, 1945–1947* (New York, 2018).

49. Mao Zedong, "Farewell, Leighton Stuart!" 18 Aug. 1949, *Selected Works of Mao Tse-tung,* vol. 4, Marxists Internet Archive, https://www.marxists.org/reference/archive/mao/selected-works/volume-4/mswv4_67.htm.

50. John Ikenberry, *Liberal Leviathan: The Origins, Crisis, and Transformation of the American World Order* (Princeton, NJ, 2011).
51. See, in particular, Xi Jinping's speech to the World Economic Forum at Davos in January 2018. The text can be found at CGTN, https://america.cgtn.com/2017/01/17/full-text-of-xi-jinping-keynote-at-the-world-economic-forum.
52. Sima and Mingbo, "Zaiping 'Dongfeng yu.'"

Conclusion: China's Long Postwar

1. Tony Judt, *Postwar: A History of Europe since 1945* (London, 2005).
2. Felix Wemheuer, *A Social History of Maoist China: Conflict and Change, 1949–1976* (Cambridge, 2019).
3. Lynn T. White III, *Policies of Chaos: The Organizational Causes of Violence in China's Cultural Revolution* (Princeton, NJ, 1989).
4. Amy King, *China-Japan Relations after World War Two: Empire, Industry and War, 1949–1971* (Cambridge, 2016).
5. On China's use of ideas of human security in international order, see Rosemary Foot, *China, the United Nations, and Human Protection: Beliefs, Power, Image* (Oxford, 2020).
6. An excellent example of the sort of memories contained within the US liberation circuit are the fine "Road to Tokyo" galleries at the National World War II Museum in New Orleans.
7. "Moment of Truth: Xi Leads War on COVID-19," Xinhuanet (10 March 2020), http://www.xinhuanet.com/english/2020-03/10/c_138863611.htm. Pieces using similar language in Chinese about victory in the People's War against the virus are here: http://www.xinhuanet.com/politics/leaders/2020-02/10/c_1125555826.htm and http://www.xinhuanet.com/politics/2020-03/10/c_1125689049.htm. On unconventional ways in which the War of Resistance is being politicized, see Hongping Annie Nie, "Gaming, Nationalism, and Ideological Work in Contemporary China: Online Games Based on the War of Resistance against Japan," *Journal of Contemporary China* (2013), 22:81, 499–517.

Acknowledgments

It was a privilege to be invited to deliver the Wiles Lectures at Queen's University Belfast in May 2014, an occasion which allowed me to develop the ideas that I expand on in this book. The Wiles Lecturer is asked "to promote the study of the history of civilisation and to encourage the extension of historical thinking into the realm of general ideas," and I have written this book in that spirit, with a full awareness of the formidable range of lecturers and topics that have made up the series since 1953. I am grateful to Peter Gray of Queen's and the Wiles Trustees, in particular Steve Smith and the late Christopher Bayly, whose conversation I still miss hugely, for making the lectures such a memorable occasion for me. I benefited greatly from the eight scholars who joined me in Belfast and gave friendly and rigorous critiques to the lectures: Jennifer Altehenger, Robert Bickers, Felix Boecking, Adam Cathcart, Lily Chang, Janet Chen, Henrietta Harrison, and Matthew Johnson.

Over the years since, various colleagues and friends at Oxford and elsewhere have been extremely helpful in making suggestions that have informed this book. On matters relating to World War II in China, I will always be in the debt of Hans van de Ven. I have learned immense amounts over the years from the conferences on the Sino-Japanese War coordinated by the indefatigable Ezra Vogel, from years of conversation on the wider historical context with Akira Iriye, Barak Kushner, and Arne Westad, and on contemporary Chinese nationalism with Kevin Rudd. I am grateful to colleagues from China who were willing to speak to me for the book and provided truly invaluable documentation; for reasons that I hope are clear, some have been anonymized, or their names have been withheld. Rosemary Foot and Graham Hutchings went well beyond the call of friendship to give detailed suggestions for the whole manuscript. I also benefited greatly from the reports of two anonymous readers. Annie Hongping Nie provided invaluable research input and was a key source of insight. Kathleen McDermott at Harvard University Press has been a helpful and inspiringly positive editor, Louise Robbins provided outstanding editing of the text, and Sarah Chalfant and James Pullen of the Wylie Agency have been exemplary agents. All responsibility for errors remains my own.

Research for the work was supported in significant part by the Leverhulme Trust, which awarded me a Research Leadership Award for 2007–2013; the support was so generous that this is the second book I have been able to write on the basis of that grant. In institutions around the world, the emerging scholars who were supported by that grant have continued to pursue research and teaching on the legacy of World War II in China.

Chapter 4 builds on ideas first discussed in my essay "China's 'Good War': Voices, Locations, and Generations in the Interpretation of the War of Resistance to Japan," in *Ruptured Histories: War, Memory, and the Post–Cold War in Asia,* edited with Sheila Miyoshi Jager and published by Harvard University Press in 2007. In Chapter 6, I expand on topics first treated in "Behind the Scenes at the Museum: Nationalism, History and Memory in the Beijing War of Resistance Museum, 1987–1997," published in *China Quarterly* in March 2000.

I could not have completed the book without the support of my family. My mother, Swasti, passed away during the writing of the book; I know she would have enjoyed reading it and miss having the chance to talk to her about it. My father, Partha; wife, Katharine; daughter, Malavika; sister, Pamina; and their various extended families have all been sources of love and support during its writing.

Index